Kentucky Votes: I

A UNIVERSITY OF
KENTUCKY STUDY

KENTUCKY VOTES

By MALCOLM E. JEWELL

UNIVERSITY OF KENTUCKY PRESS, 1963

BOONE

CAMPBELL

KENTON

GALLATIN

GRANT

CARROLL

OWEN

PENDLETON

BRACKEN

MASON

TRIMBLE

ROBERTSON

GREENUP

HARRISON

LEWIS

BOYD

OLDHAM

HENRY

NICHOLAS

FLEMING

BOURBON

CARTER

JEFFERSON

SHELBY

FRANKLIN

SCOTT

BATH

ROWAN

WOODFORD

ELLIOTT

FAYETTE

LAWRENCE

SPENCER

ANDERSON

CLARK

MONTGOMERY

MENIFEE

MORGAN

BULLITT

JESSAMINE

POWELL

JOHNSON

MARTIN

NELSON

WASHINGTON

MERCER

GARRARD

MADISON

ESTILL

WOLFE

MAGOFFIN

BOYLE

LEE

FLOYD

LARUE

MARION

LINCOLN

OWSLEY

BREATHITT

CASEY

ROCKCASTLE

JACKSON

TAYLOR

PERRY

KNOTT

PIKE

GREEN

LETCHER

PULASKI

LAUREL

CLAY

LESLIE

METCALFE

ADAIR

RUSSELL

KNOX

CUMBERLAND

HARLAN

MONROE

CLINTON

WAYNE

McCREARY

WHITLEY

BELL

Volume I

Presidential Elections, 1952-1960

U.S. Senate Primary and General Elections,

1920-1960

Acknowledgments

The compilation of these election statistics was made possible by the cooperation of the office of the Secretary of State in Frankfort, and especially Sylva Lyon of that office. Mrs. Marjorie Sanders carried out the laborious chore of typing the figures with great accuracy. I am indebted to the staff of the University of Kentucky Computing Center, and particularly Duncan White, for planning and executing the computing program that makes a project such as this feasible. Two graduate assistants in the Department of Political Science, Jack Turner and Jack Neale, assisted in the checking of figures. A grant from the University of Kentucky Research Fund Committee helped to make this publication possible.

Introduction

Kentucky Votes is being issued in three volumes. Volume 1 includes presidential elections from 1952 through 1960 and primaries and elections for the U.S. Senate from 1920 through 1960. Volume 2 includes gubernatorial primaries and elections from 1923 through 1959. Volume 3 includes primaries and elections for the U.S. House of Representatives from 1920 through 1960. In 1950 the Bureau of Government Research of the University of Kentucky published *Presidential Politics in Kentucky, 1824-1948*, by Jasper B. Shannon and Ruth McQuown, containing comparable election statistics for that period.

Accurate, detailed election statistics are one of the basic tools of political research, and yet until recent years these have not been easily accessible to scholars or others interested in political research—journalists, teachers, and political candidates, for example. In Kentucky, as in many states, these figures have been available only in the Secretary of State's office, and there has been no compilation of percentages and pluralities necessary for comparative purposes.

The Elections Research Center of the Governmental Affairs Institute in Washington has begun publishing election statistics for all the states every two years in *America Votes*. This includes county-by-county election returns, with percentages and pluralities for presidential, senatorial, and gubernatorial elections, beginning in 1952. In several other states supplementary volumes have been issued by the state universities to provide greater detail and coverage of returns for earlier years. These volumes of *Kentucky Votes* serve the same purpose. In Kentucky, where primary elections frequently overshadow general elections, it is particularly important to include primary election returns as well.

The source of all the statistics in these volumes of *Kentucky Votes* is the official records in the office of the Secretary of State in Frankfort, Kentucky. The returns were punched on IBM cards and the percentages and pluralities were calculated on the IBM 1620 at the University of Kentucky Computing Center. The use of IBM equipment for printing the results as well minimizes the possibilities of error.

The format used in these volumes necessarily differs for primaries and general elections. In each volume the elections are arranged chronologically, and for each year the Democratic and Republican primaries (if any) are listed first, followed by the general election. This format is followed in the House elections as well, with Democratic primaries in all districts where held being followed by all Republican primaries and then all general election contests, for a given year.

For the primary elections, the first column of figures is the total vote cast, and in subsequent columns the vote and percentage of total vote for each candidate are given, in declining order of their vote. It is impossible and unnecessary to include the votes for all minor candidates, but in some primary contests it is difficult to distinguish between major and minor candidates and some uniform standard must be used. The general rule that has been followed in the primaries is that the vote has been listed separately for any candidate receiving at least 10 per cent of the total vote. Where two or more candidates receive less than 10 per cent of the vote, their votes have been combined in the Other Candidates column. In a very few cases there were more than three candidates receiving 10 per cent or more of the vote. Since there was space for only four listings, in these cases all candidates below the top three were listed together in the Other Candidates column. Whenever the vote for two or more candidates has been combined in the Other Candidates column, the statewide vote for each candidate has been listed at the bottom of the page.

The same standard has been used for determining which primaries to include. Only those primaries are included in these volumes in which more than one candidate won 10 per cent of the vote. The remaining primaries are excluded because the contest at the polls was only a nominal one.

In the general elections, the first column of figures is the total vote. Thereafter, the vote and the percentage of the total vote for the Democratic candidate, the Republican candidate, and all other candidates are listed. Then the Democratic and Republican percentages of the two-party vote are listed, followed by the two-party plurality of the winner. At the bottom of the page are the names of the Democratic and Republican candidates and the names, party names, and statewide vote of all candidates whose vote is included in the Other Candidates column. Where no general election is listed for a year (as frequently occurs in House races), it is because only one party ran a candidate.

There is an occasional discrepancy between the candidate listed as the winner of a primary and the one who represents that party in the general election, because the primary winner may die or withdraw as a candidate and may or may not be replaced by the party in the general election.

County	Total Vote	Democratic Total	Per Cent	Republican Total	Per Cent	Other Vote Total	Per Cent	Per Cent of Two-Party Vote Dem	Rep	Dem-Rep Plurality
ADAIR	5,927	2,184	36.8	3,737	63.1	6	0.1	36.9	63.1	1,553 R
ALLEN	4,717	1,750	37.1	2,946	62.5	21	0.4	37.3	62.7	1,196 R
ANDERSON	3,607	2,153	59.7	1,445	40.1	9	0.2	59.8	40.2	708 D
BALLARD	3,767	2,910	77.2	851	22.6	6	0.2	77.4	22.6	2,059 D
BARREN	8,365	4,618	55.2	3,743	44.7	4		55.2	44.8	875 D
BATH	4,142	2,400	57.9	1,737	41.9	5	0.1	58.0	42.0	663 D
BELL	11,761	5,276	44.9	6,461	54.9	24	0.2	45.0	55.0	1,185 R
BOONE	4,946	2,620	53.0	2,309	46.7	17	0.3	53.2	46.8	311 D
BOURBON	5,570	3,339	59.9	2,229	40.0	2		60.0	40.0	1,110 D
BOYD	20,720	10,245	49.4	10,426	50.3	49	0.2	49.6	50.4	181 R
BOYLE	6,763	3,771	55.8	2,969	43.9	23	0.3	55.9	44.1	802 D
BRACKEN	3,444	1,753	50.9	1,690	49.1	1		50.9	49.1	63 D
BREATHITT	4,764	3,383	71.0	1,381	29.0			71.0	29.0	2,002 D
BRECKINRIDGE	5,922	2,828	47.8	3,078	52.0	16	0.3	47.9	52.1	250 R
BULLITT	3,418	2,121	62.1	1,292	37.8	5	0.1	62.1	37.9	829 D
BUTLER	4,165	1,157	27.8	2,996	71.9	12	0.3	27.9	72.1	1,839 R
CALDWELL	4,650	2,133	45.9	2,507	53.9	10	0.2	46.0	54.0	374 R
CALLOWAY	7,275	5,434	74.7	1,829	25.1	12	0.2	74.8	25.2	3,605 D
CAMPBELL	30,716	12,976	42.2	17,705	57.6	35	0.1	42.3	57.7	4,729 R
CARLISLE	2,524	1,867	74.0	656	26.0	1		74.0	26.0	1,211 D
CARROLL	3,632	2,605	71.7	1,019	28.1	8	0.2	71.9	28.1	1,586 D
CARTER	7,262	3,019	41.6	4,221	58.1	22	0.3	41.7	58.3	1,202 R
CASEY	5,366	1,522	28.4	3,831	71.4	13	0.2	28.4	71.6	2,309 R
CHRISTIAN	11,672	6,787	58.1	4,858	41.6	27	0.2	58.3	41.7	1,929 D
CLARK	6,212	3,620	58.3	2,592	41.7			58.3	41.7	1,028 D
CLAY	5,544	1,365	24.6	4,161	75.1	18	0.3	24.7	75.3	2,796 R
CLINTON	3,546	678	19.1	2,856	80.5	12	0.3	19.2	80.8	2,178 R
CRITTENDEN	3,914	1,427	36.5	2,471	63.1	16	0.4	36.6	63.4	1,044 R
CUMBERLAND	3,349	909	27.1	2,426	72.4	14	0.4	27.3	72.7	1,517 R
DAVIESS	18,010	7,522	41.8	10,462	58.1	26	0.1	41.8	58.2	2,940 R
EDMONSON	3,273	992	30.3	2,279	69.6	2	0.1	30.3	69.7	1,287 R
ELLIOTT	2,703	2,074	76.7	629	23.3			76.7	23.3	1,445 D
ESTILL	4,550	1,900	41.8	2,630	57.8	20	0.4	41.9	58.1	730 R
FAYETTE	31,789	14,275	44.9	17,376	54.7	138	0.4	45.1	54.9	3,101 R
FLEMING	5,050	2,446	48.4	2,592	51.3	12	0.2	48.6	51.4	146 R
FLOYD	13,189	8,940	67.8	4,238	32.1	11	0.1	67.8	32.2	4,702 D
FRANKLIN	10,411	7,309	70.2	3,097	29.7	5		70.2	29.8	4,212 D
FULTON	3,942	2,673	67.8	1,266	32.1	3	0.1	67.9	32.1	1,407 D
GALLATIN	1,851	1,383	74.7	465	25.1	3	0.2	74.8	25.2	918 D
GARRARD	4,331	1,927	44.5	2,398	55.4	6	0.1	44.6	55.4	471 R
GRANT	4,161	2,545	61.2	1,609	38.7	7	0.2	61.3	38.7	936 D
GRAVES	12,530	9,592	76.6	2,925	23.3	13	0.1	76.6	23.4	6,667 D
GRAYSON	6,362	2,341	36.8	4,011	63.0	10	0.2	36.9	63.1	1,670 R
GREEN	4,641	1,857	40.0	2,773	59.8	11	0.2	40.1	59.9	916 R
GREENUP	9,078	4,716	51.9	4,354	48.0	8	0.1	52.0	48.0	362 D
HANCOCK	2,525	1,177	46.6	1,341	53.1	7	0.3	46.7	53.3	164 R
HARDIN	8,558	4,599	53.7	3,914	45.7	45	0.5	54.0	46.0	685 D
HARLAN	17,330	10,025	57.8	7,284	42.0	21	0.1	57.9	42.1	2,741 D
HARRISON	5,240	3,367	64.3	1,866	35.6	7	0.1	64.3	35.7	1,501 D
HART	5,903	2,952	50.0	2,934	49.7	17	0.3	50.2	49.8	18 D
HENDERSON	10,893	5,913	54.3	4,929	45.2	51	0.5	54.5	45.5	984 D
HENRY	5,062	3,468	68.5	1,584	31.3	10	0.2	68.6	31.4	1,884 D
HICKMAN	2,865	1,988	69.4	871	30.4	6	0.2	69.5	30.5	1,117 D
HOPKINS	11,469	7,157	62.4	4,285	37.4	27	0.2	62.6	37.4	2,872 D
JACKSON	3,578	471	13.2	3,104	86.8	3	0.1	13.2	86.8	2,633 R
JEFFERSON	181,447	81,642	45.0	99,069	54.6	736	0.4	45.2	54.8	17,427 R
JESSAMINE	4,792	2,578	53.8	2,193	45.8	21	0.4	54.0	46.0	385 D
JOHNSON	7,856	2,654	33.8	5,199	66.2	3		33.8	66.2	2,545 R
KENTON	38,709	19,457	50.3	19,200	49.6	52	0.1	50.3	49.7	257 D
KNOTT	5,582	4,437	79.5	1,124	20.1	21	0.4	79.8	20.2	3,313 D
KNOX	8,253	2,766	33.5	5,470	66.3	17	0.2	33.6	66.4	2,704 R
LARUE	3,862	2,161	56.0	1,701	44.0			56.0	44.0	460 D
LAUREL	8,051	2,263	28.1	5,776	71.7	12	0.1	28.2	71.8	3,513 R
LAWRENCE	5,302	2,597	49.0	2,696	50.8	9	0.2	49.1	50.9	99 R
LEE	2,678	1,100	41.1	1,572	58.7	6	0.2	41.2	58.8	472 R

PRESIDENT — 1952

County	Total Vote	Democratic Total	Democratic Per Cent	Republican Total	Republican Per Cent	Other Vote Total	Other Vote Per Cent	Per Cent of Two-Party Vote Dem	Per Cent of Two-Party Vote Rep	Dem-Rep Plurality
LESLIE	3,959	705	17.8	3,239	81.8	15	0.4	17.9	82.1	2,534 R
LETCHER	9,786	5,097	52.1	4,689	47.9			52.1	47.9	408 D
LEWIS	4,888	1,556	31.8	3,317	67.9	15	0.3	31.9	68.1	1,761 R
LINCOLN	6,114	2,910	47.6	3,186	52.1	18	0.3	47.7	52.3	276 R
LIVINGSTON	2,657	1,554	58.5	1,102	41.5	1		58.5	41.5	452 D
LOGAN	7,690	4,917	63.9	2,758	35.9	15	0.2	64.1	35.9	2,159 D
LYON	2,158	1,404	65.1	746	34.6	8	0.4	65.3	34.7	658 D
MADISON	11,815	5,901	49.9	5,886	49.8	28	0.2	50.1	49.9	15 D
MAGOFFIN	4,342	2,243	51.7	2,093	48.2	6	0.1	51.7	48.3	150 D
MARION	5,429	3,159	58.2	2,262	41.7	8	0.1	58.3	41.7	897 D
MARSHALL	4,934	3,445	69.8	1,474	29.9	15	0.3	70.0	30.0	1,971 D
MARTIN	3,815	1,174	30.8	2,641	69.2			30.8	69.2	1,467 R
MASON	7,228	3,614	50.0	3,606	49.9	8	0.1	50.1	49.9	8 D
MC CRACKEN	18,375	12,302	66.9	6,051	32.9	22	0.1	67.0	33.0	6,251 D
MC CREARY	4,309	937	21.7	3,360	78.0	12	0.3	21.8	78.2	2,423 R
MC LEAN	3,763	1,961	52.1	1,791	47.6	11	0.3	52.3	47.7	170 D
MEADE	3,310	2,040	61.6	1,265	38.2	5	0.2	61.7	38.3	775 D
MENIFEE	1,863	1,219	65.4	638	34.2	6	0.3	65.6	34.4	581 D
MERCER	5,312	2,740	51.6	2,545	47.9	27	0.5	51.8	48.2	195 D
METCALFE	4,037	1,848	45.8	2,176	53.9	13	0.3	45.9	54.1	328 R
MONROE	4,759	1,084	22.8	3,675	77.2			22.8	77.2	2,591 R
MONTGOMERY	4,648	2,653	57.1	1,981	42.6	14	0.3	57.3	42.7	672 D
MORGAN	4,476	3,161	70.6	1,311	29.3	4	0.1	70.7	29.3	1,850 D
MUHLENBERG	9,812	5,037	51.3	4,761	48.5	14	0.1	51.4	48.6	276 D
NELSON	6,494	3,417	52.6	3,064	47.2	13	0.2	52.7	47.3	353 D
NICHOLAS	2,979	1,819	61.1	1,156	38.8	4	0.1	61.1	38.9	663 D
OHIO	7,142	2,700	37.8	4,428	62.0	14	0.2	37.9	62.1	1,728 R
OLDHAM	3,476	1,735	49.9	1,723	49.6	18	0.5	50.2	49.8	12 D
OWEN	4,000	3,174	79.4	819	20.5	7	0.2	79.5	20.5	2,355 D
OWSLEY	2,387	419	17.6	1,954	81.9	14	0.6	17.7	82.3	1,535 R
PENDLETON	3,892	1,993	51.2	1,895	48.7	4	0.1	51.3	48.7	98 D
PERRY	10,762	5,538	51.5	5,210	48.4	14	0.1	51.5	48.5	328 D
PIKE	22,576	12,761	56.5	9,778	43.3	37	0.2	56.6	43.4	2,983 D
POWELL	2,213	1,218	55.0	992	44.8	3	0.1	55.1	44.9	226 D
PULASKI	13,707	4,032	29.4	9,651	70.4	24	0.2	29.5	70.5	5,619 R
ROBERTSON	1,451	827	57.0	623	42.9	1	0.1	57.0	43.0	204 D
ROCKCASTLE	4,842	1,326	27.4	3,503	72.3	13	0.3	27.5	72.5	2,177 R
ROWAN	4,216	2,220	52.7	1,985	47.1	11	0.3	52.8	47.2	235 D
RUSSELL	4,095	1,171	28.6	2,913	71.1	11	0.3	28.7	71.3	1,742 R
SCOTT	5,261	3,171	60.3	2,077	39.5	13	0.2	60.4	39.6	1,094 D
SHELBY	6,562	4,076	62.1	2,474	37.7	12	0.2	62.2	37.8	1,602 D
SIMPSON	4,040	2,724	67.4	1,310	32.4	6	0.1	67.5	32.5	1,414 D
SPENCER	2,007	1,283	63.9	723	36.0	1		64.0	36.0	560 D
TAYLOR	5,592	2,439	43.6	3,126	55.9	27	0.5	43.8	56.2	687 R
TODD	4,416	2,995	67.8	1,401	31.7	20	0.5	68.1	31.9	1,594 D
TRIGG	3,725	2,585	69.4	1,134	30.4	6	0.2	69.5	30.5	1,451 D
TRIMBLE	2,240	1,855	82.8	370	16.5	15	0.7	83.4	16.6	1,485 D
UNION	5,422	3,445	63.5	1,967	36.3	10	0.2	63.7	36.3	1,478 D
WARREN	14,407	7,106	49.3	7,267	50.4	34	0.2	49.4	50.6	161 R
WASHINGTON	4,415	2,114	47.9	2,290	51.9	11	0.2	48.0	52.0	176 R
WAYNE	5,861	2,461	42.0	3,396	57.9	4	0.1	42.0	58.0	935 R
WEBSTER	5,386	3,516	65.3	1,858	34.5	12	0.2	65.4	34.6	1,658 D
WHITLEY	10,011	2,958	29.5	7,030	70.2	23	0.2	29.6	70.4	4,072 R
WOLFE	2,435	1,557	63.9	876	36.0	2	0.1	64.0	36.0	681 D
WOODFORD	4,171	2,319	55.6	1,845	44.2	7	0.2	55.7	44.3	474 D
TOTAL	993,148	495,729	49.9	495,029	49.8	2,390	0.2	50.0	50.0	700 D

OTHER VOTE: Eric Hass (Socialist Labor) 893
Vincent Hallinan (Progressive) 336
Stuart Hamblen (Prohibition) 1161
DEMOCRAT: Adlai E. Stevenson
REPUBLICAN: Dwight D. Eisenhower

County	Total Vote	Democratic		Republican		Other Vote		Per Cent of Two-Party Vote		Dem-Rep Plurality
		Total	Per Cent	Total	Per Cent	Total	Per Cent	Dem	Rep	
ADAIR	6,651	2,491	37.5	4,157	62.5	3		37.5	62.5	1,666 R
ALLEN	5,193	1,975	38.0	3,200	61.6	18	0.3	38.2	61.8	1,225 R
ANDERSON	3,973	2,089	52.6	1,878	47.3	6	0.2	52.7	47.3	211 D
BALLARD	3,936	3,088	78.5	838	21.3	10	0.3	78.7	21.3	2,250 D
BARREN	9,414	5,206	55.3	4,206	44.7	2		55.3	44.7	1,000 D
BATH	4,125	2,221	53.8	1,889	45.8	15	0.4	54.0	46.0	332 D
BELL	11,319	4,477	39.6	6,824	60.3	18	0.2	39.6	60.4	2,347 R
BOONE	6,090	2,933	48.2	3,139	51.5	18	0.3	48.3	51.7	206 R
BOURBON	5,790	3,263	56.4	2,475	42.7	52	0.9	56.9	43.1	788 D
BOYD	20,082	8,546	42.6	11,502	57.3	34	0.2	42.6	57.4	2,956 R
BOYLE	6,880	3,436	49.9	3,427	49.8	17	0.2	50.1	49.9	9 D
BRACKEN	3,276	1,515	46.2	1,754	53.5	7	0.2	46.3	53.7	239 R
BREATHITT	5,673	3,246	57.2	2,423	42.7	4	0.1	57.3	42.7	823 D
BRECKINRIDGE	6,671	2,867	43.0	3,784	56.7	20	0.3	43.1	56.9	917 R
BULLITT	4,290	2,279	53.1	2,007	46.8	4	0.1	53.2	46.8	272 D
BUTLER	4,513	1,202	26.6	3,303	73.2	8	0.2	26.7	73.3	2,101 R
CALDWELL	5,124	2,417	47.2	2,681	52.3	26	0.5	47.4	52.6	264 R
CALLOWAY	8,460	6,152	72.7	2,292	27.1	16	0.2	72.9	27.1	3,860 D
CAMPBELL	29,171	10,359	35.5	18,617	63.8	195	0.7	35.8	64.2	8,258 R
CARLISLE	2,676	2,063	77.1	608	22.7	5	0.2	77.2	22.8	1,455 D
CARROLL	3,316	2,169	65.4	1,130	34.1	17	0.5	65.7	34.3	1,039 D
CARTER	8,258	3,112	37.7	5,127	62.1	19	0.2	37.8	62.2	2,015 R
CASEY	5,749	1,570	27.3	4,167	72.5	12	0.2	27.4	72.6	2,597 R
CHRISTIAN	11,495	6,487	56.4	4,963	43.2	45	0.4	56.7	43.3	1,524 D
CLARK	6,663	3,609	54.2	3,030	45.5	24	0.4	54.4	45.6	579 D
CLAY	5,934	1,027	17.3	4,897	82.5	10	0.2	17.3	82.7	3,870 R
CLINTON	4,147	747	18.0	3,396	81.9	4	0.1	18.0	82.0	2,649 R
CRITTENDEN	4,068	1,494	36.7	2,548	62.6	26	0.6	37.0	63.0	1,054 R
CUMBERLAND	3,601	1,000	27.8	2,584	71.8	17	0.5	27.9	72.1	1,584 R
DAVIESS	18,373	6,674	36.3	11,491	62.5	208	1.1	36.7	63.3	4,817 R
EDMONSON	3,897	1,092	28.0	2,800	71.9	5	0.1	28.1	71.9	1,708 R
ELLIOTT	3,176	2,143	67.5	1,033	32.5			67.5	32.5	1,110 D
ESTILL	4,868	1,912	39.3	2,946	60.5	10	0.2	39.4	60.6	1,034 R
FAYETTE	35,683	13,547	38.0	21,904	61.4	232	0.7	38.2	61.8	8,357 R
FLEMING	5,280	2,519	47.7	2,744	52.0	17	0.3	47.9	52.1	225 R
FLOYD	14,088	7,907	56.1	6,166	43.8	15	0.1	56.2	43.8	1,741 D
FRANKLIN	10,553	6,412	60.8	4,047	38.3	94	0.9	61.3	38.7	2,365 D
FULTON	4,128	2,953	71.5	1,147	27.8	28	0.7	72.0	28.0	1,806 D
GALLATIN	1,771	1,223	69.1	547	30.9	1	0.1	69.1	30.9	676 D
GARRARD	4,133	1,798	43.5	2,311	55.9	24	0.6	43.8	56.2	513 R
GRANT	3,996	2,300	57.6	1,680	42.0	16	0.4	57.8	42.2	620 D
GRAVES	13,815	10,090	73.0	3,711	26.9	14	0.1	73.1	26.9	6,379 D
GRAYSON	6,592	2,021	30.7	4,565	69.3	6	0.1	30.7	69.3	2,544 R
GREEN	4,689	1,726	36.8	2,951	62.9	12	0.3	36.9	63.1	1,225 R
GREENUP	10,538	5,045	47.9	5,464	51.9	29	0.3	48.0	52.0	419 R
HANCOCK	2,346	1,022	43.6	1,317	56.1	7	0.3	43.7	56.3	295 R
HARDIN	9,430	4,325	45.9	5,050	53.6	55	0.6	46.1	53.9	725 R
HARLAN	15,761	6,915	43.9	8,820	56.0	26	0.2	43.9	56.1	1,905 R
HARRISON	5,657	3,515	62.1	2,128	37.6	14	0.2	62.3	37.7	1,387 D
HART	6,506	3,207	49.3	3,276	50.4	23	0.4	49.5	50.5	69 R
HENDERSON	10,838	5,501	50.8	5,085	46.9	252	2.3	52.0	48.0	416 D
HENRY	4,838	3,157	65.3	1,670	34.5	11	0.2	65.4	34.6	1,487 D
HICKMAN	3,163	2,367	74.8	785	24.8	11	0.3	75.1	24.9	1,582 D
HOPKINS	11,917	6,535	54.8	5,300	44.5	82	0.7	55.2	44.8	1,235 D
JACKSON	4,471	501	11.2	3,950	88.3	20	0.4	11.3	88.7	3,449 R
JEFFERSON	203,917	83,483	40.9	119,262	58.5	1,172	0.6	41.2	58.8	35,779 R
JESSAMINE	4,553	2,072	45.5	2,340	51.4	141	3.1	47.0	53.0	268 R
JOHNSON	8,165	2,356	28.9	5,802	71.1	7	0.1	28.9	71.1	3,446 R
KENTON	36,070	14,923	41.4	20,895	57.9	252	0.7	41.7	58.3	5,972 R
KNOTT	5,712	3,987	69.8	1,715	30.0	10	0.2	69.9	30.1	2,272 D
KNOX	8,882	2,539	28.6	6,341	71.4	2		28.6	71.4	3,802 R
LARUE	4,259	1,859	43.6	2,387	56.0	13	0.3	43.8	56.2	528 R
LAUREL	8,916	2,316	26.0	6,586	73.9	14	0.2	26.0	74.0	4,270 R
LAWRENCE	5,438	2,495	45.9	2,932	53.9	11	0.2	46.0	54.0	437 R
LEE	2,716	938	34.5	1,774	65.3	4	0.1	34.6	65.4	836 R

4

County	Total Vote	Democratic		Republican		Other Vote		Per Cent of Two-Party Vote		Dem-Rep Plurality
		Total	Per Cent	Total	Per Cent	Total	Per Cent	Dem	Rep	
LESLIE	4,315	531	12.3	3,770	87.4	14	0.3	12.3	87.7	3,239 R
LETCHER	9,904	4,133	41.7	5,741	58.0	30	0.3	41.9	58.1	1,608 R
LEWIS	4,927	1,585	32.2	3,333	67.6	9	0.2	32.2	67.8	1,748 R
LINCOLN	6,510	2,953	45.4	3,535	54.3	22	0.3	45.5	54.5	582 R
LIVINGSTON	3,046	1,795	58.9	1,247	40.9	4	0.1	59.0	41.0	548 D
LOGAN	8,174	5,299	64.8	2,855	34.9	20	0.2	65.0	35.0	2,444 D
LYON	2,535	1,527	60.2	989	39.0	19	0.7	60.7	39.3	538 D
MADISON	11,710	5,670	48.4	5,955	50.9	85	0.7	48.8	51.2	285 R
MAGOFFIN	4,509	2,162	47.9	2,343	52.0	4	0.1	48.0	52.0	181 R
MARION	5,892	2,927	49.7	2,945	50.0	20	0.3	49.8	50.2	18 R
MARSHALL	6,382	4,358	68.3	2,015	31.6	9	0.1	68.4	31.6	2,343 D
MARTIN	3,633	694	19.1	2,927	80.6	12	0.3	19.2	80.8	2,233 R
MASON	7,490	3,572	47.7	3,880	51.8	38	0.5	47.9	52.1	308 R
MC CRACKEN	21,258	14,103	66.3	7,076	33.3	79	0.4	66.6	33.4	7,027 D
MC CREARY	4,630	814	17.6	3,812	82.3	4	0.1	17.6	82.4	2,998 R
MC LEAN	3,870	1,965	50.8	1,886	48.7	19	0.5	51.0	49.0	79 D
MEADE	3,692	2,016	54.6	1,670	45.2	6	0.2	54.7	45.3	346 D
MENIFEE	1,985	1,185	59.7	799	40.3	1	0.1	59.7	40.3	386 D
MERCER	5,952	2,767	46.5	3,168	53.2	17	0.3	46.6	53.4	401 R
METCALFE	4,438	2,014	45.4	2,412	54.3	12	0.3	45.5	54.5	398 R
MONROE	5,014	1,255	25.0	3,759	75.0			25.0	75.0	2,504 R
MONTGOMERY	4,895	2,656	54.3	2,220	45.4	19	0.4	54.5	45.5	436 D
MORGAN	5,048	3,164	62.7	1,878	37.2	6	0.1	62.8	37.2	1,286 D
MUHLENBERG	10,113	4,752	47.0	5,323	52.6	38	0.4	47.2	52.8	571 R
NELSON	7,365	3,240	44.0	4,107	55.8	18	0.2	44.1	55.9	867 R
NICHOLAS	2,695	1,667	61.9	999	37.1	29	1.1	62.5	37.5	668 D
OHIO	7,649	2,726	35.6	4,901	64.1	22	0.3	35.7	64.3	2,175 R
OLDHAM	3,909	1,769	45.3	2,128	54.4	12	0.3	45.4	54.6	359 R
OWEN	3,791	2,928	77.2	857	22.6	6	0.2	77.4	22.6	2,071 D
OWSLEY	2,347	331	14.1	2,013	85.8	3	0.1	14.1	85.9	1,682 R
PENDLETON	4,174	1,889	45.3	2,273	54.5	12	0.3	45.4	54.6	384 R
PERRY	11,161	4,545	40.7	6,591	59.1	25	0.2	40.8	59.2	2,046 R
PIKE	23,185	11,466	49.5	11,678	50.4	41	0.2	49.5	50.5	212 R
POWELL	2,685	1,343	50.0	1,339	49.9	3	0.1	50.1	49.9	4 D
PULASKI	14,572	3,899	26.8	10,636	73.0	37	0.3	26.8	73.2	6,737 R
ROBERTSON	1,412	793	56.2	617	43.7	2	0.1	56.2	43.8	176 D
ROCKCASTLE	5,112	1,313	25.7	3,787	74.1	12	0.2	25.7	74.3	2,474 R
ROWAN	4,857	2,380	49.0	2,470	50.9	7	0.1	49.1	50.9	90 R
RUSSELL	4,358	1,284	29.5	3,065	70.3	9	0.2	29.5	70.5	1,781 R
SCOTT	4,848	2,860	59.0	1,940	40.0	48	1.0	59.6	40.4	920 D
SHELBY	6,799	4,017	59.1	2,768	40.7	14	0.2	59.2	40.8	1,249 D
SIMPSON	4,350	2,879	66.2	1,454	33.4	17	0.4	66.4	33.6	1,425 D
SPENCER	2,117	1,214	57.3	896	42.3	7	0.3	57.5	42.5	318 D
TAYLOR	6,342	2,433	38.4	3,892	61.4	17	0.3	38.5	61.5	1,459 R
TODD	4,585	3,087	67.3	1,480	32.3	18	0.4	67.6	32.4	1,607 D
TRIGG	3,855	2,517	65.3	1,329	34.5	9	0.2	65.4	34.6	1,188 D
TRIMBLE	2,310	1,792	77.6	506	21.9	12	0.5	78.0	22.0	1,286 D
UNION	5,193	2,863	55.1	1,956	37.7	374	7.2	59.4	40.6	907 D
WARREN	15,310	7,143	46.7	8,123	53.1	44	0.3	46.8	53.2	980 R
WASHINGTON	4,637	2,084	44.9	2,536	54.7	17	0.4	45.1	54.9	452 R
WAYNE	5,902	2,263	38.3	3,609	61.1	30	0.5	38.5	61.5	1,346 R
WEBSTER	5,253	3,050	58.1	1,948	37.1	255	4.9	61.0	39.0	1,102 D
WHITLEY	10,438	2,656	25.4	7,759	74.3	23	0.2	25.5	74.5	5,103 R
WOLFE	2,742	1,683	61.4	1,059	38.6			61.4	38.6	624 D
WOODFORD	4,257	2,027	47.6	2,170	51.0	60	1.4	48.3	51.7	143 R
TOTAL	1,053,805	476,453	45.2	572,192	54.3	5,160	0.5	45.4	54.6	95,739 R

OTHER VOTE: Enoch Holtwick (Prohibition) 2145
Eric Hass (Socialist Labor) 358
Harry F. Byrd (State's Rights) 2657
DEMOCRAT: Adlai E. Stevenson
REPUBLICAN: Dwight D. Eisenhower

County	Total Vote	Democratic		Republican		Per Cent of Two-Party Vote		Dem-Rep Plurality
		Total	Per Cent	Total	Per Cent	Dem	Rep	
ADAIR	6,890	2,269	32.9	4,621	67.1	32.9	67.1	2,352 R
ALLEN	5,073	1,663	32.8	3,410	67.2	32.8	67.2	1,747 R
ANDERSON	4,071	2,038	50.1	2,033	49.9	50.1	49.9	5 D
BALLARD	3,867	2,746	71.0	1,121	29.0	71.0	29.0	1,625 D
BARREN	10,133	4,946	48.8	5,187	51.2	48.8	51.2	241 R
BATH	3,954	2,066	52.3	1,888	47.7	52.3	47.7	178 D
BELL	11,986	5,181	43.2	6,805	56.8	43.2	56.8	1,624 R
BOONE	7,800	2,965	38.0	4,835	62.0	38.0	62.0	1,870 R
BOURBON	5,535	3,156	57.0	2,379	43.0	57.0	43.0	777 D
BOYD	20,399	9,094	44.6	11,305	55.4	44.6	55.4	2,211 R
BOYLE	6,932	3,308	47.7	3,624	52.3	47.7	52.3	316 R
BRACKEN	3,328	1,326	39.8	2,002	60.2	39.8	60.2	676 R
BREATHITT	5,303	3,307	62.4	1,996	37.6	62.4	37.6	1,311 D
BRECKINRIDGE	7,115	3,136	44.1	3,979	55.9	44.1	55.9	843 R
BULLITT	5,120	2,437	47.6	2,683	52.4	47.6	52.4	246 R
BUTLER	4,648	992	21.3	3,656	78.7	21.3	78.7	2,664 R
CALDWELL	5,579	2,137	38.3	3,442	61.7	38.3	61.7	1,305 R
CALLOWAY	8,049	4,693	58.3	3,356	41.7	58.3	41.7	1,337 D
CAMPBELL	32,078	14,690	45.8	17,388	54.2	45.8	54.2	2,698 R
CARLISLE	2,748	1,770	64.4	978	35.6	64.4	35.6	792 D
CARROLL	3,360	2,225	66.2	1,135	33.8	66.2	33.8	1,090 D
CARTER	8,435	3,479	41.2	4,956	58.8	41.2	58.8	1,477 R
CASEY	6,224	1,413	22.7	4,811	77.3	22.7	77.3	3,398 R
CHRISTIAN	12,125	6,874	56.7	5,251	43.3	56.7	43.3	1,623 D
CLARK	6,341	3,024	47.7	3,317	52.3	47.7	52.3	293 R
CLAY	6,303	1,381	21.9	4,922	78.1	21.9	78.1	3,541 R
CLINTON	4,190	666	15.9	3,524	84.1	15.9	84.1	2,858 R
CRITTENDEN	4,089	1,319	32.3	2,770	67.7	32.3	67.7	1,451 R
CUMBERLAND	3,537	840	23.7	2,697	76.3	23.7	76.3	1,857 R
DAVIESS	23,231	9,846	42.4	13,385	57.6	42.4	57.6	3,539 R
EDMONSON	3,960	1,076	27.2	2,884	72.8	27.2	72.8	1,808 R
ELLIOTT	2,523	1,734	68.7	789	31.3	68.7	31.3	945 D
ESTILL	4,993	1,755	35.1	3,238	64.9	35.1	64.9	1,483 R
FAYETTE	41,647	16,478	39.6	25,169	60.4	39.6	60.4	8,691 R
FLEMING	4,993	2,216	44.4	2,777	55.6	44.4	55.6	561 R
FLOYD	14,886	9,876	66.3	5,010	33.7	66.3	33.7	4,866 D
FRANKLIN	11,794	7,052	59.8	4,742	40.2	59.8	40.2	2,310 D
FULTON	4,275	2,708	63.3	1,567	36.7	63.3	36.7	1,141 D
GALLATIN	1,784	1,028	57.6	756	42.4	57.6	42.4	272 D
GARRARD	4,539	1,780	39.2	2,759	60.8	39.2	60.8	979 R
GRANT	4,062	1,899	46.8	2,163	53.2	46.8	53.2	264 R
GRAVES	12,543	7,689	61.3	4,854	38.7	61.3	38.7	2,835 D
GRAYSON	7,162	2,355	32.9	4,807	67.1	32.9	67.1	2,452 R
GREEN	5,186	1,580	30.5	3,606	69.5	30.5	69.5	2,026 R
GREENUP	11,346	5,245	46.2	6,101	53.8	46.2	53.8	856 R
HANCOCK	2,506	1,018	40.6	1,488	59.4	40.6	59.4	470 R
HARDIN	11,332	5,141	45.4	6,191	54.6	45.4	54.6	1,050 R
HARLAN	16,696	9,211	55.2	7,485	44.8	55.2	44.8	1,726 D
HARRISON	5,787	3,481	60.2	2,306	39.8	60.2	39.8	1,175 D
HART	6,739	3,129	46.4	3,610	53.6	46.4	53.6	481 R
HENDERSON	10,867	5,565	51.2	5,302	48.8	51.2	48.8	263 D
HENRY	4,683	2,969	63.4	1,714	36.6	63.4	36.6	1,255 D
HICKMAN	3,144	2,176	69.2	968	30.8	69.2	30.8	1,208 D
HOPKINS	12,010	6,436	53.6	5,574	46.4	53.6	46.4	862 D
JACKSON	4,342	419	9.6	3,923	90.4	9.6	90.4	3,504 R
JEFFERSON	235,755	117,180	49.7	118,575	50.3	49.7	50.3	1,395 R
JESSAMINE	4,809	2,022	42.0	2,787	58.0	42.0	58.0	765 R
JOHNSON	7,939	2,622	33.0	5,317	67.0	33.0	67.0	2,695 R
KENTON	41,323	19,466	47.1	21,857	52.9	47.1	52.9	2,391 R
KNOTT	5,369	3,957	73.7	1,412	26.3	73.7	26.3	2,545 D
KNOX	8,770	2,956	33.7	5,814	66.3	33.7	66.3	2,858 R
LARUE	4,381	1,713	39.1	2,668	60.9	39.1	60.9	955 R
LAUREL	9,794	2,309	23.6	7,485	76.4	23.6	76.4	5,176 R
LAWRENCE	5,540	2,510	45.3	3,030	54.7	45.3	54.7	520 R
LEE	2,970	958	32.3	2,012	67.7	32.3	67.7	1,054 R

6

PRESIDENT — 1960

County	Total Vote	Democratic Total	Per Cent	Republican Total	Per Cent	Per Cent of Two-Party Vote Dem	Rep	Dem-Rep Plurality
LESLIE	4,689	795	17.0	3,894	83.0	17.0	83.0	3,099 R
LETCHER	8,666	4,258	49.1	4,408	50.9	49.1	50.9	150 R
LEWIS	5,498	1,682	30.6	3,816	69.4	30.6	69.4	2,134 R
LINCOLN	6,128	2,381	38.9	3,747	61.1	38.9	61.1	1,366 R
LIVINGSTON	3,157	1,518	48.1	1,639	51.9	48.1	51.9	121 R
LOGAN	8,836	4,719	53.4	4,117	46.6	53.4	46.6	602 D
LYON	2,403	1,379	57.4	1,024	42.6	57.4	42.6	355 D
MADISON	12,313	5,621	45.7	6,692	54.3	45.7	54.3	1,071 R
MAGOFFIN	5,207	2,471	47.5	2,736	52.5	47.5	52.5	265 R
MARION	6,495	4,292	66.1	2,203	33.9	66.1	33.9	2,089 D
MARSHALL	6,872	3,484	50.7	3,388	49.3	50.7	49.3	96 D
MARTIN	3,925	1,116	28.4	2,809	71.6	28.4	71.6	1,693 R
MASON	7,487	3,153	42.1	4,334	57.9	42.1	57.9	1,181 R
MC CRACKEN	22,228	12,539	56.4	9,689	43.6	56.4	43.6	2,850 D
MC CREARY	4,595	924	20.1	3,671	79.9	20.1	79.9	2,747 R
MC LEAN	3,985	1,716	43.1	2,269	56.9	43.1	56.9	553 R
MEADE	4,211	2,385	56.6	1,826	43.4	56.6	43.4	559 D
MENIFEE	1,806	989	54.8	817	45.2	54.8	45.2	172 D
MERCER	6,282	2,713	43.2	3,569	56.8	43.2	56.8	856 R
METCALFE	3,699	1,553	42.0	2,146	58.0	42.0	58.0	593 R
MONROE	5,307	970	18.3	4,337	81.7	18.3	81.7	3,367 R
MONTGOMERY	5,080	2,629	51.8	2,451	48.2	51.8	48.2	178 D
MORGAN	4,628	2,910	62.9	1,718	37.1	62.9	37.1	1,192 D
MUHLENBERG	10,395	4,427	42.6	5,968	57.4	42.6	57.4	1,541 R
NELSON	7,734	4,713	60.9	3,021	39.1	60.9	39.1	1,692 D
NICHOLAS	2,513	1,455	57.9	1,058	42.1	57.9	42.1	397 D
OHIO	7,650	2,420	31.6	5,230	68.4	31.6	68.4	2,810 R
OLDHAM	4,181	1,960	46.9	2,221	53.1	46.9	53.1	261 R
OWEN	3,658	2,446	66.9	1,212	33.1	66.9	33.1	1,234 D
OWSLEY	2,515	346	13.8	2,169	86.2	13.8	86.2	1,823 R
PENDLETON	3,884	1,497	38.5	2,387	61.5	38.5	61.5	890 R
PERRY	10,725	4,971	46.3	5,754	53.7	46.3	53.7	783 R
PIKE	22,995	13,039	56.7	9,956	43.3	56.7	43.3	3,083 D
POWELL	2,630	1,122	42.7	1,508	57.3	42.7	57.3	386 R
PULASKI	14,996	3,097	20.7	11,899	79.3	20.7	79.3	8,802 R
ROBERTSON	1,246	652	52.3	594	47.7	52.3	47.7	58 D
ROCKCASTLE	5,123	1,141	22.3	3,982	77.7	22.3	77.7	2,841 R
ROWAN	4,970	2,412	48.5	2,558	51.5	48.5	51.5	146 R
RUSSELL	4,866	1,230	25.3	3,636	74.7	25.3	74.7	2,406 R
SCOTT	4,798	2,598	54.1	2,200	45.9	54.1	45.9	398 D
SHELBY	6,756	3,822	56.6	2,934	43.4	56.6	43.4	888 D
SIMPSON	4,569	2,642	57.8	1,927	42.2	57.8	42.2	715 D
SPENCER	2,182	1,048	48.0	1,134	52.0	48.0	52.0	86 R
TAYLOR	6,855	2,186	31.9	4,669	68.1	31.9	68.1	2,483 R
TODD	4,673	2,827	60.5	1,846	39.5	60.5	39.5	981 D
TRIGG	3,911	2,411	61.6	1,500	38.4	61.6	38.4	911 D
TRIMBLE	2,330	1,587	68.1	743	31.9	68.1	31.9	844 D
UNION	5,246	3,457	65.9	1,789	34.1	65.9	34.1	1,668 D
WARREN	16,531	7,457	45.1	9,074	54.9	45.1	54.9	1,617 R
WASHINGTON	5,023	2,391	47.6	2,632	52.4	47.6	52.4	241 R
WAYNE	5,937	1,964	33.1	3,973	66.9	33.1	66.9	2,009 R
WEBSTER	5,677	3,179	56.0	2,498	44.0	56.0	44.0	681 D
WHITLEY	10,514	2,961	28.2	7,553	71.8	28.2	71.8	4,592 R
WOLFE	2,813	1,554	55.2	1,259	44.8	55.2	44.8	295 D
WOODFORD	4,177	1,950	46.7	2,227	53.3	46.7	53.3	277 R
TOTAL	1,124,462	521,855	46.4	602,607	53.6	46.4	53.6	80,752 R

DEMOCRAT: John F. Kennedy
REPUBLICAN: Richard M. Nixon

County	Total Vote	Democratic		Republican		Per Cent of Two-Party Vote		Dem-Rep Plurality
		Total	Per Cent	Total	Per Cent	Dem	Rep	
ADAIR	6,202	2,703	43.6	3,499	56.4	43.6	56.4	796 R
ALLEN	5,689	2,244	39.4	3,445	60.6	39.4	60.6	1,201 R
ANDERSON	4,305	2,481	57.6	1,824	42.4	57.6	42.4	657 D
BALLARD	5,038	3,945	78.3	1,093	21.7	78.3	21.7	2,852 D
BARREN	9,430	5,482	58.1	3,948	41.9	58.1	41.9	1,534 D
BATH	4,412	2,437	55.2	1,975	44.8	55.2	44.8	462 D
BELL	8,923	2,273	25.5	6,650	74.5	25.5	74.5	4,377 R
BOONE	4,435	3,453	77.9	982	22.1	77.9	22.1	2,471 D
BOURBON	9,456	5,416	57.3	4,040	42.7	57.3	42.7	1,376 D
BOYD	11,350	4,869	42.9	6,481	57.1	42.9	57.1	1,612 R
BOYLE	7,282	4,068	55.9	3,214	44.1	55.9	44.1	854 D
BRACKEN	4,388	2,571	58.6	1,817	41.4	58.6	41.4	754 D
BREATHITT	5,276	2,860	54.2	2,416	45.8	54.2	45.8	444 D
BRECKINRIDGE	8,001	3,668	45.8	4,333	54.2	45.8	54.2	665 R
BULLITT	3,928	2,543	64.7	1,385	35.3	64.7	35.3	1,158 D
BUTLER	5,437	1,353	24.9	4,084	75.1	24.9	75.1	2,731 R
CALDWELL	5,661	2,724	48.1	2,937	51.9	48.1	51.9	213 R
CALLOWAY	6,025	4,536	75.3	1,489	24.7	75.3	24.7	3,047 D
CAMPBELL	22,829	9,927	43.5	12,902	56.5	43.5	56.5	2,975 R
CARLISLE	3,353	2,673	79.7	680	20.3	79.7	20.3	1,993 D
CARROLL	4,094	3,208	78.4	886	21.6	78.4	21.6	2,322 D
CARTER	7,307	2,749	37.6	4,558	62.4	37.6	62.4	1,809 R
CASEY	5,439	1,920	35.3	3,519	64.7	35.3	64.7	1,599 R
CHRISTIAN	15,917	7,205	45.3	8,712	54.7	45.3	54.7	1,507 R
CLARK	7,869	4,779	60.7	3,090	39.3	60.7	39.3	1,689 D
CLAY	4,910	951	19.4	3,959	80.6	19.4	80.6	3,008 R
CLINTON	2,753	429	15.6	2,324	84.4	15.6	84.4	1,895 R
CRITTENDEN	5,240	2,124	40.5	3,116	59.5	40.5	59.5	992 R
CUMBERLAND	3,256	923	28.3	2,333	71.7	28.3	71.7	1,410 R
DAVIESS	17,211	9,667	56.2	7,544	43.8	56.2	43.8	2,123 D
EDMONSON	3,496	1,165	33.3	2,331	66.7	33.3	66.7	1,166 R
ELLIOTT	2,585	1,748	67.6	837	32.4	67.6	32.4	911 D
ESTILL	4,346	1,811	41.7	2,535	58.3	41.7	58.3	724 R
FAYETTE	23,926	12,797	53.5	11,129	46.5	53.5	46.5	1,668 D
FLEMING	6,430	3,474	54.0	2,956	46.0	54.0	46.0	518 D
FLOYD	6,369	3,577	56.2	2,792	43.8	56.2	43.8	785 D
FRANKLIN	8,559	5,821	68.0	2,738	32.0	68.0	32.0	3,083 D
FULTON	5,180	3,816	73.7	1,364	26.3	73.7	26.3	2,452 D
GALLATIN	2,312	1,780	77.0	532	23.0	77.0	23.0	1,248 D
GARRARD	5,414	2,432	44.9	2,982	55.1	44.9	55.1	550 R
GRANT	4,280	2,668	62.3	1,612	37.7	62.3	37.7	1,056 D
GRAVES	12,178	8,963	73.6	3,215	26.4	73.6	26.4	5,748 D
GRAYSON	6,870	2,814	41.0	4,056	59.0	41.0	59.0	1,242 R
GREEN	4,013	1,714	42.7	2,299	57.3	42.7	57.3	585 R
GREENUP	5,822	2,724	46.8	3,098	53.2	46.8	53.2	374 R
HANCOCK	2,825	1,381	48.9	1,444	51.1	48.9	51.1	63 R
HARDIN	8,669	5,345	61.7	3,324	38.3	61.7	38.3	2,021 D
HARLAN	9,231	1,798	19.5	7,433	80.5	19.5	80.5	5,635 R
HARRISON	7,140	4,760	66.7	2,380	33.3	66.7	33.3	2,380 D
HART	6,150	2,932	47.7	3,218	52.3	47.7	52.3	286 R
HENDERSON	11,328	7,167	63.3	4,161	36.7	63.3	36.7	3,006 D
HENRY	6,813	4,621	67.8	2,192	32.2	67.8	32.2	2,429 D
HICKMAN	3,901	3,045	78.1	856	21.9	78.1	21.9	2,189 D
HOPKINS	14,449	7,785	53.9	6,664	46.1	53.9	46.1	1,121 D
JACKSON	3,404	261	7.7	3,143	92.3	7.7	92.3	2,882 R
JEFFERSON	123,471	54,710	44.3	68,761	55.7	44.3	55.7	14,051 R
JESSAMINE	5,533	3,195	57.7	2,338	42.3	57.7	42.3	857 D
JOHNSON	5,984	1,677	28.0	4,307	72.0	28.0	72.0	2,630 R
KENTON	27,913	13,398	48.0	14,515	52.0	48.0	52.0	1,117 R
KNOTT	3,044	2,247	73.8	797	26.2	73.8	26.2	1,450 D
KNOX	6,679	1,520	22.8	5,159	77.2	22.8	77.2	3,639 R
LARUE	4,181	2,355	56.3	1,826	43.7	56.3	43.7	529 D
LAUREL	5,823	1,591	27.3	4,232	72.7	27.3	72.7	2,641 R
LAWRENCE	5,365	2,545	47.4	2,820	52.6	47.4	52.6	275 R
LEE	3,045	1,233	40.5	1,812	59.5	40.5	59.5	579 R

8

County	Total Vote	Democratic		Republican		Per Cent of Two-Party Vote		Dem-Rep Plurality
		Total	Per Cent	Total	Per Cent	Dem	Rep	
LESLIE	2,669	137	5.1	2,532	94.9	5.1	94.9	2,395 R
LETCHER	6,172	1,923	31.2	4,249	68.8	31.2	68.8	2,326 R
LEWIS	5,674	1,545	27.2	4,129	72.8	27.2	72.8	2,584 R
LINCOLN	7,487	3,772	50.4	3,715	49.6	50.4	49.6	57 D
LIVINGSTON	3,695	1,917	51.9	1,778	48.1	51.9	48.1	139 D
LOGAN	10,020	6,086	60.7	3,934	39.3	60.7	39.3	2,152 D
LYON	3,223	1,966	61.0	1,257	39.0	61.0	39.0	709 D
MADISON	11,613	5,629	48.5	5,984	51.5	48.5	51.5	355 R
MAGOFFIN	3,637	1,331	36.6	2,306	63.4	36.6	63.4	975 R
MARION	6,163	3,750	60.8	2,413	39.2	60.8	39.2	1,337 D
MARSHALL	5,400	3,535	65.5	1,865	34.5	65.5	34.5	1,670 D
MARTIN	1,997	322	16.1	1,675	83.9	16.1	83.9	1,353 R
MASON	8,417	4,663	55.4	3,754	44.6	55.4	44.6	909 D
MC CRACKEN	14,503	8,405	58.0	6,098	42.0	58.0	42.0	2,307 D
MC CREARY	3,362	513	15.3	2,849	84.7	15.3	84.7	2,336 R
MC LEAN	5,151	2,752	53.4	2,399	46.6	53.4	46.6	353 D
MEADE	3,637	2,185	60.1	1,452	39.9	60.1	39.9	733 D
MENIFEE	1,708	1,133	66.3	575	33.7	66.3	33.7	558 D
MERCER	6,376	3,610	56.6	2,766	43.4	56.6	43.4	844 D
METCALFE	3,244	1,442	44.5	1,802	55.5	44.5	55.5	360 R
MONROE	4,486	1,100	24.5	3,386	75.5	24.5	75.5	2,286 R
MONTGOMERY	5,209	3,052	58.6	2,157	41.4	58.6	41.4	895 D
MORGAN	5,112	3,342	65.4	1,770	34.6	65.4	34.6	1,572 D
MUHLENBERG	11,360	4,775	42.0	6,585	58.0	42.0	58.0	1,810 R
NELSON	7,973	5,051	63.4	2,922	36.6	63.4	36.6	2,129 D
NICHOLAS	4,433	2,945	66.4	1,488	33.6	66.4	33.6	1,457 D
OHIO	9,296	3,974	42.7	5,322	57.3	42.7	57.3	1,348 R
OLDHAM	3,644	2,634	72.3	1,010	27.7	72.3	27.7	1,624 D
OWEN	5,631	4,591	81.5	1,040	18.5	81.5	18.5	3,551 D
OWSLEY	2,153	254	11.8	1,899	88.2	11.8	88.2	1,645 R
PENDLETON	4,694	2,587	55.1	2,107	44.9	55.1	44.9	480 D
PERRY	6,341	2,161	34.1	4,180	65.9	34.1	65.9	2,019 R
PIKE	13,285	5,520	41.6	7,765	58.4	41.6	58.4	2,245 R
POWELL	1,850	1,025	55.4	825	44.6	55.4	44.6	200 D
PULASKI	10,923	3,713	34.0	7,210	66.0	34.0	66.0	3,497 R
ROBERTSON	1,548	935	60.4	613	39.6	60.4	39.6	322 D
ROCKCASTLE	4,946	1,420	28.7	3,526	71.3	28.7	71.3	2,106 R
ROWAN	2,792	1,254	44.9	1,538	55.1	44.9	55.1	284 R
RUSSELL	3,694	1,140	30.9	2,554	69.1	30.9	69.1	1,414 R
SCOTT	7,595	4,958	65.3	2,637	34.7	65.3	34.7	2,321 D
SHELBY	8,823	5,411	61.3	3,412	38.7	61.3	38.7	1,999 D
SIMPSON	4,865	3,198	65.7	1,667	34.3	65.7	34.3	1,531 D
SPENCER	3,236	2,131	65.9	1,105	34.1	65.9	34.1	1,026 D
TAYLOR	4,841	2,366	48.9	2,475	51.1	48.9	51.1	109 R
TODD	5,926	3,278	55.3	2,648	44.7	55.3	44.7	630 D
TRIGG	5,442	3,044	55.9	2,398	44.1	55.9	44.1	646 D
TRIMBLE	2,419	2,056	85.0	363	15.0	85.0	15.0	1,693 D
UNION	6,803	4,880	71.7	1,923	28.3	71.7	28.3	2,957 D
WARREN	12,691	7,261	57.2	5,430	42.8	57.2	42.8	1,831 D
WASHINGTON	5,466	2,592	47.4	2,874	52.6	47.4	52.6	282 R
WAYNE	4,780	1,819	38.1	2,961	61.9	38.1	61.9	1,142 R
WEBSTER	8,328	4,812	57.8	3,516	42.2	57.8	42.2	1,296 D
WHITLEY	8,719	1,550	17.8	7,169	82.2	17.8	82.2	5,619 R
WOLFE	2,390	1,470	61.5	920	38.5	61.5	38.5	550 D
WOODFORD	5,484	3,278	59.8	2,206	40.2	59.8	40.2	1,072 D
TOTAL	903,470	449,244	49.7	454,226	50.3	49.7	50.3	4,982 R

DEMOCRAT: J. C. W. Beckham
REPUBLICAN: R. P. Ernst

County	Total Vote	A. O. Stanley		John J. Howe	
		Total	Per Cent	Total	Per Cent
ADAIR	433	267	61.7	166	38.3
ALLEN	534	260	48.7	274	51.3
ANDERSON	919	513	55.8	406	44.2
BALLARD	841	345	41.0	496	59.0
BARREN	1,437	600	41.8	837	58.2
BATH	1,006	664	66.0	342	34.0
BELL	563	360	63.9	203	36.1
BOONE	1,376	326	23.7	1,050	76.3
BOURBON	2,809	1,601	57.0	1,208	43.0
BOYD	1,980	936	47.3	1,044	52.7
BOYLE	1,441	825	57.3	616	42.7
BRACKEN	947	272	28.7	675	71.3
BREATHITT	1,456	1,224	84.1	232	15.9
BRECKINRIDGE	753	566	75.2	187	24.8
BULLITT	550	350	63.6	200	36.4
BUTLER	376	268	71.3	108	28.7
CALDWELL	999	460	46.0	539	54.0
CALLOWAY	726	297	40.9	429	59.1
CAMPBELL	3,194	2,661	83.3	533	16.7
CARLISLE	581	296	50.9	285	49.1
CARROLL	2,042	392	19.2	1,650	80.8
CARTER	1,705	790	46.3	915	53.7
CASEY	302	206	68.2	96	31.8
CHRISTIAN	1,728	783	45.3	945	54.7
CLARK	1,682	761	45.2	921	54.8
CLAY	191	128	67.0	63	33.0
CLINTON	142	103	72.5	39	27.5
CRITTENDEN	579	184	31.8	395	68.2
CUMBERLAND	185	118	63.8	67	36.2
DAVIESS	4,059	2,252	55.5	1,807	44.5
EDMONSON	268	214	79.9	54	20.1
ELLIOTT	1,433	927	64.7	506	35.3
ESTILL	561	381	67.9	180	32.1
FAYETTE	5,489	3,331	60.7	2,158	39.3
FLEMING	1,432	862	60.2	570	39.8
FLOYD	1,325	1,157	87.3	168	12.7
FRANKLIN	2,854	1,637	57.4	1,217	42.6
FULTON	1,100	787	71.5	313	28.5
GALLATIN	905	201	22.2	704	77.8
GARRARD	839	672	80.1	167	19.9
GRANT	910	324	35.6	586	64.4
GRAVES	1,690	842	49.8	848	50.2
GRAYSON	771	382	49.5	389	50.5
GREEN	247	161	65.2	86	34.8
GREENUP	582	461	79.2	121	20.8
HANCOCK	251	128	51.0	123	49.0
HARDIN	1,220	495	40.6	725	59.4
HARLAN	516	421	81.6	95	18.4
HARRISON	2,245	1,020	45.4	1,225	54.6
HART	725	397	54.8	328	45.2
HENDERSON	4,011	1,801	44.9	2,210	55.1
HENRY	2,038	787	38.6	1,251	61.4
HICKMAN	579	287	49.6	292	50.4
HOPKINS	4,234	2,267	53.5	1,967	46.5
JACKSON	45	35	77.8	10	22.2
JEFFERSON	13,780	11,902	86.4	1,878	13.6
JESSAMINE	1,440	762	52.9	678	47.1
JOHNSON	429	337	78.6	92	21.4
KENTON	6,566	4,812	73.3	1,754	26.7
KNOTT	544	412	75.7	132	24.3
KNOX	305	186	61.0	119	39.0
LARUE	305	194	63.6	111	36.4
LAUREL	440	348	79.1	92	20.9
LAWRENCE	1,535	781	50.9	754	49.1
LEE	253	189	74.7	64	25.3

County	Total Vote	A. O. Stanley Total	A. O. Stanley Per Cent	John J. Howe Total	John J. Howe Per Cent
LESLIE	54	45	83.3	9	16.7
LETCHER	378	290	76.7	88	23.3
LEWIS	586	327	55.8	259	44.2
LINCOLN	1,082	565	52.2	517	47.8
LIVINGSTON	573	174	30.4	399	69.6
LOGAN	2,522	1,502	59.6	1,020	40.4
LYON	584	265	45.4	319	54.6
MADISON	1,462	973	66.6	489	33.4
MAGOFFIN	599	565	94.3	34	5.7
MARION	816	470	57.6	346	42.4
MARSHALL	1,385	802	57.9	583	42.1
MARTIN	81	60	74.1	21	25.9
MASON	1,658	1,121	67.6	537	32.4
MC CRACKEN	3,039	1,424	46.9	1,615	53.1
MC CREARY	105	71	67.6	34	32.4
MC LEAN	873	442	50.6	431	49.4
MEADE	338	191	56.5	147	43.5
MENIFEE	380	248	65.3	132	34.7
MERCER	1,120	355	31.7	765	68.3
METCALFE	323	259	80.2	64	19.8
MONROE	249	163	65.5	86	34.5
MONTGOMERY	1,481	580	39.2	901	60.8
MORGAN	2,696	1,883	69.8	813	30.2
MUHLENBERG	1,924	1,190	61.9	734	38.1
NELSON	1,256	992	79.0	264	21.0
NICHOLAS	1,523	846	55.5	677	44.5
OHIO	679	372	54.8	307	45.2
OLDHAM	1,052	353	33.6	699	66.4
OWEN	1,705	750	44.0	955	56.0
OWSLEY	73	48	65.8	25	34.2
PENDLETON	688	301	43.8	387	56.3
PERRY	618	447	72.3	171	27.7
PIKE	1,614	1,487	92.1	127	7.9
POWELL	300	212	70.7	88	29.3
PULASKI	802	343	42.8	459	57.2
ROBERTSON	404	157	38.9	247	61.1
ROCKCASTLE	349	284	81.4	65	18.6
ROWAN	382	262	68.6	120	31.4
RUSSELL	234	173	73.9	61	26.1
SCOTT	1,687	745	44.2	942	55.8
SHELBY	1,683	619	36.8	1,064	63.2
SIMPSON	718	460	64.1	258	35.9
SPENCER	631	217	34.4	414	65.6
TAYLOR	454	230	50.7	224	49.3
TODD	893	397	44.5	496	55.5
TRIGG	826	375	45.4	451	54.6
TRIMBLE	832	249	29.9	583	70.1
UNION	1,464	942	64.3	522	35.7
WARREN	2,576	1,230	47.7	1,346	52.3
WASHINGTON	534	408	76.4	126	23.6
WAYNE	483	356	73.7	127	26.3
WEBSTER	1,811	865	47.8	946	52.2
WHITLEY	467	410	87.8	57	12.2
WOLFE	615	471	76.6	144	23.4
WOODFORD	1,167	612	52.4	555	47.6
TOTAL	150,236	88,286	58.8	61,950	41.2

County	Total Vote	Fred M. Sackett Total	Per Cent	Burgess Bethurum Total	Per Cent
ADAIR	334	249	74.6	85	25.4
ALLEN	476	357	75.0	119	25.0
ANDERSON	226	131	58.0	95	42.0
BALLARD	95	88	92.6	7	7.4
BARREN	439	292	66.5	147	33.5
BATH	301	195	64.8	106	35.2
BELL	2,160	1,374	63.6	786	36.4
BOONE	112	61	54.5	51	45.5
BOURBON	906	299	33.0	607	67.0
BOYD	1,327	624	47.0	703	53.0
BOYLE	966	329	34.1	637	65.9
BRACKEN	164	97	59.1	67	40.9
BREATHITT	282	168	59.6	114	40.4
BRECKINRIDGE	584	546	93.5	38	6.5
BULLITT	76	71	93.4	5	6.6
BUTLER	420	152	36.2	268	63.8
CALDWELL	424	279	65.8	145	34.2
CALLOWAY	175	149	85.1	26	14.9
CAMPBELL	1,308	848	64.8	460	35.2
CARLISLE	70	65	92.9	5	7.1
CARROLL	163	92	56.4	71	43.6
CARTER	612	455	74.3	157	25.7
CASEY	342	268	78.4	74	21.6
CHRISTIAN	867	754	87.0	113	13.0
CLARK	309	125	40.5	184	59.5
CLAY	1,595	1,118	70.1	477	29.9
CLINTON	1,050	390	37.1	660	62.9
CRITTENDEN	409	346	84.6	63	15.4
CUMBERLAND	439	261	59.5	178	40.5
DAVIESS	471	409	86.8	62	13.2
EDMONSON	297	131	44.1	166	55.9
ELLIOTT	89	77	86.5	12	13.5
ESTILL	292	106	36.3	186	63.7
FAYETTE	1,319	903	68.5	416	31.5
FLEMING	355	250	70.4	105	29.6
FLOYD	1,483	1,372	92.5	111	7.5
FRANKLIN	525	403	76.8	122	23.2
FULTON	59	48	81.4	11	18.6
GALLATIN	175	136	77.7	39	22.3
GARRARD	307	126	41.0	181	59.0
GRANT	154	113	73.4	41	26.6
GRAVES	377	293	77.7	84	22.3
GRAYSON	352	324	92.0	28	8.0
GREEN	191	163	85.3	28	14.7
GREENUP	573	244	42.6	329	57.4
HANCOCK	101	84	83.2	17	16.8
HARDIN	312	284	91.0	28	9.0
HARLAN	5,400	4,327	80.1	1,073	19.9
HARRISON	339	203	59.9	136	40.1
HART	277	170	61.4	107	38.6
HENDERSON	513	439	85.6	74	14.4
HENRY	309	235	76.1	74	23.9
HICKMAN	60	49	81.7	11	18.3
HOPKINS	564	443	78.5	121	21.5
JACKSON	942	528	56.1	414	43.9
JEFFERSON	16,315	14,914	91.4	1,401	8.6
JESSAMINE	840	672	80.0	168	20.0
JOHNSON	1,472	1,147	77.9	325	22.1
KENTON	827	649	78.5	178	21.5
KNOTT	227	201	88.5	26	11.5
KNOX	2,187	1,654	75.6	533	24.4
LARUE	132	113	85.6	19	14.4
LAUREL	1,381	487	35.3	894	64.7
LAWRENCE	807	560	69.4	247	30.6
LEE	239	99	41.4	140	58.6

12

County	Total Vote	Fred M. Sackett Total	Fred M. Sackett Per Cent	Burgess Bethurum Total	Burgess Bethurum Per Cent
LESLIE	1,014	894	88.2	120	11.8
LETCHER	842	502	59.6	340	40.4
LEWIS	515	301	58.4	214	41.6
LINCOLN	710	339	47.7	371	52.3
LIVINGSTON	173	117	67.6	56	32.4
LOGAN	297	240	80.8	57	19.2
LYON	201	182	90.5	19	9.5
MADISON	1,257	761	60.5	496	39.5
MAGOFFIN	1,499	1,275	85.1	224	14.9
MARION	267	230	86.1	37	13.9
MARSHALL	191	152	79.6	39	20.4
MARTIN	815	666	81.7	149	18.3
MASON	605	553	91.4	52	8.6
MC CRACKEN	524	404	77.1	120	22.9
MC CREARY	823	350	42.5	473	57.5
MC LEAN	168	136	81.0	32	19.0
MEADE	77	66	85.7	11	14.3
MENIFEE	85	37	43.5	48	56.5
MERCER	332	243	73.2	89	26.8
METCALFE	140	73	52.1	67	47.9
MONROE	686	466	67.9	220	32.1
MONTGOMERY	358	170	47.5	188	52.5
MORGAN	405	316	78.0	89	22.0
MUHLENBERG	639	523	81.8	116	18.2
NELSON	303	272	89.8	31	10.2
NICHOLAS	340	236	69.4	104	30.6
OHIO	573	489	85.3	84	14.7
OLDHAM	129	100	77.5	29	22.5
OWEN	184	107	58.2	77	41.8
OWSLEY	605	357	59.0	248	41.0
PENDLETON	166	144	86.7	22	13.3
PERRY	2,109	1,717	81.4	392	18.6
PIKE	2,997	2,536	84.6	461	15.4
POWELL	82	61	74.4	21	25.6
PULASKI	3,005	846	28.2	2,159	71.8
ROBERTSON	104	73	70.2	31	29.8
ROCKCASTLE	1,644	151	9.2	1,493	90.8
ROWAN	181	86	47.5	95	52.5
RUSSELL	724	481	66.4	243	33.6
SCOTT	599	478	79.8	121	20.2
SHELBY	675	547	81.0	128	19.0
SIMPSON	108	84	77.8	24	22.2
SPENCER	114	95	83.3	19	16.7
TAYLOR	275	264	96.0	11	4.0
TODD	115	74	64.3	41	35.7
TRIGG	420	346	82.4	74	17.6
TRIMBLE	43	35	81.4	8	18.6
UNION	109	93	85.3	16	14.7
WARREN	811	447	55.1	364	44.9
WASHINGTON	163	144	88.3	19	11.7
WAYNE	817	402	49.2	415	50.8
WEBSTER	335	231	69.0	104	31.0
WHITLEY	1,435	512	35.7	923	64.3
WOLFE	116	69	59.5	47	40.5
WOODFORD	353	174	49.3	179	50.7
TOTAL	89,151	63,186	70.9	25,965	29.1

County	Total Vote	Democratic		Republican		Per Cent of Two-Party Vote		Dem-Rep Plurality
		Total	Per Cent	Total	Per Cent	Dem	Rep	
ADAIR	5,062	2,285	45.1	2,777	54.9	45.1	54.9	492 R
ALLEN	5,468	2,321	42.4	3,147	57.6	42.4	57.6	826 R
ANDERSON	3,477	1,983	57.0	1,494	43.0	57.0	43.0	489 D
BALLARD	3,853	3,049	79.1	804	20.9	79.1	20.9	2,245 D
BARREN	7,821	4,282	54.8	3,539	45.2	54.8	45.2	743 D
BATH	3,789	2,024	53.4	1,765	46.6	53.4	46.6	259 D
BELL	7,561	2,339	30.9	5,222	69.1	30.9	69.1	2,883 R
BOONE	3,635	2,110	58.0	1,525	42.0	58.0	42.0	585 D
BOURBON	7,806	3,900	50.0	3,906	50.0	50.0	50.0	6 R
BOYD	10,613	4,455	42.0	6,158	58.0	42.0	58.0	1,703 R
BOYLE	6,026	3,285	54.5	2,741	45.5	54.5	45.5	544 D
BRACKEN	3,340	1,430	42.8	1,910	57.2	42.8	57.2	480 R
BREATHITT	4,516	2,821	62.5	1,695	37.5	62.5	37.5	1,126 D
BRECKINRIDGE	7,032	3,106	44.2	3,926	55.8	44.2	55.8	820 R
BULLITT	2,769	1,727	62.4	1,042	37.6	62.4	37.6	685 D
BUTLER	3,775	1,160	30.7	2,615	69.3	30.7	69.3	1,455 R
CALDWELL	4,754	2,137	45.0	2,617	55.0	45.0	55.0	480 R
CALLOWAY	4,726	3,708	78.5	1,018	21.5	78.5	21.5	2,690 D
CAMPBELL	22,089	10,135	45.9	11,954	54.1	45.9	54.1	1,819 R
CARLISLE	2,695	2,223	82.5	472	17.5	82.5	17.5	1,751 D
CARROLL	3,503	2,150	61.4	1,353	38.6	61.4	38.6	797 D
CARTER	6,980	2,561	36.7	4,419	63.3	36.7	63.3	1,858 R
CASEY	4,875	1,744	35.8	3,131	64.2	35.8	64.2	1,387 R
CHRISTIAN	13,662	6,307	46.2	7,355	53.8	46.2	53.8	1,048 R
CLARK	6,550	3,749	57.2	2,801	42.8	57.2	42.8	948 D
CLAY	4,754	1,115	23.5	3,639	76.5	23.5	76.5	2,524 R
CLINTON	2,595	522	20.1	2,073	79.9	20.1	79.9	1,551 R
CRITTENDEN	4,309	1,762	40.9	2,547	59.1	40.9	59.1	785 R
CUMBERLAND	3,027	866	28.6	2,161	71.4	28.6	71.4	1,295 R
DAVIESS	15,418	8,194	53.1	7,224	46.9	53.1	46.9	970 D
EDMONSON	3,185	1,157	36.3	2,028	63.7	36.3	63.7	871 R
ELLIOTT	2,296	1,673	72.9	623	27.1	72.9	27.1	1,050 D
ESTILL	4,265	2,093	49.1	2,172	50.9	49.1	50.9	79 R
FAYETTE	22,189	9,788	44.1	12,401	55.9	44.1	55.9	2,613 R
FLEMING	5,158	2,529	49.0	2,629	51.0	49.0	51.0	100 R
FLOYD	8,309	4,657	56.0	3,652	44.0	56.0	44.0	1,005 D
FRANKLIN	7,529	4,549	60.4	2,980	39.6	60.4	39.6	1,569 D
FULTON	4,212	3,289	78.1	923	21.9	78.1	21.9	2,366 D
GALLATIN	1,751	942	53.8	809	46.2	53.8	46.2	133 D
GARRARD	4,699	2,057	43.8	2,642	56.2	43.8	56.2	585 R
GRANT	3,381	1,893	56.0	1,488	44.0	56.0	44.0	405 D
GRAVES	9,501	7,133	75.1	2,368	24.9	75.1	24.9	4,765 D
GRAYSON	5,912	2,766	46.8	3,146	53.2	46.8	53.2	380 R
GREEN	3,450	1,458	42.3	1,992	57.7	42.3	57.7	534 R
GREENUP	4,767	2,174	45.6	2,593	54.4	45.6	54.4	419 R
HANCOCK	2,691	1,327	49.3	1,364	50.7	49.3	50.7	37 R
HARDIN	6,985	4,150	59.4	2,835	40.6	59.4	40.6	1,315 D
HARLAN	12,576	2,656	21.1	9,920	78.9	21.1	78.9	7,264 R
HARRISON	6,051	3,758	62.1	2,293	37.9	62.1	37.9	1,465 D
HART	5,528	2,869	51.9	2,659	48.1	51.9	48.1	210 D
HENDERSON	9,029	3,970	44.0	5,059	56.0	44.0	56.0	1,089 R
HENRY	5,556	3,502	63.0	2,054	37.0	63.0	37.0	1,448 D
HICKMAN	2,848	2,213	77.7	635	22.3	77.7	22.3	1,578 D
HOPKINS	11,335	5,753	50.8	5,582	49.2	50.8	49.2	171 D
JACKSON	2,886	278	9.6	2,608	90.4	9.6	90.4	2,330 R
JEFFERSON	112,962	50,630	44.8	62,332	55.2	44.8	55.2	11,702 R
JESSAMINE	4,740	2,310	48.7	2,430	51.3	48.7	51.3	120 R
JOHNSON	4,601	1,519	33.0	3,082	67.0	33.0	67.0	1,563 R
KENTON	26,722	13,729	51.4	12,993	48.6	51.4	48.6	736 D
KNOTT	3,126	2,216	70.9	910	29.1	70.9	29.1	1,306 D
KNOX	5,388	1,672	31.0	3,716	69.0	31.0	69.0	2,044 R
LARUE	3,349	1,948	58.2	1,401	41.8	58.2	41.8	547 D
LAUREL	4,748	1,445	30.4	3,303	69.6	30.4	69.6	1,858 R
LAWRENCE	4,887	2,322	47.5	2,565	52.5	47.5	52.5	243 R
LEE	2,659	1,322	49.7	1,337	50.3	49.7	50.3	15 R

U.S. SENATOR: GENERAL ELECTION — 1924

County	Total Vote	Democratic Total	Democratic Per Cent	Republican Total	Republican Per Cent	Per Cent of Two-Party Vote Dem	Per Cent of Two-Party Vote Rep	Dem-Rep Plurality
LESLIE	2,272	213	9.4	2,059	90.6	9.4	90.6	1,846 R
LETCHER	5,234	2,121	40.5	3,113	59.5	40.5	59.5	992 R
LEWIS	4,491	1,431	31.9	3,060	68.1	31.9	68.1	1,629 R
LINCOLN	6,059	3,047	50.3	3,012	49.7	50.3	49.7	35 D
LIVINGSTON	2,993	1,686	56.3	1,307	43.7	56.3	43.7	379 D
LOGAN	8,510	4,598	54.0	3,912	46.0	54.0	46.0	686 D
LYON	2,677	1,656	61.9	1,021	38.1	61.9	38.1	635 D
MADISON	10,119	4,757	47.0	5,362	53.0	47.0	53.0	605 R
MAGOFFIN	3,958	1,896	47.9	2,062	52.1	47.9	52.1	166 R
MARION	5,004	2,993	59.8	2,011	40.2	59.8	40.2	982 D
MARSHALL	3,935	2,694	68.5	1,241	31.5	68.5	31.5	1,453 D
MARTIN	1,902	372	19.6	1,530	80.4	19.6	80.4	1,158 R
MASON	6,977	3,480	49.9	3,497	50.1	49.9	50.1	17 R
MC CRACKEN	11,820	6,235	52.7	5,585	47.3	52.7	47.3	650 D
MC CREARY	2,851	527	18.5	2,324	81.5	18.5	81.5	1,797 R
MC LEAN	4,197	2,343	55.8	1,854	44.2	55.8	44.2	489 D
MEADE	2,839	1,703	60.0	1,136	40.0	60.0	40.0	567 D
MENIFEE	1,326	862	65.0	464	35.0	65.0	35.0	398 D
MERCER	5,379	2,539	47.2	2,840	52.8	47.2	52.8	301 R
METCALFE	2,695	1,231	45.7	1,464	54.3	45.7	54.3	233 R
MONROE	3,409	940	27.6	2,469	72.4	27.6	72.4	1,529 R
MONTGOMERY	4,297	2,265	52.7	2,032	47.3	52.7	47.3	233 D
MORGAN	5,035	3,246	64.5	1,789	35.5	64.5	35.5	1,457 D
MUHLENBERG	9,369	4,170	44.5	5,199	55.5	44.5	55.5	1,029 R
NELSON	5,913	3,850	65.1	2,063	34.9	65.1	34.9	1,787 D
NICHOLAS	3,575	2,160	60.4	1,415	39.6	60.4	39.6	745 D
OHIO	8,108	3,882	47.9	4,226	52.1	47.9	52.1	344 R
OLDHAM	2,832	1,832	64.7	1,000	35.3	64.7	35.3	832 D
OWEN	4,047	2,996	74.0	1,051	26.0	74.0	26.0	1,945 D
OWSLEY	1,725	307	17.8	1,418	82.2	17.8	82.2	1,111 R
PENDLETON	4,172	1,870	44.8	2,302	55.2	44.8	55.2	432 R
PERRY	6,969	2,594	37.2	4,375	62.8	37.2	62.8	1,781 R
PIKE	12,940	5,871	45.4	7,069	54.6	45.4	54.6	1,198 R
POWELL	1,690	906	53.6	784	46.4	53.6	46.4	122 D
PULASKI	10,057	3,496	34.8	6,561	65.2	34.8	65.2	3,065 R
ROBERTSON	1,173	621	52.9	552	47.1	52.9	47.1	69 D
ROCKCASTLE	3,991	1,306	32.7	2,685	67.3	32.7	67.3	1,379 R
ROWAN	2,372	1,030	43.4	1,342	56.6	43.4	56.6	312 R
RUSSELL	3,476	1,162	33.4	2,314	66.6	33.4	66.6	1,152 R
SCOTT	6,115	3,692	60.4	2,423	39.6	60.4	39.6	1,269 D
SHELBY	7,013	3,933	56.1	3,080	43.9	56.1	43.9	853 D
SIMPSON	3,945	2,632	66.7	1,313	33.3	66.7	33.3	1,319 D
SPENCER	2,235	1,210	54.1	1,025	45.9	54.1	45.9	185 D
TAYLOR	4,243	1,946	45.9	2,297	54.1	45.9	54.1	351 R
TODD	4,610	2,599	56.4	2,011	43.6	56.4	43.6	588 D
TRIGG	4,711	2,546	54.0	2,165	46.0	54.0	46.0	381 D
TRIMBLE	1,988	1,575	79.2	413	20.8	79.2	20.8	1,162 D
UNION	5,411	3,526	65.2	1,885	34.8	65.2	34.8	1,641 D
WARREN	12,488	6,700	53.7	5,788	46.3	53.7	46.3	912 D
WASHINGTON	4,481	2,190	48.9	2,291	51.1	48.9	51.1	101 R
WAYNE	4,410	1,971	44.7	2,439	55.3	44.7	55.3	468 R
WEBSTER	6,629	3,370	50.8	3,259	49.2	50.8	49.2	111 D
WHITLEY	6,409	1,733	27.0	4,676	73.0	27.0	73.0	2,943 R
WOLFE	2,377	1,542	64.9	835	35.1	64.9	35.1	707 D
WOODFORD	4,524	2,355	52.1	2,169	47.9	52.1	47.9	186 D
TOTAL	787,728	381,605	48.4	406,123	51.6	48.4	51.6	24,518 R

DEMOCRAT: A. O. Stanley
REPUBLICAN: Fred M. Sackett

County	Total Vote	Democratic		Republican		Per Cent of Two-Party Vote		Dem-Rep Plurality
		Total	Per Cent	Total	Per Cent	Dem	Rep	
ADAIR	2,819	1,387	49.2	1,432	50.8	49.2	50.8	45 R
ALLEN	3,541	1,538	43.4	2,003	56.6	43.4	56.6	465 R
ANDERSON	2,541	1,611	63.4	930	36.6	63.4	36.6	681 D
BALLARD	2,822	2,321	82.2	501	17.8	82.2	17.8	1,820 D
BARREN	5,692	3,473	61.0	2,219	39.0	61.0	39.0	1,254 D
BATH	2,521	1,484	58.9	1,037	41.1	58.9	41.1	447 D
BELL	5,374	1,370	25.5	4,004	74.5	25.5	74.5	2,634 R
BOONE	2,339	1,749	74.8	590	25.2	74.8	25.2	1,159 D
BOURBON	5,345	2,818	52.7	2,527	47.3	52.7	47.3	291 D
BOYD	6,234	3,265	52.4	2,969	47.6	52.4	47.6	296 D
BOYLE	4,718	2,740	58.1	1,978	41.9	58.1	41.9	762 D
BRACKEN	1,698	1,006	59.2	692	40.8	59.2	40.8	314 D
BREATHITT	2,512	1,718	68.4	794	31.6	68.4	31.6	924 D
BRECKINRIDGE	6,395	3,327	52.0	3,068	48.0	52.0	48.0	259 D
BULLITT	1,552	1,110	71.5	442	28.5	71.5	28.5	668 D
BUTLER	3,115	1,113	35.7	2,002	64.3	35.7	64.3	889 R
CALDWELL	3,192	1,686	52.8	1,506	47.2	52.8	47.2	180 D
CALLOWAY	3,914	3,164	80.8	750	19.2	80.8	19.2	2,414 D
CAMPBELL	14,401	4,738	32.9	9,663	67.1	32.9	67.1	4,925 R
CARLISLE	2,126	1,864	87.7	262	12.3	87.7	12.3	1,602 D
CARROLL	2,885	2,154	74.7	731	25.3	74.7	25.3	1,423 D
CARTER	4,536	1,984	43.7	2,552	56.3	43.7	56.3	568 R
CASEY	2,861	981	34.3	1,880	65.7	34.3	65.7	899 R
CHRISTIAN	9,001	4,327	48.1	4,674	51.9	48.1	51.9	347 R
CLARK	4,354	2,691	61.8	1,663	38.2	61.8	38.2	1,028 D
CLAY	2,453	578	23.6	1,875	76.4	23.6	76.4	1,297 R
CLINTON	1,787	365	20.4	1,422	79.6	20.4	79.6	1,057 R
CRITTENDEN	2,786	1,207	43.3	1,579	56.7	43.3	56.7	372 R
CUMBERLAND	2,041	504	24.7	1,537	75.3	24.7	75.3	1,033 R
DAVIESS	8,707	4,945	56.8	3,762	43.2	56.8	43.2	1,183 D
EDMONSON	2,640	942	35.7	1,698	64.3	35.7	64.3	756 R
ELLIOTT	1,087	846	77.8	241	22.2	77.8	22.2	605 D
ESTILL	3,455	1,750	50.7	1,705	49.3	50.7	49.3	45 D
FAYETTE	12,329	6,237	50.6	6,092	49.4	50.6	49.4	145 D
FLEMING	3,851	2,086	54.2	1,765	45.8	54.2	45.8	321 D
FLOYD	5,461	3,118	57.1	2,343	42.9	57.1	42.9	775 D
FRANKLIN	5,100	3,506	68.7	1,594	31.3	68.7	31.3	1,912 D
FULTON	2,722	2,349	86.3	373	13.7	86.3	13.7	1,976 D
GALLATIN	1,239	879	70.9	360	29.1	70.9	29.1	519 D
GARRARD	3,444	1,605	46.6	1,839	53.4	46.6	53.4	234 R
GRANT	2,315	1,427	61.6	888	38.4	61.6	38.4	539 D
GRAVES	7,473	5,880	78.7	1,593	21.3	78.7	21.3	4,287 D
GRAYSON	4,335	2,069	47.7	2,266	52.3	47.7	52.3	197 R
GREEN	2,552	1,163	45.6	1,389	54.4	45.6	54.4	226 R
GREENUP	3,474	1,881	54.1	1,593	45.9	54.1	45.9	288 D
HANCOCK	1,649	870	52.8	779	47.2	52.8	47.2	91 D
HARDIN	4,463	2,766	62.0	1,697	38.0	62.0	38.0	1,069 D
HARLAN	8,412	1,848	22.0	6,564	78.0	22.0	78.0	4,716 R
HARRISON	4,518	3,136	69.4	1,382	30.6	69.4	30.6	1,754 D
HART	3,187	1,854	58.2	1,333	41.8	58.2	41.8	521 D
HENDERSON	5,129	2,269	44.2	2,860	55.8	44.2	55.8	591 R
HENRY	3,609	2,544	70.5	1,065	29.5	70.5	29.5	1,479 D
HICKMAN	2,241	1,989	88.8	252	11.2	88.8	11.2	1,737 D
HOPKINS	8,132	4,920	60.5	3,212	39.5	60.5	39.5	1,708 D
JACKSON	1,807	208	11.5	1,599	88.5	11.5	88.5	1,391 R
JEFFERSON	95,762	45,145	47.1	50,617	52.9	47.1	52.9	5,472 R
JESSAMINE	3,455	1,934	56.0	1,521	44.0	56.0	44.0	413 D
JOHNSON	2,333	926	39.7	1,407	60.3	39.7	60.3	481 R
KENTON	20,537	8,760	42.7	11,777	57.3	42.7	57.3	3,017 R
KNOTT	2,210	1,775	80.3	435	19.7	80.3	19.7	1,340 D
KNOX	4,336	1,258	29.0	3,078	71.0	29.0	71.0	1,820 R
LARUE	2,408	1,428	59.3	980	40.7	59.3	40.7	448 D
LAUREL	3,397	1,076	31.7	2,321	68.3	31.7	68.3	1,245 R
LAWRENCE	2,807	1,500	53.4	1,307	46.6	53.4	46.6	193 D
LEE	1,661	910	54.8	751	45.2	54.8	45.2	159 D

16

County	Total Vote	Democratic		Republican		Per Cent of Two-Party Vote		Dem-Rep Plurality
		Total	Per Cent	Total	Per Cent	Dem	Rep	
LESLIE	2,007	190	9.5	1,817	90.5	9.5	90.5	1,627 R
LETCHER	4,088	1,112	27.2	2,976	72.8	27.2	72.8	1,864 R
LEWIS	2,891	1,024	35.4	1,867	64.6	35.4	64.6	843 R
LINCOLN	4,406	2,405	54.6	2,001	45.4	54.6	45.4	404 D
LIVINGSTON	1,843	1,195	64.8	648	35.2	64.8	35.2	547 D
LOGAN	6,343	4,019	63.4	2,324	36.6	63.4	36.6	1,695 D
LYON	2,362	1,601	67.8	761	32.2	67.8	32.2	840 D
MADISON	7,137	3,494	49.0	3,643	51.0	49.0	51.0	149 R
MAGOFFIN	2,723	1,297	47.6	1,426	52.4	47.6	52.4	129 R
MARION	3,592	2,351	65.5	1,241	34.5	65.5	34.5	1,110 D
MARSHALL	2,797	2,211	79.0	586	21.0	79.0	21.0	1,625 D
MARTIN	706	174	24.6	532	75.4	24.6	75.4	358 R
MASON	4,596	2,428	52.8	2,168	47.2	52.8	47.2	260 D
MC CRACKEN	6,803	4,627	68.0	2,176	32.0	68.0	32.0	2,451 D
MC CREARY	2,133	411	19.3	1,722	80.7	19.3	80.7	1,311 R
MC LEAN	2,540	1,619	63.7	921	36.3	63.7	36.3	698 D
MEADE	1,866	1,154	61.8	712	38.2	61.8	38.2	442 D
MENIFEE	802	529	66.0	273	34.0	66.0	34.0	256 D
MERCER	4,040	2,447	60.6	1,593	39.4	60.6	39.4	854 D
METCALFE	1,651	883	53.5	768	46.5	53.5	46.5	115 D
MONROE	2,568	791	30.8	1,777	69.2	30.8	69.2	986 R
MONTGOMERY	3,044	1,797	59.0	1,247	41.0	59.0	41.0	550 D
MORGAN	3,260	2,102	64.5	1,158	35.5	64.5	35.5	944 D
MUHLENBERG	6,074	3,282	54.0	2,792	46.0	54.0	46.0	490 D
NELSON	4,074	2,623	64.4	1,451	35.6	64.4	35.6	1,172 D
NICHOLAS	2,765	1,751	63.3	1,014	36.7	63.3	36.7	737 D
OHIO	5,015	2,576	51.4	2,439	48.6	51.4	48.6	137 D
OLDHAM	1,540	1,106	71.8	434	28.2	71.8	28.2	672 D
OWEN	2,961	2,402	81.1	559	18.9	81.1	18.9	1,843 D
OWSLEY	954	192	20.1	762	79.9	20.1	79.9	570 R
PENDLETON	2,833	1,732	61.1	1,101	38.9	61.1	38.9	631 D
PERRY	5,250	1,675	31.9	3,575	68.1	31.9	68.1	1,900 R
PIKE	9,773	4,897	50.1	4,876	49.9	50.1	49.9	21 D
POWELL	1,226	711	58.0	515	42.0	58.0	42.0	196 D
PULASKI	6,717	3,027	45.1	3,690	54.9	45.1	54.9	663 R
ROBERTSON	638	451	70.7	187	29.3	70.7	29.3	264 D
ROCKCASTLE	2,778	1,050	37.8	1,728	62.2	37.8	62.2	678 R
ROWAN	1,246	662	53.1	584	46.9	53.1	46.9	78 D
RUSSELL	2,457	708	28.8	1,749	71.2	28.8	71.2	1,041 R
SCOTT	4,296	2,659	61.9	1,637	38.1	61.9	38.1	1,022 D
SHELBY	4,715	3,041	64.5	1,674	35.5	64.5	35.5	1,367 D
SIMPSON	3,263	2,286	70.1	977	29.9	70.1	29.9	1,309 D
SPENCER	1,142	746	65.3	396	34.7	65.3	34.7	350 D
TAYLOR	2,973	1,528	51.4	1,445	48.6	51.4	48.6	83 D
TODD	3,536	2,246	63.5	1,290	36.5	63.5	36.5	956 D
TRIGG	3,971	2,387	60.1	1,584	39.9	60.1	39.9	803 D
TRIMBLE	1,153	1,016	88.1	137	11.9	88.1	11.9	879 D
UNION	3,105	2,299	74.0	806	26.0	74.0	26.0	1,493 D
WARREN	8,101	5,241	64.7	2,860	35.3	64.7	35.3	2,381 D
WASHINGTON	2,583	1,308	50.6	1,275	49.4	50.6	49.4	33 D
WAYNE	2,674	1,013	37.9	1,661	62.1	37.9	62.1	648 R
WEBSTER	4,387	2,510	57.2	1,877	42.8	57.2	42.8	633 D
WHITLEY	5,136	1,400	27.3	3,736	72.7	27.3	72.7	2,336 R
WOLFE	1,435	1,007	70.2	428	29.8	70.2	29.8	579 D
WOODFORD	2,893	1,532	53.0	1,361	47.0	53.0	47.0	171 D
TOTAL	553,654	286,997	51.8	266,657	48.2	51.8	48.2	20,340 D

DEMOCRAT: Alben W. Barkley
REPUBLICAN: Richard P. Ernst

17

County	Total Vote	Democratic		Republican		Per Cent of Two-Party Vote		Dem-Rep Plurality
		Total	Per Cent	Total	Per Cent	Dem	Rep	
ADAIR	4,123	1,908	46.3	2,215	53.7	46.3	53.7	307 R
ALLEN	3,607	1,691	46.9	1,916	53.1	46.9	53.1	225 R
ANDERSON	2,571	1,671	65.0	900	35.0	65.0	35.0	771 D
BALLARD	2,575	2,188	85.0	387	15.0	85.0	15.0	1,801 D
BARREN	6,621	4,013	60.6	2,608	39.4	60.6	39.4	1,405 D
BATH	2,940	1,876	63.8	1,064	36.2	63.8	36.2	812 D
BELL	6,904	2,441	35.4	4,463	64.6	35.4	64.6	2,022 R
BOONE	2,959	1,993	67.4	966	32.6	67.4	32.6	1,027 D
BOURBON	5,498	3,314	60.3	2,184	39.7	60.3	39.7	1,130 D
BOYD	9,496	4,998	52.6	4,498	47.4	52.6	47.4	500 D
BOYLE	4,673	2,971	63.6	1,702	36.4	63.6	36.4	1,269 D
BRACKEN	2,444	1,400	57.3	1,044	42.7	57.3	42.7	356 D
BREATHITT	3,859	2,562	66.4	1,297	33.6	66.4	33.6	1,265 D
BRECKINRIDGE	5,811	2,542	43.7	3,269	56.3	43.7	56.3	727 R
BULLITT	2,721	1,989	73.1	732	26.9	73.1	26.9	1,257 D
BUTLER	3,101	947	30.5	2,154	69.5	30.5	69.5	1,207 R
CALDWELL	2,886	1,435	49.7	1,451	50.3	49.7	50.3	16 R
CALLOWAY	4,245	3,523	83.0	722	17.0	83.0	17.0	2,801 D
CAMPBELL	18,903	9,897	52.4	9,006	47.6	52.4	47.6	891 D
CARLISLE	1,894	1,680	88.7	214	11.3	88.7	11.3	1,466 D
CARROLL	2,686	2,053	76.4	633	23.6	76.4	23.6	1,420 D
CARTER	6,031	2,435	40.4	3,596	59.6	40.4	59.6	1,161 R
CASEY	4,030	1,547	38.4	2,483	61.6	38.4	61.6	936 R
CHRISTIAN	7,602	3,619	47.6	3,983	52.4	47.6	52.4	364 R
CLARK	4,610	2,818	61.1	1,792	38.9	61.1	38.9	1,026 D
CLAY	4,343	1,366	31.5	2,977	68.5	31.5	68.5	1,611 R
CLINTON	2,611	587	22.5	2,024	77.5	22.5	77.5	1,437 R
CRITTENDEN	2,653	1,138	42.9	1,515	57.1	42.9	57.1	377 R
CUMBERLAND	2,753	750	27.2	2,003	72.8	27.2	72.8	1,253 R
DAVIESS	7,402	4,705	63.6	2,697	36.4	63.6	36.4	2,008 D
EDMONSON	3,687	1,742	47.2	1,945	52.8	47.2	52.8	203 R
ELLIOTT	1,799	1,358	75.5	441	24.5	75.5	24.5	917 D
ESTILL	4,262	1,981	46.5	2,281	53.5	46.5	53.5	300 R
FAYETTE	16,271	8,315	51.1	7,956	48.9	51.1	48.9	359 D
FLEMING	4,477	2,269	50.7	2,208	49.3	50.7	49.3	61 D
FLOYD	6,681	3,995	59.8	2,686	40.2	59.8	40.2	1,309 D
FRANKLIN	6,455	4,463	69.1	1,992	30.9	69.1	30.9	2,471 D
FULTON	3,763	2,927	77.8	836	22.2	77.8	22.2	2,091 D
GALLATIN	1,225	923	75.3	302	24.7	75.3	24.7	621 D
GARRARD	3,420	1,599	46.8	1,821	53.2	46.8	53.2	222 R
GRANT	3,050	1,988	65.2	1,062	34.8	65.2	34.8	926 D
GRAVES	6,708	5,371	80.1	1,337	19.9	80.1	19.9	4,034 D
GRAYSON	5,330	2,445	45.9	2,885	54.1	45.9	54.1	440 R
GREEN	3,930	1,743	44.4	2,187	55.6	44.4	55.6	444 R
GREENUP	5,324	2,604	48.9	2,720	51.1	48.9	51.1	116 R
HANCOCK	1,379	635	46.0	744	54.0	46.0	54.0	109 R
HARDIN	6,347	3,795	59.8	2,552	40.2	59.8	40.2	1,243 D
HARLAN	12,099	4,960	41.0	7,139	59.0	41.0	59.0	2,179 R
HARRISON	4,793	3,528	73.6	1,265	26.4	73.6	26.4	2,263 D
HART	5,567	2,812	50.5	2,755	49.5	50.5	49.5	57 D
HENDERSON	3,750	2,468	65.8	1,282	34.2	65.8	34.2	1,186 D
HENRY	4,133	2,836	68.6	1,297	31.4	68.6	31.4	1,539 D
HICKMAN	2,421	1,938	80.0	483	20.0	80.0	20.0	1,455 D
HOPKINS	7,513	4,499	59.9	3,014	40.1	59.9	40.1	1,485 D
JACKSON	2,546	316	12.4	2,230	87.6	12.4	87.6	1,914 R
JEFFERSON	103,479	44,379	42.9	59,100	57.1	42.9	57.1	14,721 R
JESSAMINE	3,348	2,058	61.5	1,290	38.5	61.5	38.5	768 D
JOHNSON	4,691	1,628	34.7	3,063	65.3	34.7	65.3	1,435 R
KENTON	20,955	12,708	60.6	8,247	39.4	60.6	39.4	4,461 D
KNOTT	2,585	1,902	73.6	683	26.4	73.6	26.4	1,219 D
KNOX	6,025	1,845	30.6	4,180	69.4	30.6	69.4	2,335 R
LARUE	2,915	1,762	60.4	1,153	39.6	60.4	39.6	609 D
LAUREL	5,523	1,940	35.1	3,583	64.9	35.1	64.9	1,643 R
LAWRENCE	4,389	2,306	52.5	2,083	47.5	52.5	47.5	223 D
LEE	2,341	1,052	44.9	1,289	55.1	44.9	55.1	237 R

18

County	Total Vote	Democratic		Republican		Per Cent of Two-Party Vote		Dem-Rep Plurality
		Total	Per Cent	Total	Per Cent	Dem	Rep	
LESLIE	2,376	408	17.2	1,968	82.8	17.2	82.8	1,560 R
LETCHER	5,654	2,602	46.0	3,052	54.0	46.0	54.0	450 R
LEWIS	3,625	1,243	34.3	2,382	65.7	34.3	65.7	1,139 R
LINCOLN	4,555	2,510	55.1	2,045	44.9	55.1	44.9	465 D
LIVINGSTON	1,889	1,146	60.7	743	39.3	60.7	39.3	403 D
LOGAN	5,597	3,429	61.3	2,168	38.7	61.3	38.7	1,261 D
LYON	1,964	1,277	65.0	687	35.0	65.0	35.0	590 D
MADISON	8,125	4,339	53.4	3,786	46.6	53.4	46.6	553 D
MAGOFFIN	4,286	1,794	41.9	2,492	58.1	41.9	58.1	698 R
MARION	4,457	3,162	70.9	1,295	29.1	70.9	29.1	1,867 D
MARSHALL	2,737	1,950	71.2	787	28.8	71.2	28.8	1,163 D
MARTIN	1,312	358	27.3	954	72.7	27.3	72.7	596 R
MASON	4,657	2,879	61.8	1,778	38.2	61.8	38.2	1,101 D
MC CRACKEN	6,256	3,955	63.2	2,301	36.8	63.2	36.8	1,654 D
MC CREARY	3,044	771	25.3	2,273	74.7	25.3	74.7	1,502 R
MC LEAN	2,734	1,705	62.4	1,029	37.6	62.4	37.6	676 D
MEADE	2,466	1,608	65.2	858	34.8	65.2	34.8	750 D
MENIFEE	1,251	794	63.5	457	36.5	63.5	36.5	337 D
MERCER	3,919	2,421	61.8	1,498	38.2	61.8	38.2	923 D
METCALFE	2,551	1,208	47.4	1,343	52.6	47.4	52.6	135 R
MONROE	3,228	872	27.0	2,356	73.0	27.0	73.0	1,484 R
MONTGOMERY	2,978	1,795	60.3	1,183	39.7	60.3	39.7	612 D
MORGAN	3,706	2,476	66.8	1,230	33.2	66.8	33.2	1,246 D
MUHLENBERG	7,945	3,500	44.1	4,445	55.9	44.1	55.9	945 R
NELSON	5,907	3,958	67.0	1,949	33.0	67.0	33.0	2,009 D
NICHOLAS	2,766	1,724	62.3	1,042	37.7	62.3	37.7	682 D
OHIO	6,111	2,727	44.6	3,384	55.4	44.6	55.4	657 R
OLDHAM	1,993	1,368	68.6	625	31.4	68.6	31.4	743 D
OWEN	3,260	2,648	81.2	612	18.8	81.2	18.8	2,036 D
OWSLEY	1,642	234	14.3	1,408	85.7	14.3	85.7	1,174 R
PENDLETON	2,545	1,508	59.3	1,037	40.7	59.3	40.7	471 D
PERRY	6,758	3,205	47.4	3,553	52.6	47.4	52.6	348 R
PIKE	12,935	7,188	55.6	5,747	44.4	55.6	44.4	1,441 D
POWELL	1,461	783	53.6	678	46.4	53.6	46.4	105 D
PULASKI	9,821	3,839	39.1	5,982	60.9	39.1	60.9	2,143 R
ROBERTSON	1,006	690	68.6	316	31.4	68.6	31.4	374 D
ROCKCASTLE	3,876	1,218	31.4	2,658	68.6	31.4	68.6	1,440 R
ROWAN	2,756	1,430	51.9	1,326	48.1	51.9	48.1	104 D
RUSSELL	3,610	1,171	32.4	2,439	67.6	32.4	67.6	1,268 R
SCOTT	4,021	2,569	63.9	1,452	36.1	63.9	36.1	1,117 D
SHELBY	4,650	3,172	68.2	1,478	31.8	68.2	31.8	1,694 D
SIMPSON	2,896	2,206	76.2	690	23.8	76.2	23.8	1,516 D
SPENCER	1,443	1,047	72.6	396	27.4	72.6	27.4	651 D
TAYLOR	4,108	2,009	48.9	2,099	51.1	48.9	51.1	90 R
TODD	2,982	1,959	65.7	1,023	34.3	65.7	34.3	936 D
TRIGG	3,422	1,894	55.3	1,528	44.7	55.3	44.7	366 D
TRIMBLE	1,474	1,317	89.3	157	10.7	89.3	10.7	1,160 D
UNION	2,631	2,052	78.0	579	22.0	78.0	22.0	1,473 D
WARREN	9,712	6,134	63.2	3,578	36.8	63.2	36.8	2,556 D
WASHINGTON	4,033	2,199	54.5	1,834	45.5	54.5	45.5	365 D
WAYNE	4,091	1,852	45.3	2,239	54.7	45.3	54.7	387 R
WEBSTER	4,188	2,207	52.7	1,981	47.3	52.7	47.3	226 D
WHITLEY	7,022	1,646	23.4	5,376	76.6	23.4	76.6	3,730 R
WOLFE	2,300	1,413	61.4	887	38.6	61.4	38.6	526 D
WOODFORD	3,463	2,032	58.7	1,431	41.3	58.7	41.3	601 D
TOTAL	645,928	336,748	52.1	309,180	47.9	52.1	47.9	27,568 D

DEMOCRAT: M. M. Logan
REPUBLICAN: John M. Robsion

19

County	Total Vote	Alben W. Barkley		George B. Martin		Other Vote	
		Total	Per Cent	Total	Per Cent	Total	Per Cent
ADAIR	601	321	53.4	253	42.1	27	4.5
ALLEN	1,055	919	87.1	100	9.5	36	3.4
ANDERSON	832	637	76.6	179	21.5	16	1.9
BALLARD	1,415	1,273	90.0	122	8.6	20	1.4
BARREN	2,055	1,856	90.3	157	7.6	42	2.0
BATH	1,003	530	52.8	432	43.1	41	4.1
BELL	856	563	65.8	216	25.2	77	9.0
BOONE	895	751	83.9	117	13.1	27	3.0
BOURBON	3,022	1,507	49.9	1,462	48.4	53	1.8
BOYD	3,953	645	16.3	3,134	79.3	174	4.4
BOYLE	3,208	2,384	74.3	757	23.6	67	2.1
BRACKEN	566	460	81.3	90	15.9	16	2.8
BREATHITT	2,322	2,004	86.3	217	9.3	101	4.3
BRECKINRIDGE	1,138	782	68.7	331	29.1	25	2.2
BULLITT	1,182	827	70.0	324	27.4	31	2.6
BUTLER	387	275	71.1	66	17.1	46	11.9
CALDWELL	991	889	89.7	91	9.2	11	1.1
CALLOWAY	2,263	2,129	94.1	94	4.2	40	1.8
CAMPBELL	3,951	2,015	51.0	1,844	46.7	92	2.3
CARLISLE	1,375	1,231	89.5	134	9.7	10	0.7
CARROLL	1,389	1,262	90.9	86	6.2	41	3.0
CARTER	1,518	417	27.5	978	64.4	123	8.1
CASEY	514	474	92.2	27	5.3	13	2.5
CHRISTIAN	1,489	1,157	77.7	287	19.3	45	3.0
CLARK	1,442	952	66.0	438	30.4	52	3.6
CLAY	249	180	72.3	51	20.5	18	7.2
CLINTON	220	195	88.6	23	10.5	2	0.9
CRITTENDEN	515	457	88.7	46	8.9	12	2.3
CUMBERLAND	250	221	88.4	25	10.0	4	1.6
DAVIESS	4,394	2,963	67.4	1,300	29.6	131	3.0
EDMONSON	552	478	86.6	53	9.6	21	3.8
ELLIOTT	1,150	351	30.5	754	65.6	45	3.9
ESTILL	939	764	81.4	146	15.5	29	3.1
FAYETTE	5,254	2,862	54.5	2,131	40.6	261	5.0
FLEMING	1,029	548	53.3	438	42.6	43	4.2
FLOYD	4,388	1,063	24.2	3,225	73.5	100	2.3
FRANKLIN	3,668	2,358	64.3	1,253	34.2	57	1.6
FULTON	1,408	1,169	83.0	216	15.3	23	1.6
GALLATIN	447	330	73.8	103	23.0	14	3.1
GARRARD	1,068	914	85.6	131	12.3	23	2.2
GRANT	809	682	84.3	96	11.9	31	3.8
GRAVES	4,788	4,291	89.6	421	8.8	76	1.6
GRAYSON	730	491	67.3	222	30.4	17	2.3
GREEN	349	297	85.1	50	14.3	2	0.6
GREENUP	1,870	457	24.4	239	12.8	1,174	62.8
HANCOCK	191	147	77.0	33	17.3	11	5.8
HARDIN	1,329	989	74.4	313	23.6	27	2.0
HARLAN	4,712	4,314	91.6	225	4.8	173	3.7
HARRISON	1,805	1,143	63.3	626	34.7	36	2.0
HART	909	748	82.3	150	16.5	11	1.2
HENDERSON	1,509	860	57.0	609	40.4	40	2.7
HENRY	2,026	1,729	85.3	259	12.8	38	1.9
HICKMAN	1,035	905	87.4	120	11.6	10	1.0
HOPKINS	2,436	1,884	77.3	491	20.2	61	2.5
JACKSON	87	70	80.5	13	14.9	4	4.6
JEFFERSON	18,259	10,507	57.5	7,536	41.3	216	1.2
JESSAMINE	1,057	598	56.6	391	37.0	68	6.4
JOHNSON	1,015	741	73.0	195	19.2	79	7.8
KENTON	6,145	3,127	50.9	2,891	47.0	127	2.1
KNOTT	1,451	463	31.9	891	61.4	97	6.7
KNOX	693	518	74.7	134	19.3	41	5.9
LARUE	649	507	78.1	139	21.4	3	0.5
LAUREL	1,092	1,006	92.1	71	6.5	15	1.4
LAWRENCE	1,727	184	10.7	1,485	86.0	58	3.4
LEE	619	480	77.5	117	18.9	22	3.6

20

County	Total Vote	Alben W. Barkley		George B. Martin		Other Vote	
		Total	Per Cent	Total	Per Cent	Total	Per Cent
LESLIE	118	76	64.4	20	16.9	22	18.6
LETCHER	1,929	588	30.5	782	40.5	559	29.0
LEWIS	701	264	37.7	376	53.6	61	8.7
LINCOLN	1,566	1,324	84.5	205	13.1	37	2.4
LIVINGSTON	904	841	93.0	50	5.5	13	1.4
LOGAN	3,509	3,353	95.6	109	3.1	47	1.3
LYON	951	895	94.1	47	4.9	9	0.9
MADISON	2,039	1,155	56.6	829	40.7	55	2.7
MAGOFFIN	1,651	1,045	63.3	596	36.1	10	0.6
MARION	1,091	637	58.4	440	40.3	14	1.3
MARSHALL	1,300	1,242	95.5	49	3.8	9	0.7
MARTIN	177	80	45.2	95	53.7	2	1.1
MASON	1,571	749	47.7	787	50.1	35	2.2
MC CRACKEN	3,085	2,527	81.9	503	16.3	55	1.8
MC CREARY	260	173	66.5	68	26.2	19	7.3
MC LEAN	1,112	932	83.8	142	12.8	38	3.4
MEADE	685	439	64.1	237	34.6	9	1.3
MENIFEE	367	147	40.1	203	55.3	17	4.6
MERCER	1,565	1,134	72.5	394	25.2	37	2.4
METCALFE	435	409	94.0	18	4.1	8	1.8
MONROE	353	321	90.9	26	7.4	6	1.7
MONTGOMERY	1,113	700	62.9	376	33.8	37	3.3
MORGAN	1,525	1,030	67.5	462	30.3	33	2.2
MUHLENBERG	1,496	748	50.0	709	47.4	39	2.6
NELSON	2,011	695	34.6	1,304	64.8	12	0.6
NICHOLAS	1,005	750	74.6	238	23.7	17	1.7
OHIO	1,179	907	76.9	243	20.6	29	2.5
OLDHAM	604	423	70.0	163	27.0	18	3.0
OWEN	1,358	1,052	77.5	286	21.1	20	1.5
OWSLEY	71	51	71.8	16	22.5	4	5.6
PENDLETON	570	482	84.6	55	9.6	33	5.8
PERRY	1,521	916	60.2	406	26.7	199	13.1
PIKE	4,465	3,207	71.8	970	21.7	288	6.5
POWELL	323	144	44.6	159	49.2	20	6.2
PULASKI	1,212	1,070	88.3	101	8.3	41	3.4
ROBERTSON	310	183	59.0	117	37.7	10	3.2
ROCKCASTLE	507	451	89.0	35	6.9	21	4.1
ROWAN	917	193	21.0	660	72.0	64	7.0
RUSSELL	283	256	90.5	23	8.1	4	1.4
SCOTT	1,956	1,227	62.7	675	34.5	54	2.8
SHELBY	1,610	1,209	75.1	369	22.9	32	2.0
SIMPSON	1,271	1,156	91.0	98	7.7	17	1.3
SPENCER	366	247	67.5	113	30.9	6	1.6
TAYLOR	694	427	61.5	257	37.0	10	1.4
TODD	1,392	1,286	92.4	56	4.0	50	3.6
TRIGG	1,275	1,228	96.3	42	3.3	5	0.4
TRIMBLE	694	604	87.0	67	9.7	23	3.3
UNION	1,472	1,067	72.5	364	24.7	41	2.8
WARREN	3,162	2,726	86.2	356	11.3	80	2.5
WASHINGTON	431	317	73.5	113	26.2	1	0.2
WAYNE	431	381	88.4	39	9.0	11	2.6
WEBSTER	1,351	1,111	82.2	193	14.3	47	3.5
WHITLEY	1,026	882	86.0	87	8.5	57	5.6
WOLFE	813	354	43.5	250	30.8	209	25.7
WOODFORD	1,292	713	55.2	530	41.0	49	3.8
TOTAL	187,420	124,775	66.6	55,556	29.6	7,089	3.8

OTHER VOTE: Dr. J. E. Wright 7089

County	Total Vote	Democratic		Republican		Other Vote		Per Cent of Two-Party Vote		Dem-Rep Plurality
		Total	Per Cent	Total	Per Cent	Total	Per Cent	Dem	Rep	
ADAIR	6,296	3,221	51.2	3,075	48.8			51.2	48.8	146 D
ALLEN	6,248	3,058	48.9	3,190	51.1			48.9	51.1	132 R
ANDERSON	3,584	2,387	66.6	1,193	33.3	4	0.1	66.7	33.3	1,194 D
BALLARD	3,525	2,946	83.6	568	16.1	11	0.3	83.8	16.2	2,378 D
BARREN	10,007	6,417	64.1	3,582	35.8	8	0.1	64.2	35.8	2,835 D
BATH	4,493	2,909	64.7	1,579	35.1	5	0.1	64.8	35.2	1,330 D
BELL	10,038	5,363	53.4	4,666	46.5	9	0.1	53.5	46.5	697 D
BOONE	4,894	3,528	72.1	1,349	27.6	17	0.3	72.3	27.7	2,179 D
BOURBON	7,511	4,702	62.6	2,807	37.4	2		62.6	37.4	1,895 D
BOYD	15,076	8,324	55.2	6,729	44.6	23	0.2	55.3	44.7	1,595 D
BOYLE	6,718	4,479	66.7	2,237	33.3	2		66.7	33.3	2,242 D
BRACKEN	3,843	2,380	61.9	1,452	37.8	11	0.3	62.1	37.9	928 D
BREATHITT	5,900	4,525	76.7	1,373	23.3	2		76.7	23.3	3,152 D
BRECKINRIDGE	7,017	3,765	53.7	3,249	46.3	3		53.7	46.3	516 D
BULLITT	3,962	2,869	72.4	1,090	27.5	3	0.1	72.5	27.5	1,779 D
BUTLER	4,346	1,651	38.0	2,691	61.9	4	0.1	38.0	62.0	1,040 R
CALDWELL	4,976	2,946	59.2	2,008	40.4	22	0.4	59.5	40.5	938 D
CALLOWAY	7,174	6,342	88.4	821	11.4	11	0.2	88.5	11.5	5,521 D
CAMPBELL	29,873	17,785	59.5	11,582	38.8	506	1.7	60.6	39.4	6,203 D
CARLISLE	3,253	2,849	87.6	401	12.3	3	0.1	87.7	12.3	2,448 D
CARROLL	3,766	2,996	79.6	766	20.3	4	0.1	79.6	20.4	2,230 D
CARTER	8,985	4,587	51.1	4,376	48.7	22	0.2	51.2	48.8	211 D
CASEY	6,497	2,647	40.7	3,850	59.3			40.7	59.3	1,203 R
CHRISTIAN	12,886	7,607	59.0	5,250	40.7	29	0.2	59.2	40.8	2,357 D
CLARK	6,826	4,852	71.1	1,966	28.8	8	0.1	71.2	28.8	2,886 D
CLAY	5,612	2,115	37.7	3,495	62.3	2		37.7	62.3	1,380 R
CLINTON	3,261	878	26.9	2,383	73.1			26.9	73.1	1,505 R
CRITTENDEN	4,295	2,123	49.4	2,170	50.5	2		49.5	50.5	47 R
CUMBERLAND	3,557	1,219	34.3	2,338	65.7			34.3	65.7	1,119 R
DAVIESS	16,003	10,462	65.4	5,522	34.5	19	0.1	65.5	34.5	4,940 D
EDMONSON	4,453	1,787	40.1	2,666	59.9			40.1	59.9	879 R
ELLIOTT	2,513	2,130	84.8	383	15.2			84.8	15.2	1,747 D
ESTILL	6,125	3,155	51.5	2,970	48.5			51.5	48.5	185 D
FAYETTE	27,569	15,710	57.0	11,735	42.6	124	0.4	57.2	42.8	3,975 D
FLEMING	6,047	3,417	56.5	2,624	43.4	6	0.1	56.6	43.4	793 D
FLOYD	11,752	8,381	71.3	3,360	28.6	11	0.1	71.4	28.6	5,021 D
FRANKLIN	8,339	6,269	75.2	2,050	24.6	20	0.2	75.4	24.6	4,219 D
FULTON	4,764	3,932	82.5	828	17.4	4	0.1	82.6	17.4	3,104 D
GALLATIN	2,164	1,791	82.8	373	17.2			82.8	17.2	1,418 D
GARRARD	4,868	2,584	53.1	2,284	46.9			53.1	46.9	300 D
GRANT	4,517	3,104	68.7	1,413	31.3			68.7	31.3	1,691 D
GRAVES	11,621	9,757	84.0	1,840	15.8	24	0.2	84.1	15.9	7,917 D
GRAYSON	7,542	3,829	50.8	3,712	49.2	1		50.8	49.2	117 D
GREEN	4,554	2,265	49.7	2,288	50.2	1		49.7	50.3	23 R
GREENUP	8,452	4,975	58.9	3,420	40.5	57	0.7	59.3	40.7	1,555 D
HANCOCK	2,775	1,604	57.8	1,171	42.2			57.8	42.2	433 D
HARDIN	8,833	5,990	67.8	2,814	31.9	29	0.3	68.0	32.0	3,176 D
HARLAN	20,330	9,557	47.0	10,751	52.9	22	0.1	47.1	52.9	1,194 R
HARRISON	6,709	4,882	72.8	1,826	27.2	1		72.8	27.2	3,056 D
HART	6,561	3,962	60.4	2,589	39.5	10	0.2	60.5	39.5	1,373 D
HENDERSON	8,801	6,100	69.3	2,475	28.1	226	2.6	71.1	28.9	3,625 D
HENRY	5,927	4,249	71.7	1,674	28.2	4	0.1	71.7	28.3	2,575 D
HICKMAN	3,729	3,275	87.8	452	12.1	2	0.1	87.9	12.1	2,823 D
HOPKINS	12,704	8,921	70.2	3,750	29.5	33	0.3	70.4	29.6	5,171 D
JACKSON	3,337	513	15.4	2,821	84.5	3	0.1	15.4	84.6	2,308 R
JEFFERSON	140,182	71,862	51.3	67,494	48.1	826	0.6	51.6	48.4	4,368 D
JESSAMINE	4,591	2,868	62.5	1,723	37.5			62.5	37.5	1,145 D
JOHNSON	8,008	3,154	39.4	4,854	60.6			39.4	60.6	1,700 R
KENTON	33,977	22,342	65.8	11,108	32.7	527	1.6	66.8	33.2	11,234 D
KNOTT	5,202	4,448	85.5	754	14.5			85.5	14.5	3,694 D
KNOX	7,673	3,221	42.0	4,444	57.9	8	0.1	42.0	58.0	1,223 R
LARUE	3,886	2,640	67.9	1,246	32.1			67.9	32.1	1,394 D
LAUREL	8,333	3,495	41.9	4,823	57.9	15	0.2	42.0	58.0	1,328 R
LAWRENCE	6,409	3,663	57.2	2,744	42.8	2		57.2	42.8	919 D
LEE	3,541	1,921	54.3	1,620	45.7			54.3	45.7	301 D

U.S. SENATOR: GENERAL ELECTION — 1932

County	Total Vote	Democratic Total	Democratic Per Cent	Republican Total	Republican Per Cent	Other Vote Total	Other Vote Per Cent	Per Cent of Two-Party Vote Dem	Per Cent of Two-Party Vote Rep	Dem-Rep Plurality
LESLIE	3,452	554	16.0	2,897	83.9	1		16.1	83.9	2,343 R
LETCHER	9,795	5,117	52.2	4,678	47.8			52.2	47.8	439 D
LEWIS	5,590	2,433	43.5	3,145	56.3	12	0.2	43.6	56.4	712 R
LINCOLN	7,599	4,545	59.8	3,052	40.2	2		59.8	40.2	1,493 D
LIVINGSTON	3,279	2,214	67.5	1,065	32.5			67.5	32.5	1,149 D
LOGAN	9,852	7,041	71.5	2,806	28.5	5	0.1	71.5	28.5	4,235 D
LYON	2,916	2,057	70.5	859	29.5			70.5	29.5	1,198 D
MADISON	12,718	6,898	54.2	5,792	45.5	28	0.2	54.4	45.6	1,106 D
MAGOFFIN	5,338	2,697	50.5	2,639	49.4	2		50.5	49.5	58 D
MARION	5,958	4,374	73.4	1,581	26.5	3	0.1	73.5	26.5	2,793 D
MARSHALL	5,067	4,198	82.8	858	16.9	11	0.2	83.0	17.0	3,340 D
MARTIN	2,552	754	29.5	1,791	70.2	7	0.3	29.6	70.4	1,037 R
MASON	8,211	5,028	61.2	3,174	38.7	9	0.1	61.3	38.7	1,854 D
MC CRACKEN	12,410	9,221	74.3	3,078	24.8	111	0.9	75.0	25.0	6,143 D
MC CREARY	4,449	1,151	25.9	3,287	73.9	11	0.2	25.9	74.1	2,136 R
MC LEAN	4,183	2,754	65.8	1,411	33.7	18	0.4	66.1	33.9	1,343 D
MEADE	3,517	2,451	69.7	1,054	30.0	12	0.3	69.9	30.1	1,397 D
MENIFEE	1,910	1,429	74.8	480	25.1	1	0.1	74.9	25.1	949 D
MERCER	5,713	3,753	65.7	1,960	34.3			65.7	34.3	1,793 D
METCALFE	3,657	1,946	53.2	1,710	46.8	1		53.2	46.8	236 D
MONROE	4,110	1,575	38.3	2,534	61.7	1		38.3	61.7	959 R
MONTGOMERY	4,331	2,817	65.0	1,514	35.0			65.0	35.0	1,303 D
MORGAN	5,577	4,137	74.2	1,439	25.8			74.2	25.8	2,698 D
MUHLENBERG	11,506	7,020	61.0	4,351	37.8	135	1.2	61.7	38.3	2,669 D
NELSON	7,359	5,252	71.4	2,107	28.6			71.4	28.6	3,145 D
NICHOLAS	3,936	2,699	68.6	1,237	31.4			68.6	31.4	1,462 D
OHIO	9,771	4,817	49.3	4,856	49.7	98	1.0	49.8	50.2	39 R
OLDHAM	3,177	2,262	71.2	904	28.5	11	0.3	71.4	28.6	1,358 D
OWEN	4,872	4,183	85.9	687	14.1	2		85.9	14.1	3,496 D
OWSLEY	2,466	508	20.6	1,956	79.3	2	0.1	20.6	79.4	1,448 R
PENDLETON	4,545	2,724	59.9	1,814	39.9	7	0.2	60.0	40.0	910 D
PERRY	11,451	6,274	54.8	5,171	45.2	6	0.1	54.8	45.2	1,103 D
PIKE	20,414	12,520	61.3	7,866	38.5	28	0.1	61.4	38.6	4,654 D
POWELL	2,102	1,282	61.0	820	39.0			61.0	39.0	462 D
PULASKI	11,663	4,887	41.9	6,776	58.1			41.9	58.1	1,889 R
ROBERTSON	1,585	1,042	65.7	543	34.3			65.7	34.3	499 D
ROCKCASTLE	5,452	1,940	35.6	3,511	64.4	1		35.6	64.4	1,571 R
ROWAN	4,397	2,781	63.2	1,616	36.8			63.2	36.8	1,165 D
RUSSELL	4,148	1,677	40.4	2,470	59.5	1		40.4	59.6	793 R
SCOTT	6,455	4,508	69.8	1,940	30.1	7	0.1	69.9	30.1	2,568 D
SHELBY	7,273	5,124	70.5	2,147	29.5	2		70.5	29.5	2,977 D
SIMPSON	4,820	3,604	74.8	1,213	25.2	3	0.1	74.8	25.2	2,391 D
SPENCER	2,484	1,748	70.4	735	29.6	1		70.4	29.6	1,013 D
TAYLOR	5,416	2,812	51.9	2,604	48.1			51.9	48.1	208 D
TODD	5,479	3,909	71.3	1,570	28.7			71.3	28.7	2,339 D
TRIGG	5,074	3,609	71.1	1,456	28.7	9	0.2	71.3	28.7	2,153 D
TRIMBLE	2,356	2,086	88.5	268	11.4	2	0.1	88.6	11.4	1,818 D
UNION	5,872	4,810	81.9	1,054	17.9	8	0.1	82.0	18.0	3,756 D
WARREN	13,440	8,831	65.7	4,585	34.1	24	0.2	65.8	34.2	4,246 D
WASHINGTON	5,186	2,832	54.6	2,351	45.3	3	0.1	54.6	45.4	481 D
WAYNE	5,353	2,709	50.6	2,644	49.4			50.6	49.4	65 D
WEBSTER	6,998	4,752	67.9	2,237	32.0	9	0.1	68.0	32.0	2,515 D
WHITLEY	9,646	3,530	36.6	6,116	63.4			36.6	63.4	2,586 R
WOLFE	3,195	2,289	71.6	905	28.3	1		71.7	28.3	1,384 D
WOODFORD	4,848	3,127	64.5	1,714	35.4	7	0.1	64.6	35.4	1,413 D
TOTAL	972,233	575,077	59.2	393,865	40.5	3,291	0.3	59.4	40.6	181,212 D

DEMOCRAT: Alben W. Barkley
REPUBLICAN: M. H. Thatcher
SOCIALIST: W. A. Sandefur

County	Total Vote	M. M. Logan		J. C. W. Beckham		John Y. Brown		Other Vote	
		Total	Per Cent	Total	Per Cent	Total	Per Cent	Total	Per Cent
ADAIR	2,466	1,205	48.9	1,140	46.2	104	4.2	17	0.7
ALLEN	2,137	887	41.5	1,039	48.6	165	7.7	46	2.2
ANDERSON	2,168	765	35.3	1,096	50.6	288	13.3	19	0.9
BALLARD	3,031	1,349	44.5	1,315	43.4	351	11.6	16	0.5
BARREN	4,449	2,380	53.5	1,696	38.1	318	7.1	55	1.2
BATH	2,717	987	36.3	1,482	54.5	210	7.7	38	1.4
BELL	3,367	1,353	40.2	1,336	39.7	587	17.4	91	2.7
BOONE	2,869	675	23.5	874	30.5	1,278	44.5	42	1.5
BOURBON	4,002	1,932	48.3	1,314	32.8	696	17.4	60	1.5
BOYD	6,686	3,645	54.5	1,771	26.5	968	14.5	302	4.5
BOYLE	3,905	1,133	29.0	1,358	34.8	1,370	35.1	44	1.1
BRACKEN	1,648	647	39.3	338	20.5	654	39.7	9	0.5
BREATHITT	3,604	1,894	52.6	1,372	38.1	253	7.0	85	2.4
BRECKINRIDGE	2,450	1,296	52.9	1,123	45.8	15	0.6	16	0.7
BULLITT	2,092	909	43.5	784	37.5	385	18.4	14	0.7
BUTLER	1,249	751	60.1	349	27.9	140	11.2	9	0.7
CALDWELL	2,247	976	43.4	1,129	50.2	136	6.1	6	0.3
CALLOWAY	5,484	2,579	47.0	2,618	47.7	266	4.9	21	0.4
CAMPBELL	15,585	5,041	32.3	3,208	20.6	6,735	43.2	601	3.9
CARLISLE	2,094	801	38.3	1,156	55.2	122	5.8	15	0.7
CARROLL	2,944	1,055	35.8	1,081	36.7	765	26.0	43	1.5
CARTER	2,855	670	23.5	1,676	58.7	389	13.6	120	4.2
CASEY	1,576	277	17.6	972	61.7	251	15.9	76	4.8
CHRISTIAN	5,963	1,637	27.5	3,715	62.3	591	9.9	20	0.3
CLARK	4,405	2,026	46.0	1,092	24.8	1,241	28.2	46	1.0
CLAY	1,345	447	33.2	767	57.0	99	7.4	32	2.4
CLINTON	748	203	27.1	516	69.0	25	3.3	4	0.5
CRITTENDEN	1,727	750	43.4	748	43.3	224	13.0	5	0.3
CUMBERLAND	912	224	24.6	645	70.7	26	2.9	17	1.9
DAVIESS	7,685	4,470	58.2	1,847	24.0	1,322	17.2	46	0.6
EDMONSON	1,423	1,206	84.8	133	9.3	83	5.8	1	0.1
ELLIOTT	1,900	474	24.9	1,103	58.1	294	15.5	29	1.5
ESTILL	2,089	623	29.8	955	45.7	447	21.4	64	3.1
FAYETTE	13,360	4,608	34.5	2,543	19.0	6,061	45.4	148	1.1
FLEMING	2,672	619	23.2	1,666	62.4	347	13.0	40	1.5
FLOYD	7,571	2,345	31.0	3,191	42.1	1,171	15.5	864	11.4
FRANKLIN	6,242	2,725	43.7	2,670	42.8	758	12.1	89	1.4
FULTON	2,943	1,318	44.8	1,353	46.0	264	9.0	8	0.3
GALLATIN	1,488	453	30.4	739	49.7	281	18.9	15	1.0
GARRARD	2,036	340	16.7	1,066	52.4	611	30.0	19	0.9
GRANT	2,736	882	32.2	565	20.7	1,259	46.0	30	1.1
GRAVES	9,323	4,490	48.2	4,160	44.6	654	7.0	19	0.2
GRAYSON	2,510	1,010	40.2	1,224	48.8	260	10.4	16	0.6
GREEN	1,924	1,185	61.6	650	33.8	66	3.4	23	1.2
GREENUP	3,574	2,402	67.2	750	21.0	314	8.8	108	3.0
HANCOCK	982	505	51.4	332	33.8	136	13.8	9	0.9
HARDIN	4,304	1,518	35.3	1,985	46.1	770	17.9	31	0.7
HARLAN	5,676	2,738	48.2	2,283	40.2	418	7.4	237	4.2
HARRISON	3,825	1,973	51.6	773	20.2	1,058	27.7	21	0.5
HART	2,874	1,223	42.6	1,425	49.6	198	6.9	28	1.0
HENDERSON	6,133	2,466	40.2	2,817	45.9	799	13.0	51	0.8
HENRY	3,613	1,207	33.4	1,783	49.3	582	16.1	41	1.1
HICKMAN	2,301	794	34.5	1,281	55.7	220	9.6	6	0.3
HOPKINS	7,219	3,687	51.1	2,645	36.6	837	11.6	50	0.7
JACKSON	395	196	49.6	169	42.8	21	5.3	9	2.3
JEFFERSON	48,348	19,914	41.2	22,731	47.0	5,507	11.4	196	0.4
JESSAMINE	2,890	867	30.0	766	26.5	1,213	42.0	44	1.5
JOHNSON	2,169	648	29.9	1,053	48.5	430	19.8	38	1.8
KENTON	21,303	7,969	37.4	2,815	13.2	9,984	46.9	535	2.5
KNOTT	2,758	850	30.8	899	32.6	780	28.3	229	8.3
KNOX	2,575	1,075	41.7	1,286	49.9	152	5.9	62	2.4
LARUE	2,275	919	40.4	922	40.5	419	18.4	15	0.7
LAUREL	2,274	952	41.9	1,123	49.4	175	7.7	24	1.1
LAWRENCE	2,532	1,143	45.1	1,017	40.2	258	10.2	114	4.5
LEE	1,306	407	31.2	471	36.1	367	28.1	61	4.7

County	Total Vote	M. M. Logan Total	Per Cent	J. C. W. Beckham Total	Per Cent	John Y. Brown Total	Per Cent	Other Vote Total	Per Cent
LESLIE	473	143	30.2	277	58.6	28	5.9	25	5.3
LETCHER	4,755	1,113	23.4	1,773	37.3	1,672	35.2	197	4.1
LEWIS	1,477	795	53.8	527	35.7	122	8.3	33	2.2
LINCOLN	3,456	1,378	39.9	1,387	40.1	603	17.4	88	2.5
LIVINGSTON	1,942	434	22.3	1,437	74.0	65	3.3	6	0.3
LOGAN	4,884	2,921	59.8	1,166	23.9	773	15.8	24	0.5
LYON	2,208	782	35.4	1,253	56.7	169	7.7	4	0.2
MADISON	5,237	2,223	42.4	1,325	25.3	1,591	30.4	98	1.9
MAGOFFIN	2,530	619	24.5	1,477	58.4	35	1.4	399	15.8
MARION	3,526	760	21.6	1,560	44.2	1,165	33.0	41	1.2
MARSHALL	3,104	1,567	50.5	1,278	41.2	245	7.9	14	0.5
MARTIN	593	107	18.0	442	74.5	31	5.2	13	2.2
MASON	3,797	1,628	42.9	1,354	35.7	782	20.6	33	0.9
MC CRACKEN	7,282	4,673	64.2	2,019	27.7	540	7.4	50	0.7
MC CREARY	750	278	37.1	301	40.1	154	20.5	17	2.3
MC LEAN	2,119	933	44.0	714	33.7	452	21.3	20	0.9
MEADE	2,057	671	32.6	1,120	54.4	239	11.6	27	1.3
MENIFEE	1,303	774	59.4	410	31.5	105	8.1	14	1.1
MERCER	3,278	1,187	36.2	1,389	42.4	662	20.2	40	1.2
METCALFE	1,668	627	37.6	945	56.7	70	4.2	26	1.6
MONROE	1,322	527	39.9	732	55.4	51	3.9	12	0.9
MONTGOMERY	3,289	1,599	48.6	1,213	36.9	443	13.5	34	1.0
MORGAN	3,408	1,294	38.0	1,770	51.9	273	8.0	71	2.1
MUHLENBERG	4,931	2,230	45.2	2,154	43.7	482	9.8	65	1.3
NELSON	4,545	1,534	33.8	2,041	44.9	946	20.8	24	0.5
NICHOLAS	2,119	875	41.3	783	37.0	432	20.4	29	1.4
OHIO	3,288	1,480	45.0	1,121	34.1	657	20.0	30	0.9
OLDHAM	1,561	707	45.3	617	39.5	219	14.0	18	1.2
OWEN	3,568	849	23.8	1,526	42.8	1,160	32.5	33	0.9
OWSLEY	453	154	34.0	229	50.6	49	10.8	21	4.6
PENDLETON	2,207	911	41.3	667	30.2	602	27.3	27	1.2
PERRY	4,960	732	14.8	2,224	44.8	940	19.0	1,064	21.5
PIKE	9,450	3,658	38.7	4,627	49.0	977	10.3	188	2.0
POWELL	1,099	321	29.2	665	60.5	92	8.4	21	1.9
PULASKI	4,001	1,119	28.0	2,316	57.9	538	13.4	28	0.7
ROBERTSON	791	383	48.4	252	31.9	147	18.6	9	1.1
ROCKCASTLE	1,513	421	27.8	914	60.4	165	10.9	13	0.9
ROWAN	1,621	550	33.9	759	46.8	286	17.6	26	1.6
RUSSELL	1,372	583	42.5	752	54.8	31	2.3	6	0.4
SCOTT	3,792	1,805	47.6	707	18.6	1,210	31.9	70	1.8
SHELBY	4,369	1,191	27.3	2,249	51.5	907	20.8	22	0.5
SIMPSON	2,911	947	32.5	847	29.1	1,107	38.0	10	0.3
SPENCER	1,403	380	27.1	615	43.8	395	28.2	13	0.9
TAYLOR	2,569	766	29.8	1,495	58.2	287	11.2	21	0.8
TODD	3,525	1,384	39.3	1,827	51.8	273	7.7	41	1.2
TRIGG	2,876	1,188	41.3	1,477	51.4	207	7.2	4	0.1
TRIMBLE	1,749	393	22.5	895	51.2	437	25.0	24	1.4
UNION	3,732	1,472	39.4	781	20.9	1,461	39.1	18	0.5
WARREN	8,359	4,395	52.6	2,510	30.0	1,386	16.6	68	0.8
WASHINGTON	2,060	518	25.1	1,191	57.8	341	16.6	10	0.5
WAYNE	2,463	1,010	41.0	1,354	55.0	75	3.0	24	1.0
WEBSTER	4,133	1,431	34.6	1,723	41.7	950	23.0	29	0.7
WHITLEY	1,834	972	53.0	733	40.0	101	5.5	28	1.5
WOLFE	1,667	468	28.1	988	59.3	180	10.8	31	1.9
WOODFORD	2,641	756	28.6	1,117	42.3	743	28.1	25	0.9
TOTAL	453,973	181,311	39.9	178,926	39.4	85,221	18.8	8,515	1.9

OTHER VOTE: Mont Walker 3284
Dr. K. N. Salyer 5231

County	Total Vote	Robert H. Lucas		Elmer C. Roberts		Other Vote	
		Total	Per Cent	Total	Per Cent	Total	Per Cent
ADAIR	2,106	1,269	60.3	552	26.2	285	13.5
ALLEN	1,674	1,354	80.9	50	3.0	270	16.1
ANDERSON	614	494	80.5	70	11.4	50	8.1
BALLARD	231	111	48.1	12	5.2	108	46.8
BARREN	1,670	1,132	67.8	314	18.8	224	13.4
BATH	896	805	89.8	42	4.7	49	5.5
BELL	2,640	1,371	51.9	869	32.9	400	15.2
BOONE	246	110	44.7	15	6.1	121	49.2
BOURBON	1,225	849	69.3	49	4.0	327	26.7
BOYD	4,473	3,075	68.7	498	11.1	900	20.1
BOYLE	1,238	996	80.5	31	2.5	211	17.0
BRACKEN	491	381	77.6	24	4.9	86	17.5
BREATHITT	1,200	943	78.6	152	12.7	105	8.8
BRECKINRIDGE	1,814	1,200	66.2	363	20.0	251	13.8
BULLITT	195	108	55.4	50	25.6	37	19.0
BUTLER	1,491	1,008	67.6	72	4.8	411	27.6
CALDWELL	801	439	54.8	35	4.4	327	40.8
CALLOWAY	403	263	65.3	13	3.2	127	31.5
CAMPBELL	8,342	2,793	33.5	892	10.7	4,657	55.8
CARLISLE	178	106	59.6	7	3.9	65	36.5
CARROLL	231	141	61.0	8	3.5	82	35.5
CARTER	3,116	1,886	60.5	427	13.7	803	25.8
CASEY	1,722	1,035	60.1	190	11.0	497	28.9
CHRISTIAN	2,892	1,509	52.2	134	4.6	1,249	43.2
CLARK	991	686	69.2	46	4.6	259	26.1
CLAY	2,366	712	30.1	976	41.3	678	28.7
CLINTON	1,617	948	58.6	450	27.8	219	13.5
CRITTENDEN	1,512	911	60.3	109	7.2	492	32.5
CUMBERSLAN	1,495	730	48.8	576	38.5	189	12.6
DAVIESS	1,173	797	67.9	64	5.5	312	26.6
EDMONSON	1,616	1,192	73.8	46	2.8	378	23.4
ELLIOTT	248	120	48.4	19	7.7	109	44.0
ESTILL	1,556	949	61.0	148	9.5	459	29.5
FAYETTE	3,996	2,617	65.5	174	4.4	1,205	30.2
FLEMING	1,413	1,175	83.2	64	4.5	174	12.3
FLOYD	2,553	1,331	52.1	334	13.1	888	34.8
FRANKLIN	814	630	77.4	29	3.6	155	19.0
FULTON	218	111	50.9	12	5.5	95	43.6
GALLATIN	123	82	66.7	1	0.8	40	32.5
GARRARD	1,005	833	82.9	38	3.8	134	13.3
GRANT	440	254	57.7	20	4.5	166	37.7
GRAVES	643	435	67.7	16	2.5	192	29.9
GRAYSON	1,657	990	59.7	396	23.9	271	16.4
GREEN	1,517	1,106	72.9	275	18.1	136	9.0
GREENUP	2,960	1,961	66.3	486	16.4	513	17.3
HANCOCK	441	232	52.6	112	25.4	97	22.0
HARDIN	996	660	66.3	238	23.9	98	9.8
HARLAN	6,233	3,339	53.6	1,508	24.2	1,386	22.2
HARRISON	742	651	87.7	27	3.6	64	8.6
HART	1,319	648	49.1	454	34.4	217	16.5
HENDERSON	232	144	62.1	9	3.9	79	34.1
HENRY	817	460	56.3	40	4.9	317	38.8
HICKMAN	103	66	64.1	5	4.9	32	31.1
HOPKINS	1,219	716	58.7	59	4.8	444	36.4
JACKSON	2,016	985	48.9	554	27.5	477	23.7
JEFFERSON	15,686	14,875	94.8	209	1.3	602	3.8
JESSAMINE	953	704	73.9	27	2.8	222	23.3
JOHNSON	3,047	1,333	43.7	400	13.1	1,314	43.1
KENTON	3,749	1,436	38.3	475	12.7	1,838	49.0
KNOTT	595	241	40.5	98	16.5	256	43.0
KNOX	3,099	1,779	57.4	747	24.1	573	18.5
LARUE	613	397	64.8	111	18.1	105	17.1
LAUREL	2,425	1,176	48.5	731	30.1	518	21.4
LAWRENCE	2,128	1,329	62.5	337	15.8	462	21.7
LEE	1,295	848	65.5	190	14.7	257	19.8

County	Total Vote	Robert H. Lucas		Elmer C. Roberts		Other Vote	
		Total	Per Cent	Total	Per Cent	Total	Per Cent
LESLIE	2,341	782	33.4	1,197	51.1	362	15.5
LETCHER	3,401	1,706	50.2	262	7.7	1,433	42.1
LEWIS	2,117	1,591	75.2	239	11.3	287	13.6
LINCOLN	1,751	1,343	76.7	31	1.8	377	21.5
LIVINGSTON	536	354	66.0	23	4.3	159	29.7
LOGAN	667	450	67.5	11	1.6	206	30.9
LYON	493	374	75.9	12	2.4	107	21.7
MADISON	3,407	2,494	73.2	92	2.7	821	24.1
MAGOFFIN	2,269	1,989	87.7	121	5.3	159	7.0
MARION	451	247	54.8	141	31.3	63	14.0
MARSHALL	445	340	76.4	20	4.5	85	19.1
MARTIN	1,471	513	34.9	175	11.9	783	53.2
MASON	1,397	1,166	83.5	96	6.9	135	9.7
MC CRACKEN	1,090	575	52.8	51	4.7	464	42.6
MC CREARY	2,176	631	29.0	875	40.2	670	30.8
MC LEAN	312	206	66.0	13	4.2	93	29.8
MEADE	371	234	63.1	94	25.3	43	11.6
MENIFEE	322	240	74.5	27	8.4	55	17.1
MERCER	894	654	73.2	25	2.8	215	24.0
METCALFE	974	582	59.8	217	22.3	175	18.0
MONROE	1,216	687	56.5	275	22.6	254	20.9
MONTGOMERY	709	627	88.4	39	5.5	43	6.1
MORGAN	873	628	71.9	152	17.4	93	10.7
MUHLENBERG	3,198	2,002	62.6	226	7.1	970	30.3
NELSON	885	690	78.0	150	16.9	45	5.1
NICHOLAS	671	614	91.5	22	3.3	35	5.2
OHIO	2,428	1,436	59.1	163	6.7	829	34.1
OLDHAM	269	211	78.4	3	1.1	55	20.4
OWEN	283	192	67.8	15	5.3	76	26.9
OWSLEY	1,842	1,010	54.8	616	33.4	216	11.7
PENDLETON	523	348	66.5	13	2.5	162	31.0
PERRY	3,724	1,904	51.1	555	14.9	1,265	34.0
PIKE	6,962	4,412	63.4	275	4.0	2,275	32.7
POWELL	584	389	66.6	108	18.5	87	14.9
PULASKI	3,916	2,055	52.5	1,298	33.1	563	14.4
ROBERTSON	236	180	76.3	11	4.7	45	19.1
ROCKCASTLE	2,602	1,684	64.7	573	22.0	345	13.3
ROWAN	1,028	756	73.5	159	15.5	113	11.0
RUSSELL	1,712	1,108	64.7	388	22.7	216	12.6
SCOTT	1,096	774	70.6	33	3.0	289	26.4
SHELBY	1,196	868	72.6	219	18.3	109	9.1
SIMPSON	546	398	72.9	8	1.5	140	25.6
SPENCER	228	131	57.5	73	32.0	24	10.5
TAYLOR	1,061	797	75.1	166	15.6	98	9.2
TODD	521	353	67.8	18	3.5	150	28.8
TRIGG	863	679	78.7	23	2.7	161	18.7
TRIMBLE	107	86	80.4			21	19.6
UNION	292	143	49.0	15	5.1	134	45.9
WARREN	1,732	1,152	66.5	68	3.9	512	29.6
WASHINGTON	1,060	787	74.2	175	16.5	98	9.2
WAYNE	1,853	665	35.9	907	48.9	281	15.2
WEBSTER	1,045	637	61.0	33	3.2	375	35.9
WHITLEY	4,304	1,057	24.6	743	17.3	2,504	58.2
WOLFE	698	473	67.8	190	27.2	35	5.0
WOODFORD	779	473	60.7	22	2.8	284	36.5
TOTAL	189,540	120,844	63.8	26,935	14.2	41,761	22.0

OTHER VOTE: Mrs. Helen May Young 16,059
G. Tom Hawkins 11,360
Roscoe Conklin Douglas 14,342

County	Total Vote	Democratic		Republican		Other Vote		Per Cent of Two-Party Vote		Dem-Rep Plurality
		Total	Per Cent	Total	Per Cent	Total	Per Cent	Dem	Rep	
ADAIR	6,018	2,672	44.4	3,344	55.6	2		44.4	55.6	672 R
ALLEN	5,508	2,437	44.2	3,069	55.7	2		44.3	55.7	632 R
ANDERSON	3,773	2,417	64.1	1,354	35.9	2	0.1	64.1	35.9	1,063 D
BALLARD	4,256	3,492	82.0	762	17.9	2		82.1	17.9	2,730 D
BARREN	8,416	5,104	60.6	3,307	39.3	5	0.1	60.7	39.3	1,797 D
BATH	4,489	2,786	62.1	1,701	37.9	2		62.1	37.9	1,085 D
BELL	10,319	5,777	56.0	4,537	44.0	5		56.0	44.0	1,240 D
BOONE	3,887	2,792	71.8	1,025	26.4	70	1.8	73.1	26.9	1,767 D
BOURBON	6,351	3,905	61.5	2,441	38.4	5	0.1	61.5	38.5	1,464 D
BOYD	16,384	9,724	59.4	6,611	40.4	49	0.3	59.5	40.5	3,113 D
BOYLE	6,568	4,141	63.0	2,419	36.8	8	0.1	63.1	36.9	1,722 D
BRACKEN	3,443	1,978	57.4	1,419	41.2	46	1.3	58.2	41.8	559 D
BREATHITT	5,695	3,949	69.3	1,745	30.6	1		69.4	30.6	2,204 D
BRECKINRIDGE	6,097	3,197	52.4	2,861	46.9	39	0.6	52.8	47.2	336 D
BULLITT	3,105	2,458	79.2	643	20.7	4	0.1	79.3	20.7	1,815 D
BUTLER	3,795	1,235	32.5	2,559	67.4	1		32.6	67.4	1,324 R
CALDWELL	4,814	2,694	56.0	2,099	43.6	21	0.4	56.2	43.8	595 D
CALLOWAY	6,422	5,508	85.8	910	14.2	4	0.1	85.8	14.2	4,598 D
CAMPBELL	29,973	16,800	56.1	10,330	34.5	2,843	9.5	61.9	38.1	6,470 D
CARLISLE	2,563	2,129	83.1	415	16.2	19	0.7	83.7	16.3	1,714 D
CARROLL	3,530	2,724	77.2	781	22.1	25	0.7	77.7	22.3	1,943 D
CARTER	7,717	3,382	43.8	4,325	56.0	10	0.1	43.9	56.1	943 R
CASEY	5,507	1,954	35.5	3,551	64.5	2		35.5	64.5	1,597 R
CHRISTIAN	11,766	6,467	55.0	5,299	45.0			55.0	45.0	1,168 D
CLARK	6,622	4,388	66.3	2,226	33.6	8	0.1	66.3	33.7	2,162 D
CLAY	5,663	1,575	27.8	4,088	72.2			27.8	72.2	2,513 R
CLINTON	2,797	685	24.5	2,112	75.5			24.5	75.5	1,427 R
CRITTENDEN	4,346	1,921	44.2	2,421	55.7	4	0.1	44.2	55.8	500 R
CUMBERLAND	3,027	922	30.5	2,104	69.5	1		30.5	69.5	1,182 R
DAVIESS	15,187	9,952	65.5	4,543	29.9	692	4.6	68.7	31.3	5,409 D
EDMONSON	3,810	1,358	35.6	2,448	64.3	4	0.1	35.7	64.3	1,090 R
ELLIOTT	2,010	1,543	76.8	467	23.2			76.8	23.2	1,076 D
ESTILL	5,586	2,649	47.4	2,936	52.6	1		47.4	52.6	287 R
FAYETTE	25,948	14,580	56.2	11,241	43.3	127	0.5	56.5	43.5	3,339 D
FLEMING	5,626	2,894	51.4	2,732	48.6			51.4	48.6	162 D
FLOYD	11,330	7,932	70.0	3,398	30.0			70.0	30.0	4,534 D
FRANKLIN	8,268	6,257	75.7	1,985	24.0	26	0.3	75.9	24.1	4,272 D
FULTON	4,519	3,735	82.7	776	17.2	8	0.2	82.8	17.2	2,959 D
GALLATIN	1,865	1,452	77.9	400	21.4	13	0.7	78.4	21.6	1,052 D
GARRARD	4,506	2,274	50.5	2,231	49.5	1		50.5	49.5	43 D
GRANT	3,936	2,561	65.1	1,352	34.3	23	0.6	65.4	34.6	1,209 D
GRAVES	10,991	9,226	83.9	1,641	14.9	124	1.1	84.9	15.1	7,585 D
GRAYSON	5,547	2,678	48.3	2,860	51.6	9	0.2	48.4	51.6	182 R
GREEN	4,284	1,973	46.1	2,307	53.9	4	0.1	46.1	53.9	334 R
GREENUP	8,668	4,707	54.3	3,961	45.7			54.3	45.7	746 D
HANCOCK	2,397	1,311	54.7	1,081	45.1	5	0.2	54.8	45.2	230 D
HARDIN	6,782	4,478	66.0	2,271	33.5	33	0.5	66.4	33.6	2,207 D
HARLAN	18,317	10,827	59.1	7,490	40.9			59.1	40.9	3,337 D
HARRISON	6,095	4,376	71.8	1,717	28.2	2		71.8	28.2	2,659 D
HART	6,428	3,327	51.8	3,092	48.1	9	0.1	51.8	48.2	235 D
HENDERSON	8,731	6,814	78.0	1,746	20.0	171	2.0	79.6	20.4	5,068 D
HENRY	5,028	3,523	70.1	1,502	29.9	3	0.1	70.1	29.9	2,021 D
HICKMAN	2,929	2,532	86.4	381	13.0	16	0.5	86.9	13.1	2,151 D
HOPKINS	11,664	8,114	69.6	3,531	30.3	19	0.2	69.7	30.3	4,583 D
JACKSON	3,815	424	11.1	3,391	88.9			11.1	88.9	2,967 R
JEFFERSON	141,376	85,129	60.2	52,882	37.4	3,365	2.4	61.7	38.3	32,247 D
JESSAMINE	4,843	2,813	58.1	2,028	41.9	2		58.1	41.9	785 D
JOHNSON	7,313	3,023	41.3	4,279	58.5	11	0.2	41.4	58.6	1,256 R
KENTON	34,386	22,046	64.1	8,705	25.3	3,635	10.6	71.7	28.3	13,341 D
KNOTT	4,369	3,504	80.2	865	19.8			80.2	19.8	2,639 D
KNOX	8,232	3,362	40.8	4,869	59.1	1		40.8	59.2	1,507 R
LARUE	3,426	2,307	67.3	1,111	32.4	8	0.2	67.5	32.5	1,196 D
LAUREL	7,453	2,649	35.5	4,798	64.4	6	0.1	35.5	64.4	2,149 R
LAWRENCE	6,049	3,144	52.0	2,900	47.9	5	0.1	52.0	48.0	244 D
LEE	3,226	1,430	44.3	1,796	55.7			44.3	55.7	366 R

County	Total Vote	Democratic		Republican		Other Vote		Per Cent of Two-Party Vote		Dem-Rep Plurality
		Total	Per Cent	Total	Per Cent	Total	Per Cent	Dem	Rep	
LESLIE	3,334	618	18.5	2,716	81.5			18.5	81.5	2,098 R
LETCHER	10,010	6,152	61.5	3,848	38.4	10	0.1	61.5	38.5	2,304 R
LEWIS	5,174	1,955	37.8	3,210	62.0	9	0.2	37.9	62.1	1,255 R
LINCOLN	6,817	3,610	53.0	3,205	47.0	2		53.0	47.0	405 D
LIVINGSTON	2,907	1,874	64.5	1,028	35.4	5	0.2	64.6	35.4	846 D
LOGAN	6,737	4,923	73.1	1,813	26.9	1		73.1	26.9	3,110 D
LYON	2,744	1,827	66.6	915	33.3	2	0.1	66.6	33.4	912 D
MADISON	12,247	6,234	50.9	5,948	48.6	65	0.5	51.2	48.8	286 D
MAGOFFIN	5,107	2,550	49.9	2,554	50.0	3	0.1	50.0	50.0	4 R
MARION	5,093	3,503	68.8	1,551	30.5	39	0.8	69.3	30.7	1,952 D
MARSHALL	4,673	3,534	75.6	1,131	24.2	8	0.2	75.8	24.2	2,403 D
MARTIN	2,804	794	28.3	2,010	71.7			28.3	71.7	1,216 R
MASON	7,911	4,539	57.4	3,266	41.3	106	1.3	58.2	41.8	1,273 D
MC CRACKEN	13,668	10,505	76.9	3,083	22.6	80	0.6	77.3	22.7	7,422 D
MC CREARY	4,009	1,096	27.3	2,905	72.5	8	0.2	27.4	72.6	1,809 R
MC LEAN	3,825	2,468	64.5	1,327	34.7	30	0.8	65.0	35.0	1,141 D
MEADE	2,928	2,080	71.0	778	26.6	70	2.4	72.8	27.2	1,302 D
MENIFEE	1,697	1,141	67.2	556	32.8			67.2	32.8	585 D
MERCER	5,792	3,649	63.0	2,133	36.8	10	0.2	63.1	36.9	1,516 D
METCALFE	3,478	1,723	49.5	1,753	50.4	2	0.1	49.6	50.4	30 R
MONROE	3,654	1,328	36.3	2,321	63.5	5	0.1	36.4	63.6	993 R
MONTGOMERY	4,245	2,625	61.8	1,594	37.6	26	0.6	62.2	37.8	1,031 D
MORGAN	4,455	3,214	72.1	1,241	27.9			72.1	27.9	1,973 D
MUHLENBERG	10,565	6,352	60.1	4,130	39.1	83	0.8	60.6	39.4	2,222 D
NELSON	6,213	4,150	66.8	1,893	30.5	170	2.7	68.7	31.3	2,257 D
NICHOLAS	3,589	2,323	64.7	1,254	34.9	12	0.3	64.9	35.1	1,069 D
OHIO	8,520	4,039	47.4	4,470	52.5	11	0.1	47.5	52.5	431 R
OLDHAM	2,768	2,003	72.4	754	27.2	11	0.4	72.7	27.3	1,249 D
OWEN	4,029	3,377	83.8	647	16.1	5	0.1	83.9	16.1	2,730 D
OWSLEY	2,729	458	16.8	2,271	83.2			16.8	83.2	1,813 R
PENDLETON	4,263	2,443	57.3	1,811	42.5	9	0.2	57.4	42.6	632 D
PERRY	11,371	6,756	59.4	4,608	40.5	7	0.1	59.5	40.5	2,148 D
PIKE	19,499	11,326	58.1	8,165	41.9	8		58.1	41.9	3,161 D
POWELL	2,155	1,181	54.8	974	45.2			54.8	45.2	207 D
PULASKI	12,121	4,687	38.7	7,426	61.3	8	0.1	38.7	61.3	2,739 R
ROBERTSON	1,383	892	64.5	490	35.4	1	0.1	64.5	35.5	402 D
ROCKCASTLE	5,399	1,557	28.8	3,842	71.2			28.8	71.2	2,285 R
ROWAN	3,649	2,000	54.8	1,649	45.2			54.8	45.2	351 D
RUSSELL	3,810	1,199	31.5	2,611	68.5			31.5	68.5	1,412 R
SCOTT	5,784	3,952	68.3	1,828	31.6	4	0.1	68.4	31.6	2,124 D
SHELBY	6,209	4,349	70.0	1,850	29.8	10	0.2	70.2	29.8	2,499 D
SIMPSON	4,258	3,024	71.0	1,234	29.0			71.0	29.0	1,790 D
SPENCER	2,297	1,653	72.0	638	27.8	6	0.3	72.2	27.8	1,015 D
TAYLOR	5,466	2,756	50.4	2,707	49.5	3	0.1	50.4	49.6	49 D
TODD	4,158	2,980	71.7	1,176	28.3	2		71.7	28.3	1,804 D
TRIGG	4,390	2,883	65.7	1,496	34.1	11	0.3	65.8	34.2	1,387 D
TRIMBLE	1,934	1,665	86.1	265	13.7	4	0.2	86.3	13.7	1,400 D
UNION	5,694	4,663	81.9	920	16.2	111	1.9	83.5	16.5	3,743 D
WARREN	12,432	8,147	65.5	4,271	34.4	14	0.1	65.6	34.4	3,876 D
WASHINGTON	4,919	2,526	51.4	2,388	48.5	5	0.1	51.4	48.6	138 D
WAYNE	5,404	2,496	46.2	2,900	53.7	8	0.1	46.3	53.7	404 R
WEBSTER	6,705	4,748	70.8	1,945	29.0	12	0.2	70.9	29.1	2,803 D
WHITLEY	8,863	3,171	35.8	5,686	64.2	6	0.1	35.8	64.2	2,515 R
WOLFE	2,550	1,580	62.0	970	38.0			62.0	38.0	610 D
WOODFORD	4,100	2,573	62.8	1,524	37.2	3	0.1	62.8	37.2	1,049 D
TOTAL	918,339	539,968	58.8	365,850	39.8	12,521	1.4	59.6	40.4	174,118 D

OTHER VOTE: William M. Likins (Union) 11,709
Ferdinand Zimmer (Socialist Labor) 271
W. A. Sandefur (Socialist) 541
DEMOCRAT: M. M. Logan
REPUBLICAN: Robert M. Lucas

County	Total Vote	Alben W. Barkley		A. B. Chandler		Other Vote	
		Total	Per Cent	Total	Per Cent	Total	Per Cent
ADAIR	2,689	1,379	51.3	1,277	47.5	33	1.2
ALLEN	2,175	1,210	55.6	924	42.5	41	1.9
ANDERSON	2,608	1,338	51.3	1,233	47.3	37	1.4
BALLARD	3,847	2,656	69.0	1,184	30.8	7	0.2
BARREN	5,017	2,490	49.6	2,397	47.8	130	2.6
BATH	3,354	1,458	43.5	1,794	53.5	102	3.0
BELL	2,938	1,856	63.2	1,031	35.1	51	1.7
BOONE	3,113	1,407	45.2	1,677	53.9	29	0.9
BOURBON	3,873	1,925	49.7	1,878	48.5	70	1.8
BOYD	8,360	4,762	57.0	3,480	41.6	118	1.4
BOYLE	4,573	2,361	51.6	2,128	46.5	84	1.8
BRACKEN	2,205	699	31.7	1,477	67.0	29	1.3
BREATHITT	4,656	2,679	57.5	1,857	39.9	120	2.6
BRECKINRIDGE	3,228	1,254	38.8	1,923	59.6	51	1.6
BULLITT	2,704	1,372	50.7	1,288	47.6	44	1.6
BUTLER	1,317	634	48.1	660	50.1	23	1.7
CALDWELL	2,948	1,741	59.1	1,194	40.5	13	0.4
CALLOWAY	6,518	3,859	59.2	2,642	40.5	17	0.3
CAMPBELL	11,826	5,267	44.5	6,469	54.7	90	0.8
CARLISLE	2,933	2,137	72.9	785	26.8	11	0.4
CARROLL	3,271	1,640	50.1	1,574	48.1	57	1.7
CARTER	3,139	1,680	53.5	1,390	44.3	69	2.2
CASEY	1,842	757	41.1	1,044	56.7	41	2.2
CHRISTIAN	6,350	3,491	55.0	2,836	44.7	23	0.4
CLARK	4,677	2,272	48.6	2,293	49.0	112	2.4
CLAY	1,440	625	43.4	779	54.1	36	2.5
CLINTON	788	241	30.6	534	67.8	13	1.6
CRITTENDEN	1,940	1,071	55.2	863	44.5	6	0.3
CUMBERLAND	941	431	45.8	500	53.1	10	1.1
DAVIESS	9,082	5,022	55.3	3,957	43.6	103	1.1
EDMONSON	1,554	657	42.3	865	55.7	32	2.1
ELLIOTT	2,506	1,372	54.7	1,080	43.1	54	2.2
ESTILL	2,294	1,163	50.7	1,091	47.6	40	1.7
FAYETTE	12,730	6,991	54.9	5,595	44.0	144	1.1
FLEMING	3,483	1,142	32.8	2,297	65.9	44	1.3
FLOYD	7,575	5,090	67.2	2,419	31.9	66	0.9
FRANKLIN	6,776	2,928	43.2	3,703	54.6	145	2.1
FULTON	4,007	2,724	68.0	1,260	31.4	23	0.6
GALLATIN	1,679	629	37.5	1,017	60.6	33	2.0
GARRARD	2,189	1,114	50.9	1,029	47.0	46	2.1
GRANT	3,576	1,810	50.6	1,711	47.8	55	1.5
GRAVES	11,385	6,503	57.1	4,832	42.4	50	0.4
GRAYSON	2,837	1,490	52.5	1,310	46.2	37	1.3
GREEN	2,078	974	46.9	1,081	52.0	23	1.1
GREENUP	4,189	2,420	57.8	1,683	40.2	86	2.1
HANCOCK	1,202	659	54.8	533	44.3	10	0.8
HARDIN	5,715	2,676	46.8	2,921	51.1	118	2.1
HARLAN	6,149	2,209	35.9	3,816	62.1	124	2.0
HARRISON	4,142	2,299	55.5	1,794	43.3	49	1.2
HART	3,316	1,504	45.4	1,739	52.4	73	2.2
HENDERSON	7,803	4,271	54.7	3,429	43.9	103	1.3
HENRY	4,043	2,093	51.8	1,901	47.0	49	1.2
HICKMAN	3,617	2,150	59.4	1,444	39.9	23	0.6
HOPKINS	8,220	5,337	64.9	2,767	33.7	116	1.4
JACKSON	482	230	47.7	242	50.2	10	2.1
JEFFERSON	69,158	49,568	71.7	19,170	27.7	420	0.6
JESSAMINE	3,225	1,429	44.3	1,724	53.5	72	2.2
JOHNSON	2,174	1,268	58.3	861	39.6	45	2.1
KENTON	19,282	9,960	51.7	9,206	47.7	116	0.6
KNOTT	3,706	2,235	60.3	1,370	37.0	101	2.7
KNOX	2,642	1,513	57.3	1,086	41.1	43	1.6
LARUE	3,051	1,388	45.5	1,609	52.7	54	1.8
LAUREL	2,257	1,462	64.8	764	33.9	31	1.4
LAWRENCE	2,784	1,566	56.3	1,178	42.3	40	1.4
LEE	1,367	762	55.7	577	42.2	28	2.0

County	Total Vote	Alben W. Barkley Total	Per Cent	A. B. Chandler Total	Per Cent	Other Vote Total	Per Cent
LESLIE	419	128	30.5	281	67.1	10	2.4
LETCHER	4,231	3,125	73.9	990	23.4	116	2.7
LEWIS	1,840	752	40.9	1,024	55.7	64	3.5
LINCOLN	3,880	1,753	45.2	2,025	52.2	102	2.6
LIVINGSTON	2,516	1,308	52.0	1,197	47.6	11	0.4
LOGAN	6,220	4,090	65.8	2,038	32.8	92	1.5
LYON	2,775	1,541	55.5	1,210	43.6	24	0.9
MADISON	5,687	3,158	55.5	2,417	42.5	112	2.0
MAGOFFIN	2,692	1,312	48.7	1,349	50.1	31	1.2
MARION	4,518	2,318	51.3	2,120	46.9	80	1.8
MARSHALL	4,039	2,700	66.8	1,333	33.0	6	0.1
MARTIN	862	436	50.6	409	47.4	17	2.0
MASON	4,597	1,857	40.4	2,688	58.5	52	1.1
MC CRACKEN	11,068	8,668	78.3	2,368	21.4	32	0.3
MC CREARY	787	428	54.4	349	44.3	10	1.3
MC LEAN	2,828	1,435	50.7	1,366	48.3	27	1.0
MEADE	2,677	1,197	44.7	1,441	53.8	39	1.5
MENIFEE	1,328	773	58.2	514	38.7	41	3.1
MERCER	3,757	2,038	54.2	1,648	43.9	71	1.9
METCALFE	1,964	957	48.7	977	49.7	30	1.5
MONROE	1,500	707	47.1	754	50.3	39	2.6
MONTGOMERY	3,478	2,013	57.9	1,369	39.4	96	2.8
MORGAN	3,926	2,128	54.2	1,757	44.8	41	1.0
MUHLENBERG	4,681	3,460	73.9	1,140	24.4	81	1.7
NELSON	5,327	2,320	43.6	2,930	55.0	77	1.4
NICHOLAS	2,450	988	40.3	1,412	57.6	50	2.0
OHIO	3,303	2,061	62.4	1,192	36.1	50	1.5
OLDHAM	2,034	780	38.3	1,232	60.6	22	1.1
OWEN	3,950	2,073	52.5	1,793	45.4	84	2.1
OWSLEY	459	166	36.2	274	59.7	19	4.1
PENDLETON	2,788	1,116	40.0	1,635	58.6	37	1.3
PERRY	4,736	2,988	63.1	1,597	33.7	151	3.2
PIKE	10,543	6,145	58.3	3,999	37.9	399	3.8
POWELL	1,132	610	53.9	460	40.6	62	5.5
PULASKI	4,771	2,177	45.6	2,512	52.7	82	1.7
ROBERTSON	1,208	513	42.5	672	55.6	23	1.9
ROCKCASTLE	1,547	765	49.5	764	49.4	18	1.2
ROWAN	2,351	1,175	50.0	1,127	47.9	49	2.1
RUSSELL	1,461	793	54.3	633	43.3	35	2.4
SCOTT	4,102	2,457	59.9	1,580	38.5	65	1.6
SHELBY	4,710	2,307	49.0	2,353	50.0	50	1.1
SIMPSON	3,161	1,893	59.9	1,227	38.8	41	1.3
SPENCER	1,661	741	44.6	902	54.3	18	1.1
TAYLOR	2,916	1,158	39.7	1,703	58.4	55	1.9
TODD	4,424	2,427	54.9	1,870	42.3	127	2.9
TRIGG	3,147	2,022	64.3	1,112	35.3	13	0.4
TRIMBLE	2,033	903	44.4	1,098	54.0	32	1.6
UNION	4,904	2,809	57.3	2,046	41.7	49	1.0
WARREN	9,563	4,585	47.9	4,835	50.6	143	1.5
WASHINGTON	2,609	1,326	50.8	1,247	47.8	36	1.4
WAYNE	2,474	1,429	57.8	962	38.9	83	3.4
WEBSTER	4,719	2,779	58.9	1,870	39.6	70	1.5
WHITLEY	1,857	1,039	56.0	799	43.0	19	1.0
WOLFE	2,446	1,434	58.6	1,005	41.1	7	0.3
WOODFORD	2,956	1,001	33.9	1,913	64.7	42	1.4
TOTAL	525,554	294,562	56.0	223,690	42.6	7,302	1.4

OTHER VOTE: Stuart Lampe 397
G. A. Hendon, Jr. 854   John E. Trager 163
John H. Dougherty 586   John L. Sullivan 175
Hugh K. Bullitt 2636   J. Ward Lehigh 411
Frank Coyle 702   Edward L. Macky 424
Munnell Wilson 759   W. T. McNally 195

County	Total Vote	John P. Haswell Total	Per Cent	Andrew O. Ritchie Total	Per Cent	G. Tom Hawkins Total	Per Cent	Other Vote Total	Per Cent
ADAIR	413	329	79.7	33	8.0	22	5.3	29	7.0
ALLEN	360	344	95.6	3	0.8	7	1.9	6	1.7
ANDERSON	127	102	80.3	18	14.2	5	3.9	2	1.6
BALLARD	45	26	57.8	1	2.2	4	8.9	14	31.1
BARREN	348	246	70.7	59	17.0	17	4.9	26	7.5
BATH	84	60	71.4	11	13.1	9	10.7	4	4.8
BELL	720	236	32.8	277	38.5	53	7.4	154	21.4
BOONE	54	20	37.0	1	1.9	4	7.4	29	53.7
BOURBON	55	34	61.8	7	12.7	5	9.1	9	16.4
BOYD	1,145	683	59.7	104	9.1	263	23.0	95	8.3
BOYLE	104	49	47.1	26	25.0	12	11.5	17	16.3
BRACKEN	114	37	32.5	33	28.9	35	30.7	9	7.9
BREATHITT	217	61	28.1	36	16.6	33	15.2	87	40.1
BRECKINRIDGE	1,042	1,023	98.2	15	1.4	1	0.1	3	0.3
BULLITT	66	35	53.0	14	21.2	11	16.7	6	9.1
BUTLER	432	342	79.2	35	8.1	36	8.3	19	4.4
CALDWELL	351	282	80.3	7	2.0	9	2.6	53	15.1
CALLOWAY	106	56	52.8	10	9.4	10	9.4	30	28.3
CAMPBELL	2,465	816	33.1	295	12.0	508	20.6	846	34.3
CARLISLE	53	33	62.3	4	7.5	2	3.8	14	26.4
CARROLL	38	14	36.8	15	39.5	1	2.6	8	21.1
CARTER	875	650	74.3	37	4.2	141	16.1	47	5.4
CASEY	458	373	81.4	29	6.3	21	4.6	35	7.6
CHRISTIAN	150	73	48.7	18	12.0	13	8.7	46	30.7
CLARK	168	66	39.3	35	20.8	14	8.3	53	31.5
CLAY	954	540	56.6	174	18.2	52	5.5	188	19.7
CLINTON	304	87	28.6	118	38.8	33	10.9	66	21.7
CRITTENDEN	267	184	68.9	1	0.4	28	10.5	54	20.2
CUMBERLAND	226	90	39.8	52	23.0	23	10.2	61	27.0
DAVIESS	349	288	82.5	32	9.2	14	4.0	15	4.3
EDMONSON	396	364	91.9	5	1.3	20	5.1	7	1.8
ELLIOTT	47	13	27.7	13	27.7	14	29.8	7	14.9
ESTILL	247	138	55.9	39	15.8	9	3.6	61	24.7
FAYETTE	453	230	50.8	151	33.3	20	4.4	52	11.5
FLEMING	264	125	47.3	89	33.7	33	12.5	17	6.4
FLOYD	1,201	645	53.7	103	8.6	202	16.8	251	20.9
FRANKLIN	194	138	71.1	30	15.5	3	1.5	23	11.9
FULTON	55	32	58.2			9	16.4	14	25.5
GALLATIN	38	17	44.7	11	28.9	6	15.8	4	10.5
GARRARD	121	78	64.5	31	25.6	2	1.7	10	8.3
GRANT	89	26	29.2	15	16.9	10	11.2	38	42.7
GRAVES	144	75	52.1	11	7.6	17	11.8	41	28.5
GRAYSON	514	462	89.9	34	6.6	6	1.2	12	2.3
GREEN	275	207	75.3	32	11.6	17	6.2	19	6.9
GREENUP	668	177	26.5	148	22.2	252	37.7	91	13.6
HANCOCK	155	122	78.7	19	12.3	9	5.8	5	3.2
HARDIN	251	198	78.9	34	13.5	10	4.0	9	3.6
HARLAN	1,679	784	46.7	371	22.1	150	8.9	374	22.3
HARRISON	140	92	65.7	13	9.3	30	21.4	5	3.6
HART	801	657	82.0	72	9.0	44	5.5	28	3.5
HENDERSON	67	35	52.2	10	14.9	8	11.9	14	20.9
HENRY	137	72	52.6	13	9.5	13	9.5	39	28.5
HICKMAN	23	13	56.5	1	4.3			9	39.1
HOPKINS	224	141	62.9	15	6.7	42	18.8	26	11.6
JACKSON	605	142	23.5	344	56.9	38	6.3	81	13.4
JEFFERSON	10,132	8,905	87.9	390	3.8	616	6.1	221	2.2
JESSAMINE	115	68	59.1	29	25.2	8	7.0	10	8.7
JOHNSON	1,115	532	47.7	91	8.2	319	28.6	173	15.5
KENTON	618	191	30.9	112	18.1	71	11.5	244	39.5
KNOTT	169	55	32.5	41	24.3	27	16.0	46	27.2
KNOX	1,724	677	39.3	383	22.2	218	12.6	446	25.9
LARUE	144	121	84.0	13	9.0	6	4.2	4	2.8
LAUREL	772	254	32.9	221	28.6	56	7.3	241	31.2
LAWRENCE	787	226	28.7	139	17.7	287	36.5	135	17.2
LEE	280	108	38.6	29	10.4	22	7.9	121	43.2

County	Total Vote	John P. Haswell		Andrew O. Ritchie		G. Tom Hawkins		Other Vote	
		Total	Per Cent	Total	Per Cent	Total	Per Cent	Total	Per Cent
LESLIE	568	311	54.8	83	14.6	18	3.2	156	27.5
LETCHER	1,134	339	29.9	455	40.1	193	17.0	147	13.0
LEWIS	645	490	76.0	49	7.6	90	14.0	16	2.5
LINCOLN	374	321	85.8	23	6.1	7	1.9	23	6.1
LIVINGSTON	186	125	67.2	2	1.1	17	9.1	42	22.6
LOGAN	71	57	80.3	3	4.2	9	12.7	2	2.8
LYON	93	76	81.7			1	1.1	16	17.2
MADISON	216	106	49.1	72	33.3	13	6.0	25	11.6
MAGOFFIN	1,163	731	62.9	209	18.0	44	3.8	179	15.4
MARION	91	53	58.2	20	22.0	5	5.5	13	14.3
MARSHALL	174	156	89.7	4	2.3	5	2.9	9	5.2
MARTIN	494	281	56.9	33	6.7	114	23.1	66	13.4
MASON	274	198	72.3	25	9.1	49	17.9	2	0.7
MC CRACKEN	232	121	52.2	38	16.4	18	7.8	55	23.7
MC CREARY	1,137	258	22.7	245	21.5	140	12.3	494	43.4
MC LEAN	151	130	86.1	8	5.3	10	6.6	3	2.0
MEADE	117	104	88.9	8	6.8			5	4.3
MENIFEE	87	12	13.8	50	57.5	9	10.3	16	18.4
MERCER	126	80	63.5	21	16.7	16	12.7	9	7.1
METCALFE	311	261	83.9	16	5.1	16	5.1	18	5.8
MONROE	379	252	66.5	39	10.3			88	23.2
MONTGOMERY	111	46	41.4	36	32.4	18	16.2	11	9.9
MORGAN	253	58	22.9	114	45.1	34	13.4	47	18.6
MUHLENBERG	662	510	77.0	62	9.4	61	9.2	29	4.4
NELSON	186	160	86.0	11	5.9	8	4.3	7	3.8
NICHOLAS	207	153	73.9	31	15.0	15	7.2	8	3.9
OHIO	608	526	86.5	36	5.9	30	4.9	16	2.6
OLDHAM	63	35	55.6	9	14.3	3	4.8	16	25.4
OWEN	80	43	53.8	6	7.5	8	10.0	23	28.8
OWSLEY	444	271	61.0	68	15.3	42	9.5	63	14.2
PENDLETON	87	39	44.8	35	40.2	4	4.6	9	10.3
PERRY	958	382	39.9	263	27.5	86	9.0	227	23.7
PIKE	2,028	1,046	51.6	268	13.2	623	30.7	91	4.5
POWELL	160	38	23.8	61	38.1	38	23.8	23	14.4
PULASKI	1,712	1,302	76.1	137	8.0	68	4.0	205	12.0
ROBERTSON	77	50	64.9	15	19.5	7	9.1	5	6.5
ROCKCASTLE	458	215	46.9	168	36.7	34	7.4	41	9.0
ROWAN	433	275	63.5	73	16.9	28	6.5	57	13.2
RUSSELL	543	370	68.1	65	12.0	36	6.6	72	13.3
SCOTT	214	174	81.3	20	9.3	5	2.3	15	7.0
SHELBY	166	54	32.5	81	48.8	13	7.8	18	10.8
SIMPSON	87	72	82.8	5	5.7	6	6.9	4	4.6
SPENCER	48	19	39.6	19	39.6	3	6.3	7	14.6
TAYLOR	240	168	70.0	54	22.5	9	3.8	9	3.8
TODD	74	51	68.9	6	8.1	13	17.6	4	5.4
TRIGG	197	153	77.7	8	4.1	8	4.1	28	14.2
TRIMBLE	25	7	28.0	12	48.0	1	4.0	5	20.0
UNION	71	53	74.6	9	12.7	1	1.4	8	11.3
WARREN	280	236	84.3	11	3.9	29	10.4	4	1.4
WASHINGTON	122	85	69.7	25	20.5	11	9.0	1	0.8
WAYNE	491	311	63.3	69	14.1	36	7.3	75	15.3
WEBSTER	227	144	63.4	15	6.6	31	13.7	37	16.3
WHITLEY	3,129	158	5.0	472	15.1	117	3.7	2,382	76.1
WOLFE	235	46	19.6	45	19.1	36	15.3	108	46.0
WOODFORD	78	60	76.9	3	3.8	3	3.8	12	15.4
TOTAL	59,468	34,971	58.8	8,267	13.9	6,219	10.5	10,011	16.8

OTHER VOTE: Roscoe Conklin Douglas 5157
Elmer C. Roberts 4854

County	Total Vote	Democratic		Republican		Per Cent of Two-Party Vote		Dem-Rep Plurality
		Total	Per Cent	Total	Per Cent	Dem	Rep	
ADAIR	3,468	1,631	47.0	1,837	53.0	47.0	53.0	206 R
ALLEN	2,523	1,066	42.3	1,457	57.7	42.3	57.7	391 R
ANDERSON	2,078	1,497	72.0	581	28.0	72.0	28.0	916 D
BALLARD	2,456	2,176	88.6	280	11.4	88.6	11.4	1,896 D
BARREN	4,501	2,670	59.3	1,831	40.7	59.3	40.7	839 D
BATH	2,460	1,693	68.8	767	31.2	68.8	31.2	926 D
BELL	5,638	3,405	60.4	2,233	39.6	60.4	39.6	1,172 D
BOONE	1,902	1,446	76.0	456	24.0	76.0	24.0	990 D
BOURBON	3,123	2,222	71.1	901	28.9	71.1	28.9	1,321 D
BOYD	12,127	6,827	56.3	5,300	43.7	56.3	43.7	1,527 D
BOYLE	3,110	2,164	69.6	946	30.4	69.6	30.4	1,218 D
BRACKEN	1,507	913	60.6	594	39.4	60.6	39.4	319 D
BREATHITT	2,947	2,399	81.4	548	18.6	81.4	18.6	1,851 D
BRECKINRIDGE	4,265	2,270	53.2	1,995	46.8	53.2	46.8	275 D
BULLITT	1,620	1,253	77.3	367	22.7	77.3	22.7	886 D
BUTLER	2,495	915	36.7	1,580	63.3	36.7	63.3	665 R
CALDWELL	2,978	1,847	62.0	1,131	38.0	62.0	38.0	716 D
CALLOWAY	3,657	3,252	88.9	405	11.1	88.9	11.1	2,847 D
CAMPBELL	14,812	7,677	51.8	7,135	48.2	51.8	48.2	542 D
CARLISLE	1,908	1,675	87.8	233	12.2	87.8	12.2	1,442 D
CARROLL	1,785	1,487	83.3	298	16.7	83.3	16.7	1,189 D
CARTER	4,754	2,104	44.3	2,650	55.7	44.3	55.7	546 R
CASEY	2,532	974	38.5	1,558	61.5	38.5	61.5	584 R
CHRISTIAN	7,165	3,823	53.4	3,342	46.6	53.4	46.6	481 D
CLARK	3,007	2,114	70.3	893	29.7	70.3	29.7	1,221 D
CLAY	3,036	1,101	36.3	1,935	63.7	36.3	63.7	834 R
CLINTON	1,366	411	30.1	955	69.9	30.1	69.9	544 R
CRITTENDEN	2,431	1,210	49.8	1,221	50.2	49.8	50.2	11 R
CUMBERLAND	1,342	537	40.0	805	60.0	40.0	60.0	268 R
DAVIESS	8,491	5,623	66.2	2,868	33.8	66.2	33.8	2,755 D
EDMONSON	2,428	951	39.2	1,477	60.8	39.2	60.8	526 R
ELLIOTT	2,023	1,651	81.6	372	18.4	81.6	18.4	1,279 D
ESTILL	2,524	1,353	53.6	1,171	46.4	53.6	46.4	182 D
FAYETTE	9,378	5,756	61.4	3,622	38.6	61.4	38.6	2,134 D
FLEMING	3,835	2,281	59.5	1,554	40.5	59.5	40.5	727 D
FLOYD	10,415	7,676	73.7	2,739	26.3	73.7	26.3	4,937 D
FRANKLIN	4,972	4,201	84.5	771	15.5	84.5	15.5	3,430 D
FULTON	2,952	2,586	87.6	366	12.4	87.6	12.4	2,220 D
GALLATIN	846	670	79.2	176	20.8	79.2	20.8	494 D
GARRARD	2,079	1,213	58.3	866	41.7	58.3	41.7	347 D
GRANT	2,452	1,853	75.6	599	24.4	75.6	24.4	1,254 D
GRAVES	6,579	5,777	87.8	802	12.2	87.8	12.2	4,975 D
GRAYSON	4,044	2,063	51.0	1,981	49.0	51.0	49.0	82 D
GREEN	2,727	1,268	46.5	1,459	53.5	46.5	53.5	191 R
GREENUP	6,813	3,850	56.5	2,963	43.5	56.5	43.5	887 D
HANCOCK	1,576	949	60.2	627	39.8	60.2	39.8	322 D
HARDIN	3,404	2,290	67.3	1,114	32.7	67.3	32.7	1,176 D
HARLAN	15,392	8,069	52.4	7,323	47.6	52.4	47.6	746 D
HARRISON	2,857	2,123	74.3	734	25.7	74.3	25.7	1,389 D
HART	4,500	2,251	50.0	2,249	50.0	50.0	50.0	2 D
HENDERSON	4,333	3,504	80.9	829	19.1	80.9	19.1	2,675 D
HENRY	2,784	2,140	76.9	644	23.1	76.9	23.1	1,496 D
HICKMAN	2,366	2,130	90.0	236	10.0	90.0	10.0	1,894 D
HOPKINS	6,430	4,747	73.8	1,683	26.2	73.8	26.2	3,064 D
JACKSON	2,666	495	18.6	2,171	81.4	18.6	81.4	1,676 R
JEFFERSON	97,207	61,612	63.4	35,595	36.6	63.4	36.6	26,017 D
JESSAMINE	3,057	1,961	64.1	1,096	35.9	64.1	35.9	865 D
JOHNSON	4,289	1,942	45.3	2,347	54.7	45.3	54.7	405 R
KENTON	15,829	10,725	67.8	5,104	32.2	67.8	32.2	5,621 D
KNOTT	3,617	2,928	81.0	689	19.0	81.0	19.0	2,239 D
KNOX	3,703	1,580	42.7	2,123	57.3	42.7	57.3	543 R
LARUE	2,623	1,880	71.7	743	28.3	71.7	28.3	1,137 D
LAUREL	5,158	2,299	44.6	2,859	55.4	44.6	55.4	560 R
LAWRENCE	4,004	2,244	56.0	1,760	44.0	56.0	44.0	484 D
LEE	2,257	1,237	54.8	1,020	45.2	54.8	45.2	217 D

34

County	Total Vote	Democratic		Republican		Per Cent of Two-Party Vote		Dem-Rep Plurality
		Total	Per Cent	Total	Per Cent	Dem	Rep	
LESLIE	1,376	381	27.7	995	72.3	27.7	72.3	614 R
LETCHER	6,685	4,096	61.3	2,589	38.7	61.3	38.7	1,507 D
LEWIS	3,608	1,394	38.6	2,214	61.4	38.6	61.4	820 R
LINCOLN	4,441	2,508	56.5	1,933	43.5	56.5	43.5	575 D
LIVINGSTON	2,071	1,499	72.4	572	27.6	72.4	27.6	927 D
LOGAN	4,975	3,859	77.6	1,116	22.4	77.6	22.4	2,743 D
LYON	2,197	1,674	76.2	523	23.8	76.2	23.8	1,151 D
MADISON	7,746	4,583	59.2	3,163	40.8	59.2	40.8	1,420 D
MAGOFFIN	4,170	2,418	58.0	1,752	42.0	58.0	42.0	666 D
MARION	3,420	2,498	73.0	922	27.0	73.0	27.0	1,576 D
MARSHALL	2,119	1,734	81.8	385	18.2	81.8	18.2	1,349 D
MARTIN	1,520	625	41.1	895	58.9	41.1	58.9	270 R
MASON	4,175	2,371	56.8	1,804	43.2	56.8	43.2	567 D
MC CRACKEN	8,707	7,209	82.8	1,498	17.2	82.8	17.2	5,711 D
MC CREARY	2,390	661	27.7	1,729	72.3	27.7	72.3	1,068 R
MC LEAN	2,336	1,523	65.2	813	34.8	65.2	34.8	710 D
MEADE	1,964	1,359	69.2	605	30.8	69.2	30.8	754 D
MENIFEE	857	662	77.2	195	22.8	77.2	22.8	467 D
MERCER	3,398	2,318	68.2	1,080	31.8	68.2	31.8	1,238 D
METCALFE	2,799	1,230	43.9	1,569	56.1	43.9	56.1	339 R
MONROE	3,193	1,218	38.1	1,975	61.9	38.1	61.9	757 R
MONTGOMERY	3,403	2,435	71.6	968	28.4	71.6	28.4	1,467 D
MORGAN	3,129	2,375	75.9	754	24.1	75.9	24.1	1,621 D
MUHLENBERG	6,188	3,538	57.2	2,650	42.8	57.2	42.8	888 D
NELSON	3,788	2,902	76.6	886	23.4	76.6	23.4	2,016 D
NICHOLAS	1,918	1,262	65.8	656	34.2	65.8	34.2	606 D
OHIO	4,416	2,181	49.4	2,235	50.6	49.4	50.6	54 R
OLDHAM	1,177	929	78.9	248	21.1	78.9	21.1	681 D
OWEN	2,096	1,851	88.3	245	11.7	88.3	11.7	1,606 D
OWSLEY	2,190	446	20.4	1,744	79.6	20.4	79.6	1,298 R
PENDLETON	2,164	1,275	58.9	889	41.1	58.9	41.1	386 D
PERRY	6,422	3,741	58.3	2,681	41.7	58.3	41.7	1,060 D
PIKE	15,201	9,381	61.7	5,820	38.3	61.7	38.3	3,561 D
POWELL	1,495	927	62.0	568	38.0	62.0	38.0	359 D
PULASKI	6,468	2,953	45.7	3,515	54.3	45.7	54.3	562 R
ROBERTSON	1,001	575	57.4	426	42.6	57.4	42.6	149 D
ROCKCASTLE	2,592	984	38.0	1,608	62.0	38.0	62.0	624 R
ROWAN	3,228	1,832	56.8	1,396	43.2	56.8	43.2	436 D
RUSSELL	2,413	947	39.2	1,466	60.8	39.2	60.8	519 R
SCOTT	3,206	2,398	74.8	808	25.2	74.8	25.2	1,590 D
SHELBY	3,157	2,371	75.1	786	24.9	75.1	24.9	1,585 D
SIMPSON	2,106	1,642	78.0	464	22.0	78.0	22.0	1,178 D
SPENCER	1,222	926	75.8	296	24.2	75.8	24.2	630 D
TAYLOR	3,413	1,813	53.1	1,600	46.9	53.1	46.9	213 D
TODD	3,236	2,279	70.4	957	29.6	70.4	29.6	1,322 D
TRIGG	2,838	1,976	69.6	862	30.4	69.6	30.4	1,114 D
TRIMBLE	1,193	1,070	89.7	123	10.3	89.7	10.3	947 D
UNION	3,156	2,688	85.2	468	14.8	85.2	14.8	2,220 D
WARREN	6,551	4,500	68.7	2,051	31.3	68.7	31.3	2,449 D
WASHINGTON	2,769	1,541	55.7	1,228	44.3	55.7	44.3	313 D
WAYNE	2,951	1,466	49.7	1,485	50.3	49.7	50.3	19 R
WEBSTER	2,734	2,033	74.4	701	25.6	74.4	25.6	1,332 D
WHITLEY	4,903	1,909	38.9	2,994	61.1	38.9	61.1	1,085 R
WOLFE	2,650	1,911	72.1	739	27.9	72.1	27.9	1,172 D
WOODFORD	1,877	1,221	65.1	656	34.9	65.1	34.9	565 D
TOTAL	559,001	346,735	62.0	212,266	38.0	62.0	38.0	134,469 D

DEMOCRAT: Alben W. Barkley
REPUBLICAN: John P. Haswell

County	Total Vote	A. B. Chandler		Charles P. Farnsley		Other Vote	
		Total	Per Cent	Total	Per Cent	Total	Per Cent
ADAIR	1,052	916	87.1	59	5.6	77	7.3
ALLEN	459	372	81.0	54	11.8	33	7.2
ANDERSON	1,152	980	85.1	96	8.3	76	6.6
BALLARD	2,304	1,621	70.4	278	12.1	405	17.6
BARREN	1,982	1,602	80.8	190	9.6	190	9.6
BATH	1,194	998	83.6	115	9.6	81	6.8
BELL	1,153	972	84.3	28	2.4	153	13.3
BOONE	1,070	839	78.4	119	11.1	112	10.5
BOURBON	1,097	997	90.9	50	4.6	50	4.6
BOYD	3,502	2,804	80.1	342	9.8	356	10.2
BOYLE	1,403	1,136	81.0	166	11.8	101	7.2
BRACKEN	723	634	87.7	63	8.7	26	3.6
BREATHITT	2,863	2,287	79.9	303	10.6	273	9.5
BRECKINRIDGE	1,481	1,313	88.7	72	4.9	96	6.5
BULLITT	999	778	77.9	98	9.8	123	12.3
BUTLER	433	350	80.8	66	15.2	17	3.9
CALDWELL	984	845	85.9	78	7.9	61	6.2
CALLOWAY	2,489	1,941	78.0	170	6.8	378	15.2
CAMPBELL	5,256	4,055	77.1	363	6.9	838	15.9
CARLISLE	1,408	888	63.1	243	17.3	277	19.7
CARROLL	1,646	1,153	70.0	281	17.1	212	12.9
CARTER	1,168	966	82.7	97	8.3	105	9.0
CASEY	568	512	90.1	26	4.6	30	5.3
CHRISTION	2,303	1,830	79.5	253	11.0	220	9.6
CLARK	859	672	78.2	114	13.3	73	8.5
CLAY	597	550	92.1	9	1.5	38	6.4
CLINTON	299	286	95.7	6	2.0	7	2.3
CRITTENDEN	761	564	74.1	151	19.8	46	6.0
CUMBERLAND	262	237	90.5	10	3.8	15	5.7
DAVIESS	1,808	1,501	83.0	230	12.7	77	4.3
EDMONSON	688	622	90.4	41	6.0	25	3.6
ELLIOTT	1,082	767	70.9	60	5.5	255	23.6
ESTILL	776	751	96.8	12	1.5	13	1.7
FAYETTE	6,259	4,989	79.7	707	11.3	563	9.0
FLEMING	1,984	1,812	91.3	122	6.1	50	2.5
FLOYD	3,594	2,766	77.0	257	7.2	571	15.9
FRANKLIN	3,038	2,727	89.8	201	6.6	110	3.6
FULTON	1,328	1,073	80.8	152	11.4	103	7.8
GALLATIN	736	634	86.1	46	6.3	56	7.6
GARRARD	689	618	89.7	42	6.1	29	4.2
GRANT	1,273	917	72.0	207	16.3	149	11.7
GRAVES	5,346	4,285	80.2	553	10.3	508	9.5
GRAYSON	1,111	876	78.8	134	12.1	101	9.1
GREEN	875	807	92.2	27	3.1	41	4.7
GREENUP	2,447	1,910	78.1	186	7.6	351	14.3
HANCOCK	427	328	76.8	49	11.5	50	11.7
HARDIN	2,552	2,147	84.1	166	6.5	239	9.4
HARLAN	6,112	5,880	96.2	38	0.6	194	3.2
HARRISON	1,285	957	74.5	247	19.2	81	6.3
HART	1,365	1,164	85.3	119	8.7	82	6.0
HENDERSON	2,386	1,913	80.2	258	10.8	215	9.0
HENRY	1,354	1,149	84.9	130	9.6	75	5.5
HICKMAN	990	677	68.4	211	21.3	102	10.3
HOPKINS	4,523	3,180	70.3	739	16.3	604	13.4
JACKSON	148	128	86.5	4	2.7	16	10.8
JEFFERSON	39,115	32,071	82.0	4,734	12.1	2,310	5.9
JESSAMINE	2,090	1,708	81.7	212	10.1	170	8.1
JOHNSON	926	754	81.4	50	5.4	122	13.2
KENTON	6,373	4,132	64.8	849	13.3	1,392	21.8
KNOTT	1,863	1,261	67.7	114	6.1	488	26.2
KNOX	682	529	77.6	48	7.0	105	15.4
LARUE	1,972	1,653	83.8	142	7.2	177	9.0
LAUREL	541	462	85.4	34	6.3	45	8.3
LAWRENCE	1,153	925	80.2	119	10.3	109	9.5
LEE	395	308	78.0	16	4.1	71	18.0

36

County	Total Vote	A. B. Chandler Total	Per Cent	Charles P. Farnsley Total	Per Cent	Other Vote Total	Per Cent
LESLIE	211	160	75.8	15	7.1	36	17.1
LETCHER	2,005	1,207	60.2	531	26.5	267	13.3
LEWIS	808	658	81.4	76	9.4	74	9.2
LINCOLN	1,088	918	84.4	104	9.6	66	6.1
LIVINGSTON	977	760	77.8	157	16.1	60	6.1
LOGAN	3,789	440	11.6	3,322	87.7	27	0.7
LYON	1,214	992	81.7	130	10.7	92	7.6
MADISON	3,099	2,537	81.9	237	7.6	325	10.5
MAGOFFIN	1,881	1,707	90.7	37	2.0	137	7.3
MARION	1,594	1,334	83.7	144	9.0	116	7.3
MARSHALL	1,507	1,252	83.1	124	8.2	131	8.7
MARTIN	397	330	83.1	33	8.3	34	8.6
MASON	1,352	1,112	82.2	161	11.9	79	5.8
MC CRACKEN	4,368	3,019	69.1	609	13.9	740	16.9
MC CREARY	343	264	77.0	38	11.1	41	12.0
MC LEAN	894	690	77.2	144	16.1	60	6.7
MEADE	1,186	1,010	85.2	67	5.6	109	9.2
MENIFEE	567	421	74.3	56	9.9	90	15.9
MERCER	920	743	80.8	116	12.6	61	6.6
METCALFE	971	837	86.2	72	7.4	62	6.4
MONROE	351	302	86.0	31	8.8	18	5.1
MONTGOMERY	1,171	786	67.1	290	24.8	95	8.1
MORGAN	2,186	1,676	76.7	212	9.7	298	13.6
MUHLENBERG	1,150	838	72.9	200	17.4	112	9.7
NELSON	2,411	2,016	83.6	184	7.6	211	8.8
NICHOLAS	908	751	82.7	96	10.6	61	6.7
OHIO	915	759	83.0	111	12.1	45	4.9
OLDHAM	857	747	87.2	71	8.3	39	4.6
OWEN	1,485	1,198	80.7	140	9.4	147	9.9
OWSLEY	165	143	86.7	6	3.6	16	9.7
PENDLETON	853	696	81.6	53	6.2	104	12.2
PERRY	1,527	1,122	73.5	148	9.7	257	16.8
PIKE	3,875	3,011	77.7	433	11.2	431	11.1
POWELL	489	399	81.6	54	11.0	36	7.4
PULASKI	1,684	1,505	89.4	74	4.4	105	6.2
ROBERTSON	377	280	74.3	64	17.0	33	8.8
ROCKCASTLE	649	599	92.3	27	4.2	23	3.5
ROWAN	967	734	75.9	136	14.1	97	10.0
RUSSELL	381	330	86.6	19	5.0	32	8.4
SCOTT	1,115	884	79.3	132	11.8	99	8.9
SHELBY	2,128	1,872	88.0	150	7.0	106	5.0
SIMPSON	1,077	827	76.8	163	15.1	87	8.1
SPENCER	623	516	82.8	53	8.5	54	8.7
TAYLOR	1,298	1,145	88.2	69	5.3	84	6.5
TODD	1,140	776	68.1	290	25.4	74	6.5
TRIGG	1,424	1,242	87.2	115	8.1	67	4.7
TRIMBLE	874	738	84.4	48	5.5	88	10.1
UNION	1,363	787	57.7	470	34.5	106	7.8
WARREN	3,318	2,706	81.6	410	12.4	202	6.1
WASHINGTON	1,161	1,048	90.3	59	5.1	54	4.7
WAYNE	507	422	83.2	35	6.9	50	9.9
WEBSTER	1,093	831	76.0	162	14.8	100	9.1
WHITLEY	786	678	86.3	34	4.3	74	9.4
WOLFE	1,131	920	81.3	101	8.9	110	9.7
WOODFORD	1,503	1,366	90.9	92	6.1	45	3.0
TOTAL	222,906	176,520	79.2	26,061	11.7	20,325	9.1

OTHER VOTE: Joseph G. Thornbury 4909
John J. Thobe 3439
M. E. Gilbert 7788
Jack Harrod 4189

County	Total Vote	Democratic		Republican		Per Cent of Two-Party Vote		Dem-Rep Plurality
		Total	Per Cent	Total	Per Cent	Dem	Rep	
ADAIR	6,322	2,703	42.8	3,619	57.2	42.8	57.2	916 R
ALLEN	5,201	2,004	38.5	3,197	61.5	38.5	61.5	1,193 R
ANDERSON	3,734	2,500	67.0	1,234	33.0	67.0	33.0	1,266 D
BALLARD	3,891	3,171	81.5	720	18.5	81.5	18.5	2,451 D
BARREN	8,034	4,827	60.1	3,207	39.9	60.1	39.9	1,620 D
BATH	4,125	2,513	60.9	1,612	39.1	60.9	39.1	901 D
BELL	10,812	5,599	51.8	5,213	48.2	51.8	48.2	386 D
BOONE	3,881	2,619	67.5	1,262	32.5	67.5	32.5	1,357 D
BOURBON	6,983	4,334	62.1	2,649	37.9	62.1	37.9	1,685 D
BOYD	17,158	10,099	58.9	7,059	41.1	58.9	41.1	3,040 D
BOYLE	6,283	4,084	65.0	2,199	35.0	65.0	35.0	1,885 D
BRACKEN	3,496	2,009	57.5	1,487	42.5	57.5	42.5	522 D
BREATHITT	5,469	3,940	72.0	1,529	28.0	72.0	28.0	2,411 D
BRECKINRIDGE	6,470	3,254	50.3	3,216	49.7	50.3	49.7	38 D
BULLITT	3,180	2,373	74.6	807	25.4	74.6	25.4	1,566 D
BUTLER	4,573	1,450	31.7	3,123	68.3	31.7	68.3	1,673 R
CALDWELL	5,091	2,868	56.3	2,223	43.7	56.3	43.7	645 D
CALLOWAY	6,872	5,971	86.9	901	13.1	86.9	13.1	5,070 D
CAMPBELL	29,814	16,505	55.4	13,309	44.6	55.4	44.6	3,196 D
CARLISLE	2,833	2,344	82.7	489	17.3	82.7	17.3	1,855 D
CARROLL	3,743	2,914	77.9	829	22.1	77.9	22.1	2,085 D
CARTER	7,949	3,497	44.0	4,452	56.0	44.0	56.0	955 R
CASEY	5,678	1,849	32.6	3,829	67.4	32.6	67.4	1,980 R
CHRISTIAN	13,187	6,628	50.3	6,559	49.7	50.3	49.7	69 D
CLARK	6,057	4,000	66.0	2,057	34.0	66.0	34.0	1,943 D
CLAY	6,004	1,624	27.0	4,380	73.0	27.0	73.0	2,756 R
CLINTON	3,312	751	22.7	2,561	77.3	22.7	77.3	1,810 R
CRITTENDEN	4,417	1,855	42.0	2,562	58.0	42.0	58.0	707 R
CUMBERLAND	3,326	853	25.6	2,473	74.4	25.6	74.4	1,620 R
DAVIESS	14,912	9,529	63.9	5,383	36.1	63.9	36.1	4,146 D
EDMONSON	3,944	1,353	34.3	2,591	65.7	34.3	65.7	1,238 R
ELLIOTT	2,616	1,986	75.9	630	24.1	75.9	24.1	1,356 D
ESTILL	5,432	2,592	47.7	2,840	52.3	47.7	52.3	248 R
FAYETTE	28,267	16,406	58.0	11,861	42.0	58.0	42.0	4,545 D
FLEMING	5,911	3,079	52.1	2,832	47.9	52.1	47.9	247 D
FLOYD	12,659	8,962	70.8	3,697	29.2	70.8	29.2	5,265 D
FRANKLIN	8,822	7,042	79.8	1,780	20.2	79.8	20.2	5,262 D
FULTON	4,414	3,634	82.3	780	17.7	82.3	17.7	2,854 D
GALLATIN	1,964	1,487	75.7	477	24.3	75.7	24.3	1,010 D
GARRARD	4,358	2,196	50.4	2,162	49.6	50.4	49.6	34 D
GRANT	4,226	2,740	64.8	1,486	35.2	64.8	35.2	1,254 D
GRAVES	11,808	9,745	82.5	2,063	17.5	82.5	17.5	7,682 D
GRAYSON	5,777	2,640	45.7	3,137	54.3	45.7	54.3	497 R
GREEN	4,463	1,999	44.8	2,464	55.2	44.8	55.2	465 R
GREENUP	8,715	4,710	54.0	4,005	46.0	54.0	46.0	705 D
HANCOCK	2,757	1,358	49.3	1,399	50.7	49.3	50.7	41 R
HARDIN	7,038	4,739	67.3	2,299	32.7	67.3	32.7	2,440 D
HARLAN	16,261	10,660	65.6	5,601	34.4	65.6	34.4	5,059 D
HARRISON	5,889	4,244	72.1	1,645	27.9	72.1	27.9	2,599 D
HART	6,082	3,255	53.5	2,827	46.5	53.5	46.5	428 D
HENDERSON	9,121	6,803	74.6	2,318	25.4	74.6	25.4	4,485 D
HENRY	5,280	3,864	73.2	1,416	26.8	73.2	26.8	2,448 D
HICKMAN	3,202	2,715	84.8	487	15.2	84.8	15.2	2,228 D
HOPKINS	12,462	8,676	69.6	3,786	30.4	69.6	30.4	4,890 D
JACKSON	4,136	468	11.3	3,668	88.7	11.3	88.7	3,200 R
JEFFERSON	160,412	96,082	59.9	64,330	40.1	59.9	40.1	31,752 D
JESSAMINE	4,648	2,851	61.3	1,797	38.7	61.3	38.7	1,054 D
JOHNSON	8,043	3,007	37.4	5,036	62.6	37.4	62.6	2,029 R
KENTON	32,323	20,118	62.2	12,205	37.8	62.2	37.8	7,913 D
KNOTT	5,245	4,448	84.8	797	15.2	84.8	15.2	3,651 D
KNOX	8,236	3,245	39.4	4,991	60.6	39.4	60.6	1,746 R
LARUE	3,746	2,467	65.9	1,279	34.1	65.9	34.1	1,188 D
LAUREL	8,044	2,862	35.6	5,182	64.4	35.6	64.4	2,320 R
LAWRENCE	6,186	3,165	51.2	3,021	48.8	51.2	48.8	144 D
LEE	3,432	1,609	46.9	1,823	53.1	46.9	53.1	214 R

38

County	Total Vote	Democratic		Republican			Per Cent of Two-Party Vote		Dem-Rep Plurality
		Total	Per Cent	Total	Per Cent		Dem	Rep	
LESLIE	3,894	621	15.9	3,273	84.1		15.9	84.1	2,652 R
LETCHER	10,352	5,946	57.4	4,406	42.6		57.4	42.6	1,540 D
LEWIS	5,161	1,853	35.9	3,308	64.1		35.9	64.1	1,455 R
LINCOLN	6,666	3,623	54.4	3,043	45.6		54.4	45.6	580 D
LIVINGSTON	3,164	2,000	63.2	1,164	36.8		63.2	36.8	836 D
LOGAN	8,892	6,632	74.6	2,260	25.4		74.6	25.4	4,372 D
LYON	2,871	1,964	68.4	907	31.6		68.4	31.6	1,057 D
MADISON	12,171	6,471	53.2	5,700	46.8		53.2	46.8	771 D
MAGOFFIN	5,490	2,824	51.4	2,666	48.6		51.4	48.6	158 D
MARION	5,192	3,454	66.5	1,738	33.5		66.5	33.5	1,716 D
MARSHALL	4,506	3,414	75.8	1,092	24.2		75.8	24.2	2,322 D
MARTIN	3,034	809	26.7	2,225	73.3		26.7	73.3	1,416 R
MASON	8,055	4,438	55.1	3,617	44.9		55.1	44.9	821 D
MC CRACKEN	14,984	11,481	76.6	3,503	23.4		76.6	23.4	7,978 D
MC CREARY	4,347	1,196	27.5	3,151	72.5		27.5	72.5	1,955 R
MC LEAN	4,336	2,669	61.6	1,667	38.4		61.6	38.4	1,002 D
MEADE	2,977	2,104	70.7	873	29.3		70.7	29.3	1,231 D
MENIFEE	1,660	1,161	69.9	499	30.1		69.9	30.1	662 D
MERCER	5,421	3,617	66.7	1,804	33.3		66.7	33.3	1,813 D
METCALFE	3,973	1,800	45.3	2,173	54.7		45.3	54.7	373 R
MONROE	4,739	1,400	29.5	3,339	70.5		29.5	70.5	1,939 R
MONTGOMERY	4,369	2,742	62.8	1,627	37.2		62.8	37.2	1,115 D
MORGAN	5,635	4,170	74.0	1,465	26.0		74.0	26.0	2,705 D
MUHLENBERG	10,329	5,074	49.1	5,255	50.9		49.1	50.9	181 R
NELSON	6,253	4,225	67.6	2,028	32.4		67.6	32.4	2,197 D
NICHOLAS	3,388	2,183	64.4	1,205	35.6		64.4	35.6	978 D
OHIO	8,123	3,692	45.5	4,431	54.5		45.5	54.5	739 R
OLDHAM	2,830	2,006	70.9	824	29.1		70.9	29.1	1,182 D
OWEN	4,161	3,589	86.3	572	13.7		86.3	13.7	3,017 D
OWSLEY	3,201	583	18.2	2,618	81.8		18.2	81.8	2,035 R
PENDLETON	4,191	2,239	53.4	1,952	46.6		53.4	46.6	287 D
PERRY	11,426	6,837	59.8	4,589	40.2		59.8	40.2	2,248 D
PIKE	21,037	12,121	57.6	8,916	42.4		57.6	42.4	3,205 D
POWELL	2,220	1,251	56.4	969	43.6		56.4	43.6	282 D
PULASKI	13,269	4,877	36.8	8,392	63.2		36.8	63.2	3,515 R
ROBERTSON	1,410	845	59.9	565	40.1		59.9	40.1	280 D
ROCKCASTLE	5,115	1,627	31.8	3,488	68.2		31.8	68.2	1,861 R
ROWAN	4,175	2,266	54.3	1,909	45.7		54.3	45.7	357 D
RUSSELL	4,246	1,236	29.1	3,010	70.9		29.1	70.9	1,774 R
SCOTT	5,730	4,013	70.0	1,717	30.0		70.0	30.0	2,296 D
SHELBY	6,615	4,810	72.7	1,805	27.3		72.7	27.3	3,005 D
SIMPSON	3,887	2,922	75.2	965	24.8		75.2	24.8	1,957 D
SPENCER	2,322	1,751	75.4	571	24.6		75.4	24.6	1,180 D
TAYLOR	5,546	2,794	50.4	2,752	49.6		50.4	49.6	42 D
TODD	4,713	3,299	70.0	1,414	30.0		70.0	30.0	1,885 D
TRIGG	4,389	2,901	66.1	1,488	33.9		66.1	33.9	1,413 D
TRIMBLE	2,140	1,894	88.5	246	11.5		88.5	11.5	1,648 D
UNION	5,370	4,329	80.6	1,041	19.4		80.6	19.4	3,288 D
WARREN	11,667	7,548	64.7	4,119	35.3		64.7	35.3	3,429 D
WASHINGTON	4,939	2,612	52.9	2,327	47.1		52.9	47.1	285 D
WAYNE	5,591	2,478	44.3	3,113	55.7		44.3	55.7	635 R
WEBSTER	6,258	4,195	67.0	2,063	33.0		67.0	33.0	2,132 D
WHITLEY	10,345	3,743	36.2	6,602	63.8		36.2	63.8	2,859 R
WOLFE	3,269	2,240	68.5	1,029	31.5		68.5	31.5	1,211 D
WOODFORD	4,193	2,708	64.6	1,485	35.4		64.6	35.4	1,223 D
TOTAL	962,963	561,151	58.3	401,812	41.7		58.3	41.7	159,339 D

DEMOCRAT: A. B. Chandler
REPUBLICAN: Walter B. Smith

County	Total Vote	A. B. Chandler		John Y. Brown	
		Total	Per Cent	Total	Per Cent
ADAIR	874	702	80.3	172	19.7
ALLEN	518	355	68.5	163	31.5
ANDERSON	1,188	773	65.1	415	34.9
BALLARD	1,039	526	50.6	513	49.4
BARREN	1,556	960	61.7	596	38.3
BATH	1,395	1,156	82.9	239	17.1
BELL	1,393	1,230	88.3	163	11.7
BOONE	856	591	69.0	265	31.0
BOURBON	1,669	1,387	83.1	282	16.9
BOYD	2,151	1,574	73.2	577	26.8
BOYLE	2,087	1,337	64.1	750	35.9
BRACKEN	669	512	76.5	157	23.5
BREATHITT	1,249	1,064	85.2	185	14.8
BRECKINRIDGE	1,127	823	73.0	304	27.0
BULLITT	796	507	63.7	289	36.3
BUTLER	504	376	74.6	128	25.4
CALDWELL	979	675	68.9	304	31.1
CALLOWAY	1,469	988	67.3	481	32.7
CAMPBELL	3,488	2,391	68.5	1,097	31.5
CARLISLE	666	385	57.8	281	42.2
CARROLL	1,504	940	62.5	564	37.5
CARTER	688	538	78.2	150	21.8
CASEY	697	580	83.2	117	16.8
CHRISTIAN	2,140	1,495	69.9	645	30.1
CLARK	1,249	853	68.3	396	31.7
CLAY	548	414	75.5	134	24.5
CLINTON	355	297	83.7	58	16.3
CRITTENDEN	536	346	64.6	190	35.4
CUMBERLAND	390	288	73.8	102	26.2
DAVIESS	2,466	1,710	69.3	756	30.7
EDMONSON	473	319	67.4	154	32.6
ELLIOTT	750	506	67.5	244	32.5
ESTILL	614	503	81.9	111	18.1
FAYETTE	6,187	4,255	68.8	1,932	31.2
FLEMING	1,620	1,392	85.9	228	14.1
FLOYD	2,258	1,209	53.5	1,049	46.5
FRANKLIN	3,833	2,913	76.0	920	24.0
FULTON	812	492	60.6	320	39.4
GALLATIN	595	423	71.1	172	28.9
GARRARD	883	623	70.6	260	29.4
GRANT	1,284	736	57.3	548	42.7
GRAVES	2,888	1,676	58.0	1,212	42.0
GRAYSON	923	567	61.4	356	38.6
GREEN	630	518	82.2	112	17.8
GREENUP	1,553	1,172	75.5	381	24.5
HANCOCK	335	217	64.8	118	35.2
HARDIN	1,593	1,123	70.5	470	29.5
HARLAN	4,562	4,291	94.1	271	5.9
HARRISON	1,520	1,010	66.4	510	33.6
HART	1,446	1,081	74.8	365	25.2
HENDERSON	2,869	2,135	74.4	734	25.6
HENRY	1,739	1,064	61.2	675	38.8
HICKMAN	927	516	55.7	411	44.3
HOPKINS	2,266	1,607	70.9	659	29.1
JACKSON	172	137	79.7	35	20.3
JEFFERSON	28,527	22,312	78.2	6,215	21.8
JESSAMINE	1,458	1,032	70.8	426	29.2
JOHNSON	499	294	58.9	205	41.1
KENTON	5,449	3,340	61.3	2,109	38.7
KNOTT	1,018	672	66.0	346	34.0
KNOX	785	586	74.6	199	25.4
LARUE	1,267	862	68.0	405	32.0
LAUREL	769	637	82.8	132	17.2
LAWRENCE	805	738	91.7	67	8.3
LEE	415	312	75.2	103	24.8

County	Total Vote	A. B. Chandler		John Y. Brown	
		Total	Per Cent	Total	Per Cent
LESLIE	201	163	81.1	38	18.9
LETCHER	1,201	588	49.0	613	51.0
LEWIS	524	422	80.5	102	19.5
LINCOLN	1,453	1,013	69.7	440	30.3
LIVINGSTON	787	467	59.3	320	40.7
LOGAN	4,211	3,782	89.8	429	10.2
LYON	936	620	66.2	316	33.8
MADISON	2,314	1,865	80.6	449	19.4
MAGOFFIN	591	427	72.3	164	27.7
MARION	1,547	960	62.1	587	37.9
MARSHALL	1,027	717	69.8	310	30.2
MARTIN	225	193	85.8	32	14.2
MASON	1,701	1,178	69.3	523	30.7
MC CRACKEN	2,435	1,377	56.6	1,058	43.4
MC CREARY	294	211	71.8	83	28.2
MC LEAN	784	529	67.5	255	32.5
MEADE	769	523	68.0	246	32.0
MENIFEE	403	258	64.0	145	36.0
MERCER	1,886	1,107	58.7	779	41.3
METCALFE	805	530	65.8	275	34.2
MONROE	575	397	69.0	178	31.0
MONTGOMERY	1,484	1,051	70.8	433	29.2
MORGAN	1,761	1,529	86.8	232	13.2
MUHLENBERG	914	492	53.8	422	46.2
NELSON	2,053	1,439	70.1	614	29.9
NICHOLAS	1,069	805	75.3	264	24.7
OHIO	888	611	68.8	277	31.2
OLDHAM	936	724	77.4	212	22.6
OWEN	1,729	1,126	65.1	603	34.9
OWSLEY	212	196	92.5	16	7.5
PENDLETON	757	525	69.4	232	30.6
PERRY	1,223	739	60.4	484	39.6
PIKE	2,797	1,809	64.7	988	35.3
POWELL	413	304	73.6	109	26.4
PULASKI	1,928	1,615	83.8	313	16.2
ROBERTSON	463	291	62.9	172	37.1
ROCKCASTLE	578	470	81.3	108	18.7
ROWAN	622	471	75.7	151	24.3
RUSSELL	484	372	76.9	112	23.1
SCOTT	1,745	1,199	68.7	546	31.3
SHELBY	2,309	1,713	74.2	596	25.8
SIMPSON	1,106	687	62.1	419	37.9
SPENCER	784	490	62.5	294	37.5
TAYLOR	1,269	1,033	81.4	236	18.6
TODD	1,150	820	71.3	330	28.7
TRIGG	882	544	61.7	338	38.3
TRIMBLE	968	651	67.3	317	32.7
UNION	1,145	618	54.0	527	46.0
WARREN	4,989	3,386	67.9	1,603	32.1
WASHINGTON	1,154	829	71.8	325	28.2
WAYNE	608	411	67.6	197	32.4
WEBSTER	1,099	668	60.8	431	39.2
WHITLEY	620	424	68.4	196	31.6
WOLFE	1,088	875	80.4	213	19.6
WOODFORD	1,781	1,388	77.9	393	22.1
TOTAL	187,547	134,675	71.8	52,872	28.2

County	Total Vote	Richard J. Colbert		Charles Chandler		Hector Johnson		G. Tom Hawkins	
		Total	Per Cent	Total	Per Cent	Total	Per Cent	Total	Per Cent
ADAIR	225	96	42.7	31	13.8	72	32.0	26	11.6
ALLEN	196	177	90.3	8	4.1	7	3.6	4	2.0
ANDERSON	65	48	73.8	6	9.2	6	9.2	5	7.7
BALLARD	27	13	48.1	13	48.1			1	3.7
BARREN	169	84	49.7	25	14.8	32	18.9	28	16.6
BATH	123	97	78.9	10	8.1	16	13.0		
BELL	1,400	566	40.4	591	42.2	132	9.4	111	7.9
BOONE	42	17	40.5	17	40.5	3	7.1	5	11.9
BOURBON	93	74	79.6	13	14.0	3	3.2	3	3.2
BOYD	775	558	72.0	59	7.6	71	9.2	87	11.2
BOYLE	92	79	85.9	11	12.0			2	2.2
BRACKEN	77	54	70.1	9	11.7	7	9.1	7	9.1
BREATHITT	123	78	63.4	6	4.9	32	26.0	7	5.7
BRECKINRIDGE	553	220	39.8	95	17.2	128	23.1	110	19.9
BULLITT	40	11	27.5	14	35.0	7	17.5	8	20.0
BUTLER	264	117	44.3	131	49.6	4	1.5	12	4.5
CALDWELL	176	112	63.6	49	27.8	5	2.8	10	5.7
CALLOWAY	75	31	41.3	33	44.0	5	6.7	6	8.0
CAMPBELL	1,011	318	31.5	364	36.0	101	10.0	228	22.6
CARLISLE	27	12	44.4	11	40.7			4	14.8
CARROLL	34	23	67.6	10	29.4	1	2.9		
CARTER	360	183	50.8	46	12.8	74	20.6	57	15.8
CASEY	335	236	70.4	74	22.1	8	2.4	17	5.1
CHRISTIAN	229	95	41.5	109	47.6	12	5.2	13	5.7
CLARK	109	99	90.8	5	4.6	1	0.9	4	3.7
CLAY	1,148	285	24.8	382	33.3	388	33.8	93	8.1
CLINTON	372	134	36.0	145	39.0	47	12.6	46	12.4
CRITTENDEN	152	94	61.8	34	22.4	10	6.6	14	9.2
CUMBERLAND	442	166	37.6	217	49.1	35	7.9	24	5.4
DAVIESS	202	171	84.7	19	9.4	3	1.5	9	4.5
EDMONSON	201	163	81.1	23	11.4	5	2.5	10	5.0
ELLIOTT	16	9	56.3	3	18.8	3	18.8	1	6.3
ESTILL	206	156	75.7	15	7.3	24	11.7	11	5.3
FAYETTE	642	603	93.9	19	3.0	9	1.4	11	1.7
FLEMING	167	108	64.7	25	15.0	26	15.6	8	4.8
FLOYD	612	127	20.8	115	18.8	154	25.2	216	35.3
FRANKLIN	120	102	85.0	3	2.5	4	3.3	11	9.2
FULTON	19	4	21.1	7	36.8	5	26.3	3	15.8
GALLATIN	29	20	69.0	6	20.7	1	3.4	2	6.9
GARRARD	136	114	83.8	10	7.4	12	8.8		
GRANT	50	18	36.0	19	38.0	2	4.0	11	22.0
GRAVES	109	45	41.3	38	34.9	15	13.8	11	10.1
GRAYSON	269	152	56.5	46	17.1	47	17.5	24	8.9
GREEN	119	74	62.2	14	11.8	21	17.6	10	8.4
GREENUP	296	100	33.8	57	19.3	76	25.7	63	21.3
HANCOCK	132	86	65.2	15	11.4	18	13.6	13	9.8
HARDIN	116	80	69.0	20	17.2	12	10.3	4	3.4
HARLAN	2,775	1,770	63.8	610	22.0	161	5.8	234	8.4
HARRISON	88	60	68.2	11	12.5	7	8.0	10	11.4
HART	270	188	69.6	24	8.9	45	16.7	13	4.8
HENDERSON	44	30	68.2	4	9.1	1	2.3	9	20.5
HENRY	106	73	68.9	19	17.9	6	5.7	8	7.5
HICKMAN	15	10	66.7	2	13.3			3	20.0
HOPKINS	130	78	60.0	14	10.8	9	6.9	29	22.3
JACKSON	1,007	140	13.9	183	18.2	608	60.4	76	7.5
JEFFERSON	5,191	4,300	82.8	332	6.4	114	2.2	445	8.6
JESSAMINE	119	101	84.9	9	7.6	6	5.0	3	2.5
JOHNSON	630	219	34.8	141	22.4	66	10.5	204	32.4
KENTON	321	99	30.8	120	37.4	49	15.3	53	16.5
KNOTT	52	8	15.4	11	21.2	9	17.3	24	46.2
KNOX	1,255	251	20.0	630	50.2	209	16.7	165	13.1
LARUE	73	37	50.7	12	16.4	16	21.9	8	11.0
LAUREL	1,173	318	27.1	503	42.9	275	23.4	77	6.6
LAWRENCE	255	126	49.4	47	18.4	39	15.3	43	16.9
LEE	188	134	71.3	22	11.7	23	12.2	9	4.8

County	Total Vote	Richard J. Colbert Total	Per Cent	Charles Chandler Total	Per Cent	Hector Johnson Total	Per Cent	G. Tom Hawkins Total	Per Cent
LESLIE	839	176	21.0	345	41.1	93	11.1	225	26.8
LETCHER	680	209	30.7	128	18.8	87	12.8	256	37.6
LEWIS	309	133	43.0	50	16.2	71	23.0	55	17.8
LINCOLN	259	234	90.3	19	7.3	3	1.2	3	1.2
LIVINGSTON	71	31	43.7	33	46.5	4	5.6	3	4.2
LOGAN	34	17	50.0	3	8.8	1	2.9	13	38.2
LYON	57	46	80.7	7	12.3	1	1.8	3	5.3
MADISON	233	192	82.4	12	5.2	21	9.0	8	3.4
MAGOFFIN	370	209	56.5	79	21.4	11	3.0	71	19.2
MARION	66	33	50.0	2	3.0	23	34.8	8	12.1
MARSHALL	52	24	46.2	20	38.5	5	9.6	3	5.8
MARTIN	372	82	22.0	128	34.4	46	12.4	116	31.2
MASON	213	163	76.5	19	8.9	20	9.4	11	5.2
MC CRACKEN	134	54	40.3	53	39.6	16	11.9	11	8.2
MC CREARY	803	172	21.4	531	66.1	67	8.3	33	4.1
MC LEAN	89	63	70.8	7	7.9	1	1.1	18	20.2
MEADE	41	18	43.9	4	9.8	13	31.7	6	14.6
MENIFEE	33	17	51.5	5	15.2	8	24.2	3	9.1
MERCER	108	81	75.0	7	6.5	12	11.1	8	7.4
METCALFE	161	134	83.2	9	5.6	12	7.5	6	3.7
MONTOE	657	359	54.6	149	22.7	84	12.8	65	9.9
MONTGOMERY	76	57	75.0	7	9.2	10	13.2	2	2.6
MORGAN	222	200	90.1	9	4.1	11	5.0	2	0.9
MUHLENBERG	332	225	67.8	24	7.2	16	4.8	67	20.2
NELSON	95	42	44.2	16	16.8	26	27.4	11	11.6
NICHOLAS	74	63	85.1	5	6.8	5	6.8	1	1.4
OHIO	306	206	67.3	55	18.0	14	4.6	31	10.1
OLDHAM	51	29	56.9	20	39.2	1	2.0	1	2.0
OWEN	50	25	50.0	6	12.0	2	4.0	17	34.0
OWSLEY	415	84	20.2	133	32.0	148	35.7	50	12.0
PENDLETON	89	55	61.8	20	22.5	3	3.4	11	12.4
PERRY	890	250	28.1	163	18.3	216	24.3	261	29.3
PIKE	1,164	509	43.7	165	14.2	91	7.8	399	34.3
POWELL	76	29	38.2	12	15.8	24	31.6	11	14.5
PULASKI	2,532	1,096	43.3	1,177	46.5	155	6.1	104	4.1
ROBERTSON	48	27	56.3	6	12.5	11	22.9	4	8.3
ROCKCASTLE	686	256	37.3	251	36.6	151	22.0	28	4.1
ROWAN	154	88	57.1	20	13.0	31	20.1	15	9.7
RUSSELL	521	222	42.6	224	43.0	49	9.4	26	5.0
SCOTT	94	85	90.4	5	5.3	2	2.1	2	2.1
SHELBY	105	68	64.8	21	20.0	11	10.5	5	4.8
SIMPSON	50	39	78.0	6	12.0			5	10.0
SPENCER	37	21	56.8	9	24.3	3	8.1	4	10.8
TAYLOR	181	129	71.3	37	20.4	13	7.2	2	1.1
TODD	27	20	74.1	4	14.8			3	11.1
TRIGG	115	75	65.2	31	27.0	2	1.7	7	6.1
TRIMBLE	18	12	66.7	4	22.2	1	5.6	1	5.6
UNION	31	17	54.8	6	19.4	2	6.5	6	19.4
WARREN	165	130	78.8	15	9.1	5	3.0	15	9.1
WASHINGTON	80	53	66.3	13	16.3	12	15.0	2	2.5
WAYNE	518	124	23.9	249	48.1	83	16.0	62	12.0
WEBSTER	623	595	95.5	13	2.1	3	0.5	12	1.9
WHITLEY	1,766	395	22.4	947	53.6	272	15.4	152	8.6
WOLFE	121	62	51.2	36	29.8	19	15.7	4	3.3
WOODFORD	89	85	95.5	3	3.4	1	1.1		
TOTAL	43,249	21,971	50.8	10,988	25.4	5,279	12.2	5,011	11.6

43

County	Total Vote	Democratic		Republican		Per Cent of Two-Party Vote		Dem-Rep Plurality
		Total	Per Cent	Total	Per Cent	Dem	Rep	
ADAIR	2,937	1,134	38.6	1,803	61.4	38.6	61.4	669 R
ALLEN	1,521	513	33.7	1,008	66.3	33.7	66.3	495 R
ANDERSON	1,564	992	63.4	572	36.6	63.4	36.6	420 D
BALLARD	1,438	1,215	84.5	223	15.5	84.5	15.5	992 D
BARREN	2,905	1,688	58.1	1,217	41.9	58.1	41.9	471 D
BATH	1,416	820	57.9	596	42.1	57.9	42.1	224 D
BELL	3,552	2,058	57.9	1,494	42.1	57.9	42.1	564 D
BOONE	1,310	920	70.2	390	29.8	70.2	29.8	530 D
BOURBON	2,082	1,413	67.9	669	32.1	67.9	32.1	744 D
BOYD	7,087	3,700	52.2	3,387	47.8	52.2	47.8	313 D
BOYLE	2,290	1,346	58.8	944	41.2	58.8	41.2	402 D
BRACKEN	1,049	619	59.0	430	41.0	59.0	41.0	189 D
BREATHITT	1,626	1,194	73.4	432	26.6	73.4	26.6	762 D
BRECKINRIDGE	3,352	1,585	47.3	1,767	52.7	47.3	52.7	182 R
BULLITT	1,135	793	69.9	342	30.1	69.9	30.1	451 D
BUTLER	2,395	617	25.8	1,778	74.2	25.8	74.2	1,161 R
CALDWELL	2,320	1,075	46.3	1,245	53.7	46.3	53.7	170 R
CALLOWAY	1,629	1,328	81.5	301	18.5	81.5	18.5	1,027 D
CAMPBELL	14,307	6,624	46.3	7,683	53.7	46.3	53.7	1,059 R
CARLISLE	786	658	83.7	128	16.3	83.7	16.3	530 D
CARROLL	1,353	1,019	75.3	334	24.7	75.3	24.7	685 D
CARTER	2,734	1,120	41.0	1,614	59.0	41.0	59.0	494 R
CASEY	2,255	670	29.7	1,585	70.3	29.7	70.3	915 R
CHRISTIAN	4,403	2,374	53.9	2,029	46.1	53.9	46.1	345 D
CLARK	2,044	1,318	64.5	726	35.5	64.5	35.5	592 D
CLAY	2,008	540	26.9	1,468	73.1	26.9	73.1	928 R
CLINTON	1,417	371	26.2	1,046	73.8	26.2	73.8	675 R
CRITTENDEN	1,794	568	31.7	1,226	68.3	31.7	68.3	658 R
CUMBERLAND	1,263	343	27.2	920	72.8	27.2	72.8	577 R
DAVIESS	4,370	2,653	60.7	1,717	39.3	60.7	39.3	936 D
EDMONSON	1,453	459	31.6	994	68.4	31.6	68.4	535 R
ELLIOTT	596	477	80.0	119	20.0	80.0	20.0	358 D
ESTILL	1,878	826	44.0	1,052	56.0	44.0	56.0	226 R
FAYETTE	9,591	5,339	55.7	4,252	44.3	55.7	44.3	1,087 D
FLEMING	3,308	1,963	59.3	1,345	40.7	59.3	40.7	618 D
FLOYD	7,237	4,755	65.7	2,482	34.3	65.7	34.3	2,273 D
FRANKLIN	3,952	3,283	83.1	669	16.9	83.1	16.9	2,614 D
FULTON	962	819	85.1	143	14.9	85.1	14.9	676 D
GALLATIN	707	511	72.3	196	27.7	72.3	27.7	315 D
GARRARD	1,933	904	46.8	1,029	53.2	46.8	53.2	125 R
GRANT	1,487	919	61.8	568	38.2	61.8	38.2	351 D
GRAVES	3,027	2,430	80.3	597	19.7	80.3	19.7	1,833 D
GRAYSON	3,248	1,268	39.0	1,980	61.0	39.0	61.0	712 R
GREEN	1,956	812	41.5	1,144	58.5	41.5	58.5	332 R
GREENUP	3,881	2,108	54.3	1,773	45.7	54.3	45.7	335 D
HANCOCK	1,211	550	45.4	661	54.6	45.4	54.6	111 R
HARDIN	2,614	1,691	64.7	923	35.3	64.7	35.3	768 D
HARLAN	12,713	11,228	88.3	1,485	11.7	88.3	11.7	9,743 D
HARRISON	2,041	1,409	69.0	632	31.0	69.0	31.0	777 D
HART	2,903	1,544	53.2	1,359	46.8	53.2	46.8	185 D
HENDERSON	2,587	2,001	77.3	586	22.7	77.3	22.7	1,415 D
HENRY	2,067	1,435	69.4	632	30.6	69.4	30.6	803 D
HICKMAN	843	695	82.4	148	17.6	82.4	17.6	547 D
HOPKINS	3,237	2,270	70.1	967	29.9	70.1	29.9	1,303 D
JACKSON	1,900	296	15.6	1,604	84.4	15.6	84.4	1,308 R
JEFFERSON	72,734	39,065	53.7	33,669	46.3	53.7	46.3	5,396 D
JESSAMINE	2,021	1,126	55.7	895	44.3	55.7	44.3	231 D
JOHNSON	4,318	1,382	32.0	2,936	68.0	32.0	68.0	1,554 R
KENTON	11,074	6,337	57.2	4,737	42.8	57.2	42.8	1,600 D
KNOTT	2,593	2,079	80.2	514	19.8	80.2	19.8	1,565 D
KNOX	2,528	826	32.7	1,702	67.3	32.7	67.3	876 R
LARUE	2,051	1,392	67.9	659	32.1	67.9	32.1	733 D
LAUREL	3,021	1,057	35.0	1,964	65.0	35.0	65.0	907 R
LAWRENCE	1,942	942	48.5	1,000	51.5	48.5	51.5	58 R
LEE	1,157	459	39.7	698	60.3	39.7	60.3	239 R

County	Total Vote	Democratic Total	Democratic Per Cent	Republican Total	Republican Per Cent	Per Cent of Two-Party Vote Dem	Per Cent of Two-Party Vote Rep	Dem-Rep Plurality
LESLIE	1,459	290	19.9	1,169	80.1	19.9	80.1	879 R
LETCHER	5,595	2,710	48.4	2,885	51.6	48.4	51.6	175 R
LEWIS	1,986	661	33.3	1,325	66.7	33.3	66.7	664 R
LINCOLN	2,733	1,340	49.0	1,393	51.0	49.0	51.0	53 R
LIVINGSTON	1,094	680	62.2	414	37.8	62.2	37.8	266 D
LOGAN	4,149	3,622	87.3	527	12.7	87.3	12.7	3,095 D
LYON	1,285	841	65.4	444	34.6	65.4	34.6	397 D
MADISON	5,259	2,878	54.7	2,381	45.3	54.7	45.3	497 D
MAGOFFIN	3,022	1,626	53.8	1,396	46.2	53.8	46.2	230 D
MARION	2,522	1,369	54.3	1,153	45.7	54.3	45.7	216 D
MARSHALL	1,307	943	72.1	364	27.9	72.1	27.9	579 D
MARTIN	1,773	426	24.0	1,347	76.0	24.0	76.0	921 R
MASON	3,534	1,652	46.7	1,882	53.3	46.7	53.3	230 R
MC CRACKEN	3,280	2,419	73.8	861	26.3	73.8	26.3	1,558 D
MC CREARY	1,232	272	22.1	960	77.9	22.1	77.9	688 R
MC LEAN	1,378	807	58.6	571	41.4	58.6	41.4	236 D
MEADE	1,310	881	67.3	429	32.7	67.3	32.7	452 D
MENIFEE	494	315	63.8	179	36.2	63.8	36.2	136 D
MERCER	2,431	1,296	53.3	1,135	46.7	53.3	46.7	161 D
METCALFE	1,753	721	41.1	1,032	58.9	41.1	58.9	311 R
MONROE	1,522	435	28.6	1,087	71.4	28.6	71.4	652 R
MONTGOMERY	1,625	952	58.6	673	41.4	58.6	41.4	279 D
MORGAN	2,267	1,655	73.0	612	27.0	73.0	27.0	1,043 D
MUHLENBERG	2,972	1,208	40.6	1,764	59.4	40.6	59.4	556 R
NELSON	3,191	2,176	68.2	1,015	31.8	68.2	31.8	1,161 D
NICHOLAS	1,280	808	63.1	472	36.9	63.1	36.9	336 D
OHIO	2,905	1,200	41.3	1,705	58.7	41.3	58.7	505 R
OLDHAM	1,223	856	70.0	367	30.0	70.0	30.0	489 D
OWEN	1,513	1,206	79.7	307	20.3	79.7	20.3	899 D
OWSLEY	1,314	256	19.5	1,058	80.5	19.5	80.5	802 R
PENDLETON	1,529	796	52.1	733	47.9	52.1	47.9	63 D
PERRY	6,206	3,061	49.3	3,145	50.7	49.3	50.7	84 R
PIKE	11,727	6,699	57.1	5,028	42.9	57.1	42.9	1,671 D
POWELL	755	407	53.9	348	46.1	53.9	46.1	59 D
PULASKI	5,905	2,217	37.5	3,688	62.5	37.5	62.5	1,471 R
ROBERTSON	697	401	57.5	296	42.5	57.5	42.5	105 D
ROCKCASTLE	2,456	797	32.5	1,659	67.5	32.5	67.5	862 R
ROWAN	1,424	731	51.3	693	48.7	51.3	48.7	38 D
RUSSELL	1,688	591	35.0	1,097	65.0	35.0	65.0	506 R
SCOTT	2,185	1,407	64.4	778	35.6	64.4	35.6	629 D
SHELBY	2,787	2,083	74.7	704	25.3	74.7	25.3	1,379 D
SIMPSON	855	643	75.2	212	24.8	75.2	24.8	431 D
SPENCER	1,040	703	67.6	337	32.4	67.6	32.4	366 D
TAYLOR	2,886	1,470	50.9	1,416	49.1	50.9	49.1	54 D
TODD	1,660	1,089	65.6	571	34.4	65.6	34.4	518 D
TRIGG	1,576	967	61.4	609	38.6	61.4	38.6	358 D
TRIMBLE	800	644	80.5	156	19.5	80.5	19.5	488 D
UNION	1,007	737	73.2	270	26.8	73.2	26.8	467 D
WARREN	4,572	3,276	71.7	1,296	28.3	71.7	28.3	1,980 D
WASHINGTON	2,195	1,010	46.0	1,185	54.0	46.0	54.0	175 R
WAYNE	1,883	782	41.5	1,101	58.5	41.5	58.5	319 R
WEBSTER	1,429	964	67.5	465	32.5	67.5	32.5	499 D
WHITLEY	2,850	844	29.6	2,006	70.4	29.6	70.4	1,162 R
WOLFE	1,288	909	70.6	379	29.4	70.6	29.4	530 D
WOODFORD	2,118	1,304	61.6	814	38.4	61.6	38.4	490 D
TOTAL	392,039	216,958	55.3	175,081	44.7	55.3	44.7	41,877 D

DEMOCRAT: A. B. Chandler
REPUBLICAN: Richard J. Colbert

County	Total Vote	James Park		Clarence Bartlett		Other Vote	
		Total	Per Cent	Total	Per Cent	Total	Per Cent
ADAIR	1,340	730	54.5	308	23.0	302	22.5
ALLEN	381	254	66.7	64	16.8	63	16.5
ANDERSON	397	361	90.9	11	2.8	25	6.3
BALLARD	95	66	69.5	24	25.3	5	5.3
BARREN	621	139	22.4	346	55.7	136	21.9
BATH	193	156	80.8	16	8.3	21	10.9
BELL	2,177	1,776	81.6	228	10.5	173	7.9
BOONE	94	49	52.1	36	38.3	9	9.6
BOURBON	299	284	95.0	1	0.3	14	4.7
BOYD	1,352	1,034	76.5	196	14.5	122	9.0
BOYLE	486	418	86.0	16	3.3	52	10.7
BRACKEN	134	84	62.7	16	11.9	34	25.4
BREATHITT	174	112	64.4	22	12.6	40	23.0
BRECKINRIDGE	998	652	65.3	248	24.8	98	9.8
BULLITT	97	35	36.1	36	37.1	26	26.8
BUTLER	1,462	44	3.0	1,355	92.7	63	4.3
CALDWELL	319	209	65.5	97	30.4	13	4.1
CALLOWAY	118	106	89.8	9	7.6	3	2.5
CAMPBELL	3,519	1,092	31.0	2,083	59.2	344	9.8
CARLISLE	84	61	72.6	17	20.2	6	7.1
CARROLL	74	34	45.9	38	51.4	2	2.7
CARTER	1,362	940	69.0	183	13.4	239	17.5
CASEY	872	760	87.2	36	4.1	76	8.7
CHRISTIAN	501	390	77.8	78	15.6	33	6.6
CLARK	272	232	85.3	9	3.3	31	11.4
CLAY	2,009	1,321	65.8	543	27.0	145	7.2
CLINTON	496	294	59.3	135	27.2	67	13.5
CRITTENDEN	288	175	60.8	89	30.9	24	8.3
CUMBERLAND	564	321	56.9	163	28.9	80	14.2
DAVIESS	555	249	44.9	278	50.1	28	5.0
EDMONSON	767	54	7.0	654	85.3	59	7.7
ELLIOTT	35	17	48.6	5	14.3	13	37.1
ESTILL	445	372	83.6	15	3.4	58	13.0
FAYETTE	4,639	4,569	98.5	22	0.5	48	1.0
FLEMING	362	295	81.5	14	3.9	53	14.6
FLOYD	433	252	58.2	121	27.9	60	13.9
FRANKLIN	438	189	43.2	221	50.5	28	6.4
FULTON	75	49	65.3	21	28.0	5	6.7
GALLATIN	49	28	57.1	17	34.7	4	8.2
GARRARD	429	405	94.4	7	1.6	17	4.0
GRANT	176	98	55.7	67	38.1	11	6.3
GRAVES	384	349	90.9	23	6.0	12	3.1
GRAYSON	1,629	211	13.0	1,203	73.8	215	13.2
GREEN	752	279	37.1	389	51.7	84	11.2
GREENUP	748	218	29.1	417	55.7	113	15.1
HANCOCK	320	132	41.3	147	45.9	41	12.8
HARDIN	499	378	75.8	64	12.8	57	11.4
HARLAN	2,198	1,663	75.7	326	14.8	209	9.5
HARRISON	412	381	92.5	5	1.2	26	6.3
HART	913	202	22.1	572	62.7	139	15.2
HENDERSON	138	116	84.1	6	4.3	16	11.6
HENRY	237	201	84.8	10	4.2	26	11.0
HICKMAN	37	32	86.5	4	10.8	1	2.7
HOPKINS	854	472	55.3	299	35.0	83	9.7
JACKSON	1,042	783	75.1	195	18.7	64	6.1
JEFFERSON	8,280	7,573	91.5	547	6.6	160	1.9
JESSAMINE	375	316	84.3	13	3.5	46	12.3
JOHNSON	818	360	44.0	381	46.6	77	9.4
KENTON	835	395	47.3	337	40.4	103	12.3
KNOTT	84	84	100.0				
KNOX	1,898	1,409	74.2	266	14.0	223	11.7
LARUE	216	108	50.0	68	31.5	40	18.5
LAUREL	1,219	979	80.3	183	15.0	57	4.7
LAWRENCE	464	348	75.0	42	9.1	74	15.9
LEE	255	200	78.4	3	1.2	52	20.4

46

County	Total Vote	James Park		Clarence Bartlett		Other Vote	
		Total	Per Cent	Total	Per Cent	Total	Per Cent
LESLIE	921	328	35.6	310	33.7	283	30.7
LETCHER	757	617	81.5	61	8.1	79	10.4
LEWIS	778	609	78.3	57	7.3	112	14.4
LINCOLN	422	357	84.6	11	2.6	54	12.8
LIVINGSTON	159	116	73.0	30	18.9	13	8.2
LOGAN	195	23	11.8	166	85.1	6	3.1
LYON	152	138	90.8	6	3.9	8	5.3
MADISON	1,883	1,752	93.0	17	0.9	114	6.1
MAGOFFIN	459	333	72.5	86	18.7	40	8.7
MARION	278	126	45.3	71	25.5	81	29.1
MARSHALL	148	115	77.7	25	16.9	8	5.4
MARTIN	274	223	81.4	15	5.5	36	13.1
MASON	450	392	87.1	11	2.4	47	10.4
MC CRACKEN	484	408	84.3	61	12.6	15	3.1
MC CREARY	607	443	73.0	39	6.4	125	20.6
MC LEAN	230	15	6.5	193	83.9	22	9.6
MEADE	225	25	11.1	177	78.7	23	10.2
MENIFEE	61	41	67.2	4	6.6	16	26.2
MERCER	386	361	93.5	13	3.4	12	3.1
METCALFE	495	286	57.8	89	18.0	120	24.2
MONROE	887	526	59.3	291	32.8	70	7.9
MONTGOMERY	173	148	85.5	9	5.2	16	9.2
MORGAN	197	171	86.8	11	5.6	15	7.6
MUHLENBERG	1,654	21	1.3	1,575	95.2	58	3.5
NELSON	467	383	82.0	27	5.8	57	12.2
NICHOLAS	182	168	92.3	3	1.6	11	6.0
OHIO	1,939	35	1.8	1,835	94.6	69	3.6
OLDHAM	96	69	71.9	24	25.0	3	3.1
OWEN	112	96	85.7	2	1.8	14	12.5
OWSLEY	491	398	81.1	59	12.0	34	6.9
PENDLETON	180	117	65.0	55	30.6	8	4.4
PERRY	909	749	82.4	98	10.8	62	6.8
PIKE	1,152	820	71.2	135	11.7	197	17.1
POWELL	115	70	60.9	19	16.5	26	22.6
PULASKI	2,399	938	39.1	1,343	56.0	118	4.9
ROBERTSON	115	88	76.5	4	3.5	23	20.0
ROCKCASTLE	912	717	78.6	147	16.1	48	5.3
ROWAN	592	413	69.8	57	9.6	122	20.6
RUSSELL	657	348	53.0	73	11.1	236	35.9
SCOTT	266	234	88.0	2	0.8	30	11.3
SHELBY	564	234	41.5	292	51.8	38	6.7
SIMPSON	196	153	78.1	24	12.2	19	9.7
SPENCER	113	68	60.2	19	16.8	26	23.0
TAYLOR	782	652	83.4	56	7.2	74	9.5
TODD	89	18	20.2	26	29.2	45	50.6
TRIGG	230	185	80.4	36	15.7	9	3.9
TRIMBLE	30	17	56.7	10	33.3	3	10.0
UNION	70	28	40.0	16	22.9	26	37.1
WARREN	545	137	25.1	341	62.6	67	12.3
WASHINGTON	406	337	83.0	18	4.4	51	12.6
WAYNE	400	143	35.8	201	50.3	56	14.0
WEBSTER	185	125	67.6	30	16.2	30	16.2
WHITLEY	1,491	1,040	69.8	301	20.2	150	10.1
WOLFE	141	81	57.4	29	20.6	31	22.0
WOODFORD	597	556	93.1	4	0.7	37	6.2
TOTAL	82,486	52,886	64.1	21,959	26.6	7,641	9.3

OTHER VOTE: G. Tom Hawkins 3397
Silas A. Sullivan 4244

County	Total Vote	Democratic		Republican		Other Vote		Per Cent of Two-Party Vote		Dem-Rep Plurality
		Total	Per Cent	Total	Per Cent	Total	Per Cent	Dem	Rep	
ADAIR	5,671	2,361	41.6	3,293	58.1	17	0.3	41.8	58.2	932 R
ALLEN	4,785	1,717	35.9	3,033	63.4	35	0.7	36.1	63.9	1,316 R
ANDERSON	3,500	2,085	59.6	1,391	39.7	24	0.7	60.0	40.0	694 D
BALLARD	3,372	2,754	81.7	612	18.1	6	0.2	81.8	18.2	2,142 D
BARREN	7,509	4,358	58.0	3,151	42.0			58.0	42.0	1,207 D
BATH	3,680	2,136	58.0	1,539	41.8	5	0.1	58.1	41.9	597 D
BELL	9,055	4,388	48.5	4,627	51.1	40	0.4	48.7	51.3	239 R
BOONE	3,826	2,437	63.7	1,378	36.0	11	0.3	63.9	36.1	1,059 D
BOURBON	5,692	3,768	66.2	1,917	33.7	7	0.1	66.3	33.7	1,851 D
BOYD	14,726	7,959	54.0	6,742	45.8	25	0.2	54.1	45.9	1,217 D
BOYLE	5,598	3,436	61.4	2,143	38.3	19	0.3	61.6	38.4	1,293 D
BRACKEN	3,335	1,894	56.8	1,424	42.7	17	0.5	57.1	42.9	470 D
BREATHITT	4,073	2,865	70.3	1,186	29.1	22	0.5	70.7	29.3	1,679 D
BRECKINRIDGE	6,034	2,817	46.7	3,186	52.8	31	0.5	46.9	53.1	369 R
BULLITT	2,894	2,047	70.7	843	29.1	4	0.1	70.8	29.2	1,204 D
BUTLER	4,307	1,105	25.7	3,197	74.2	5	0.1	25.7	74.3	2,092 R
CALDWELL	4,603	2,420	52.6	2,178	47.3	5	0.1	52.6	47.4	242 D
CALLOWAY	5,807	4,741	81.6	1,048	18.0	18	0.3	81.9	18.1	3,693 D
CAMPBELL	26,254	12,940	49.3	13,274	50.6	40	0.2	49.4	50.6	334 R
CARLISLE	2,475	1,981	80.0	489	19.8	5	0.2	80.2	19.8	1,492 D
CARROLL	3,364	2,623	78.0	729	21.7	12	0.4	78.3	21.7	1,894 D
CARTER	6,664	2,625	39.4	4,035	60.5	4	0.1	39.4	60.6	1,410 R
CASEY	5,290	1,494	28.2	3,778	71.4	18	0.3	28.3	71.7	2,284 R
CHRISTIAN	10,635	6,214	58.4	4,396	41.3	25	0.2	58.6	41.4	1,818 D
CLARK	5,431	3,556	65.5	1,852	34.1	23	0.4	65.8	34.2	1,704 D
CLAY	5,270	1,125	21.3	4,139	78.5	6	0.1	21.4	78.6	3,014 R
CLINTON	3,086	558	18.1	2,525	81.8	3	0.1	18.1	81.9	1,967 R
CRITTENDEN	4,150	1,533	36.9	2,601	62.7	16	0.4	37.1	62.9	1,068 R
CUMBERLAND	3,213	698	21.7	2,507	78.0	8	0.2	21.8	78.2	1,809 R
DAVIESS	13,909	8,040	57.8	5,815	41.8	54	0.4	58.0	42.0	2,225 D
EDMONSON	3,467	1,019	29.4	2,439	70.3	9	0.3	29.5	70.5	1,420 R
ELLIOTT	2,097	1,599	76.3	498	23.7			76.3	23.7	1,101 D
ESTILL	4,460	1,961	44.0	2,490	55.8	9	0.2	44.1	55.9	529 R
FAYETTE	24,442	13,155	53.8	11,160	45.7	127	0.5	54.1	45.9	1,995 D
FLEMING	5,211	2,583	49.6	2,616	50.2	12	0.2	49.7	50.3	33 R
FLOYD	10,498	7,455	71.0	3,042	29.0	1		71.0	29.0	4,413 D
FRANKLIN	8,357	6,297	75.4	2,016	24.1	44	0.5	75.7	24.3	4,281 D
FULTON	3,533	2,916	82.5	604	17.1	13	0.4	82.8	17.2	2,312 D
GALLATIN	1,823	1,329	72.9	483	26.5	11	0.6	73.3	26.7	846 D
GARRARD	3,798	1,759	46.3	2,032	53.5	7	0.2	46.4	53.6	273 R
GRANT	3,917	2,350	60.0	1,559	39.8	8	0.2	60.1	39.9	791 D
GRAVES	9,981	7,892	79.1	2,080	20.8	9	0.1	79.1	20.9	5,812 D
GRAYSON	5,899	2,349	39.8	3,536	59.9	14	0.2	39.9	60.1	1,187 R
GREEN	4,133	1,782	43.1	2,321	56.2	30	0.7	43.4	56.6	539 R
GREENUP	7,406	3,776	51.0	3,628	49.0	2		51.0	49.0	148 D
HANCOCK	2,454	1,120	45.6	1,326	54.0	8	0.3	45.8	54.2	206 R
HARDIN	7,101	4,355	61.3	2,737	38.5	9	0.1	61.4	38.6	1,618 D
HARLAN	13,303	7,670	57.7	5,617	42.2	16	0.1	57.7	42.3	2,053 D
HARRISON	5,122	3,657	71.4	1,465	28.6			71.4	28.6	2,192 D
HART	6,025	3,070	51.0	2,951	49.0	4	0.1	51.0	49.0	119 D
HENDERSON	8,215	5,753	70.0	2,444	29.8	18	0.2	70.2	29.8	3,309 D
HENRY	4,898	3,423	69.9	1,462	29.8	13	0.3	70.1	29.9	1,961 D
HICKMAN	2,489	1,964	78.9	515	20.7	10	0.4	79.2	20.8	1,449 D
HOPKINS	10,838	7,184	66.3	3,628	33.5	26	0.2	66.4	33.6	3,556 D
JACKSON	3,734	309	8.3	3,424	91.7	1		8.3	91.7	3,115 R
JEFFERSON	139,904	79,855	57.1	59,619	42.6	430	0.3	57.3	42.7	20,236 D
JESSAMINE	4,144	2,347	56.6	1,773	42.8	24	0.6	57.0	43.0	574 D
JOHNSON	6,553	2,113	32.2	4,434	67.7	6	0.1	32.3	67.7	2,321 R
KENTON	29,863	17,965	60.2	11,874	39.8	24	0.1	60.2	39.8	6,091 D
KNOTT	4,416	3,690	83.6	726	16.4			83.6	16.4	2,964 D
KNOX	7,371	2,296	31.1	5,071	68.8	4	0.1	31.2	68.8	2,775 R
LARUE	3,474	2,011	57.9	1,446	41.6	17	0.5	58.2	41.8	565 D
LAUREL	6,912	1,992	28.8	4,918	71.2	2		28.8	71.2	2,926 R
LAWRENCE	4,956	2,340	47.2	2,606	52.6	10	0.2	47.3	52.7	266 R
LEE	2,473	1,038	42.0	1,431	57.9	4	0.2	42.0	58.0	393 R

County	Total Vote	Democratic Total	Democratic Per Cent	Republican Total	Republican Per Cent	Other Vote Total	Other Vote Per Cent	Per Cent of Two-Party Vote Dem	Per Cent of Two-Party Vote Rep	Dem-Rep Plurality
LESLIE	3,031	457	15.1	2,574	84.9			15.1	84.9	2,117 R
LETCHER	8,255	4,328	52.4	3,909	47.4	18	0.2	52.5	47.5	419 D
LEWIS	4,512	1,361	30.2	3,148	69.8	3	0.1	30.2	69.8	1,787 R
LINCOLN	5,798	3,014	52.0	2,746	47.4	38	0.7	52.3	47.7	268 D
LIVINGSTON	2,835	1,668	58.8	1,163	41.0	4	0.1	58.9	41.1	505 D
LOGAN	7,228	5,056	70.0	2,163	29.9	9	0.1	70.0	30.0	2,893 D
LYON	2,587	1,691	65.4	891	34.4	5	0.2	65.5	34.5	800 D
MADISON	11,099	5,597	50.4	5,457	49.2	45	0.4	50.6	49.4	140 D
MAGOFFIN	4,104	2,004	48.8	2,100	51.2			48.8	51.2	96 R
MARION	4,510	2,939	65.2	1,555	34.5	16	0.4	65.4	34.6	1,384 D
MARSHALL	4,129	2,879	69.7	1,240	30.0	10	0.2	69.9	30.1	1,639 D
MARTIN	2,518	557	22.1	1,961	77.9			22.1	77.9	1,404 R
MASON	6,975	3,779	54.2	3,170	45.4	26	0.4	54.4	45.6	609 D
MC CRACKEN	14,605	10,765	73.7	3,799	26.0	41	0.3	73.9	26.1	6,966 D
MC CREARY	3,963	800	20.2	3,163	79.8			20.2	79.8	2,363 R
MC LEAN	3,847	2,154	56.0	1,671	43.4	22	0.6	56.3	43.7	483 D
MEADE	2,800	1,791	64.0	1,009	36.0			64.0	36.0	782 D
MENIFEE	1,449	915	63.1	532	36.7	2	0.1	63.2	36.8	383 D
MERCER	4,965	2,943	59.3	2,007	40.4	15	0.3	59.5	40.5	936 D
METCALFE	3,906	1,649	42.2	2,247	57.5	10	0.3	42.3	57.7	598 R
MONROE	4,752	1,081	22.7	3,671	77.3			22.7	77.3	2,590 R
MONTGOMERY	3,769	2,310	61.3	1,456	38.6	3	0.1	61.3	38.7	854 D
MORGAN	4,323	3,154	73.0	1,165	26.9	4	0.1	73.0	27.0	1,989 D
MUHLENBERG	8,134	3,623	44.5	4,493	55.2	18	0.2	44.6	55.4	870 R
NELSON	5,660	3,668	64.8	1,971	34.8	21	0.4	65.0	35.0	1,697 D
NICHOLAS	2,823	1,787	63.3	1,025	36.3	11	0.4	63.5	36.5	762 D
OHIO	7,476	3,080	41.2	4,383	58.6	13	0.2	41.3	58.7	1,303 R
OLDHAM	2,897	1,887	65.1	993	34.3	17	0.6	65.5	34.5	894 D
OWEN	3,718	3,098	83.3	620	16.7			83.3	16.7	2,478 D
OWSLEY	2,337	324	13.9	2,005	85.8	8	0.3	13.9	86.1	1,681 R
PENDLETON	3,998	2,079	52.0	1,904	47.6	15	0.4	52.2	47.8	175 D
PERRY	9,494	5,273	55.5	4,221	44.5			55.5	44.5	1,052 D
PIKE	17,459	9,550	54.7	7,888	45.2	21	0.1	54.8	45.2	1,662 D
POWELL	1,882	1,006	53.5	872	46.3	4	0.2	53.6	46.4	134 D
PULASKI	11,871	3,838	32.3	7,979	67.2	54	0.5	32.5	67.5	4,141 R
ROBERTSON	1,373	821	59.8	547	39.8	5	0.4	60.0	40.0	274 D
ROCKCASTLE	4,969	1,285	25.9	3,684	74.1			25.9	74.1	2,399 R
ROWAN	3,538	1,813	51.2	1,720	48.6	5	0.1	51.3	48.7	93 D
RUSSELL	4,031	1,148	28.5	2,873	71.3	10	0.2	28.6	71.4	1,725 R
SCOTT	5,150	3,539	68.7	1,575	30.6	36	0.7	69.2	30.8	1,964 D
SHELBY	6,259	4,302	68.7	1,928	30.8	29	0.5	69.1	30.9	2,374 D
SIMPSON	3,704	2,727	73.6	963	26.0	14	0.4	73.9	26.1	1,764 D
SPENCER	2,041	1,410	69.1	628	30.8	3	0.1	69.2	30.8	782 D
TAYLOR	5,000	2,425	48.5	2,538	50.8	37	0.7	48.9	51.1	113 R
TODD	4,169	2,861	68.6	1,292	31.0	16	0.4	68.9	31.1	1,569 D
TRIGG	3,715	2,424	65.2	1,284	34.6	7	0.2	65.4	34.6	1,140 D
TRIMBLE	2,139	1,865	87.2	253	11.8	21	1.0	88.1	11.9	1,612 D
UNION	4,251	3,430	80.7	817	19.2	4	0.1	80.8	19.2	2,613 D
WARREN	12,201	7,391	60.6	4,769	39.1	41	0.3	60.8	39.2	2,622 D
WASHINGTON	4,587	2,256	49.2	2,320	50.6	11	0.2	49.3	50.7	64 R
WAYNE	4,875	2,078	42.6	2,797	57.4			42.6	57.4	719 R
WEBSTER	5,078	3,297	64.9	1,765	34.8	16	0.3	65.1	34.9	1,532 D
WHITLEY	8,619	2,323	27.0	6,296	73.0			27.0	73.0	3,973 R
WOLFE	2,257	1,410	62.5	847	37.5			62.5	37.5	563 D
WOODFORD	3,486	2,094	60.1	1,379	39.6	13	0.4	60.3	39.7	715 D
TOTAL	846,626	464,053	54.8	380,425	44.9	2,148	0.3	55.0	45.0	83,628 D

OTHER VOTE: Robert H. Garrison (Prohibition) 1808
Yona M. Marret (Socialist Labor) 340
DEMOCRAT: Alben W. Barkley
REPUBLICAN: James Park

County	Total Vote	John Y. Brown		Philip P. Ardery		Other Vote	
		Total	Per Cent	Total	Per Cent	Total	Per Cent
ADAIR	602	308	51.2	157	26.1	137	22.8
ALLEN	281	130	46.3	38	13.5	113	40.2
ANDERSON	774	381	49.2	298	38.5	95	12.3
BALLARD	590	157	26.6	252	42.7	181	30.7
BARREN	1,173	637	54.3	236	20.1	300	25.6
BATH	1,028	420	40.9	437	42.5	171	16.6
BELL	436	199	45.6	198	45.4	39	8.9
BOONE	628	337	53.7	166	26.4	125	19.9
BOURBON	2,188	134	6.1	1,939	88.6	115	5.3
BOYD	2,218	1,066	48.1	331	14.9	821	37.0
BOYLE	1,466	590	40.2	620	42.3	256	17.5
BRACKEN	516	234	45.3	176	34.1	106	20.5
BREATHITT	1,392	841	60.4	385	27.7	166	11.9
BRECKINRIDGE	743	453	61.0	136	18.3	154	20.7
BULLITT	521	197	37.8	241	46.3	83	15.9
BUTLER	258	106	41.1	19	7.4	133	51.6
CALDWELL	468	143	30.6	96	20.5	229	48.9
CALLOWAY	744	218	29.3	379	50.9	147	19.8
CAMPBELL	3,038	1,028	33.8	1,497	49.3	513	16.9
CARLISLE	284	104	36.6	139	48.9	41	14.4
CARROLL	977	306	31.3	497	50.9	174	17.8
CARTER	713	445	62.4	117	16.4	151	21.2
CASEY	296	131	44.3	104	35.1	61	20.6
CHRISTIAN	1,149	275	23.9	363	31.6	511	44.5
CLARK	1,091	568	52.1	384	35.2	139	12.7
CLAY	172	93	54.1	43	25.0	36	20.9
CLINTON	160	78	48.8	62	38.8	20	12.5
CRITTENDEN	313	180	57.5	91	29.1	42	13.4
CUMBERLAND	135	48	35.6	67	49.6	20	14.8
DAVIESS	1,912	722	37.8	712	37.2	478	25.0
EDMONSON	292	32	11.0	16	5.5	244	83.6
ELLIOTT	754	582	77.2	50	6.6	122	16.2
ESTILL	492	256	52.0	92	18.7	144	29.3
FAYETTE	5,923	2,470	41.7	2,622	44.3	831	14.0
FLEMING	650	322	49.5	225	34.6	103	15.8
FLOYD	2,111	1,327	62.9	93	4.4	691	32.7
FRANKLIN	2,712	536	19.8	1,938	71.5	238	8.8
FULTON	384	95	24.7	186	48.4	103	26.8
GALLATIN	318	174	54.7	87	27.4	57	17.9
GARRARD	528	203	38.4	188	35.6	137	25.9
GRANT	918	421	45.9	99	10.8	398	43.4
GRAVES	1,213	441	36.4	451	37.2	321	26.5
GRAYSON	584	193	33.0	90	15.4	301	51.5
GREEN	357	158	44.3	156	43.7	43	12.0
GREENUP	1,424	1,021	71.7	127	8.9	276	19.4
HANCOCK	199	82	41.2	57	28.6	60	30.2
HARDIN	1,138	380	33.4	530	46.6	228	20.0
HARLAN	1,183	829	70.1	153	12.9	201	17.0
HARRISON	985	334	33.9	444	45.1	207	21.0
HART	521	256	49.1	141	27.1	124	23.8
HENDERSON	1,016	415	40.8	277	27.3	324	31.9
HENRY	1,228	385	31.4	460	37.5	383	31.2
HICKMAN	493	85	17.2	370	75.1	38	7.7
HOPKINS	1,991	855	42.9	222	11.2	914	45.9
JACKSON	104	36	34.6	62	59.6	6	5.8
JEFFERSON	18,129	6,695	36.9	6,770	37.3	4,664	25.7
JESSAMINE	1,238	684	55.3	314	25.4	240	19.4
JOHNSON	337	230	68.2	49	14.5	58	17.2
KENTON	4,563	2,111	46.3	1,160	25.4	1,292	28.3
KNOTT	762	534	70.1	101	13.3	127	16.7
KNOX	467	178	38.1	244	52.2	45	9.6
LARUE	788	190	24.1	539	68.4	59	7.5
LAUREL	388	200	51.5	163	42.0	25	6.4
LAWRENCE	554	336	60.6	43	7.8	175	31.6
LEE	572	14	2.4	9	1.6	549	96.0

50

County	Total Vote	John Y. Brown Total	Per Cent	Philip P. Ardery Total	Per Cent	Other Vote Total	Per Cent
LESLIE	101	46	45.5	27	26.7	28	27.7
LETCHER	996	707	71.0	81	8.1	208	20.9
LEWIS	294	134	45.6	84	28.6	76	25.9
LINCOLN	889	372	41.8	351	39.5	166	18.7
LIVINGSTON	501	157	31.3	173	34.5	171	34.1
LOGAN	2,931	2,675	91.3	40	1.4	216	7.4
LYON	456	115	25.2	272	59.6	69	15.1
MADISON	1,543	666	43.2	538	34.9	339	22.0
MAGOFFIN	726	239	32.9	373	51.4	114	15.7
MARION	863	387	44.8	336	38.9	140	16.2
MARSHALL	472	140	29.7	239	50.6	93	19.7
MARTIN	96	69	71.9	7	7.3	20	20.8
MASON	718	347	48.3	269	37.5	102	14.2
MC CRACKEN	1,710	453	26.5	647	37.8	610	35.7
MC CREARY	173	102	59.0	47	27.2	24	13.9
MC LEAN	607	193	31.8	289	47.6	125	20.6
MEADE	639	118	18.5	294	46.0	227	35.5
MENIFEE	246	156	63.4	37	15.0	53	21.5
MERCER	782	299	38.2	303	38.7	180	23.0
METCALFE	508	343	67.5	83	16.3	82	16.1
MONROE	240	178	74.2	51	21.3	11	4.6
MONTGOMERY	989	294	29.7	501	50.7	194	19.6
MORGAN	1,220	316	25.9	148	12.1	756	62.0
MUHLENBERG	724	420	58.0	117	16.2	187	25.8
NELSON	1,227	407	33.2	624	50.9	196	16.0
NICHOLAS	638	265	41.5	310	48.6	63	9.9
OHIO	657	313	47.6	252	38.4	92	14.0
OLDHAM	521	151	29.0	157	30.1	213	40.9
OWEN	1,186	537	45.3	328	27.7	321	27.1
OWSLEY	74	15	20.3	6	8.1	53	71.6
PENDLETON	469	202	43.1	200	42.6	67	14.3
PERRY	1,224	999	81.6	72	5.9	153	12.5
PIKE	2,465	2,043	82.9	160	6.5	262	10.6
POWELL	236	54	22.9	113	47.9	69	29.2
PULASKI	955	219	22.9	666	69.7	70	7.3
ROBERTSON	335	163	48.7	125	37.3	47	14.0
ROCKCASTLE	354	138	39.0	189	53.4	27	7.6
ROWAN	1,164	405	34.8	315	27.1	444	38.1
RUSSELL	207	119	57.5	67	32.4	21	10.1
SCOTT	1,673	465	27.8	865	51.7	343	20.5
SHELBY	1,092	252	23.1	525	48.1	315	28.8
SIMPSON	665	397	59.7	63	9.5	205	30.8
SPENCER	363	129	35.5	127	35.0	107	29.5
TAYLOR	996	314	31.5	614	61.6	68	6.8
TODD	624	352	56.4	61	9.8	211	33.8
TRIGG	805	576	71.6	157	19.5	72	8.9
TRIMBLE	593	109	18.4	427	72.0	57	9.6
UNION	1,114	489	43.9	498	44.7	127	11.4
WARREN	3,496	2,116	60.5	188	5.4	1,192	34.1
WASHINGTON	545	290	53.2	136	25.0	119	21.8
WAYNE	300	159	53.0	91	30.3	50	16.7
WEBSTER	732	407	55.6	120	16.4	205	28.0
WHITLEY	294	171	58.2	98	33.3	25	8.5
WOLFE	665	282	42.4	234	35.2	149	22.4
WOODFORD	1,022	244	23.9	620	60.7	158	15.5
TOTAL	126,698	55,297	43.6	42,423	33.5	28,978	22.9

OTHER VOTE: Norris Brooks Vincent 7253
Henry C. Stephens, Jr. 1656
John J. Thobe 1826
James Delk 1245
George T. Smith 2444
Blakey Helm 9864
Tom Logan 4690

County	Total Vote	John S. Cooper Total	John S. Cooper Per Cent	Roscoe C. Douglas Total	Roscoe C. Douglas Per Cent
ADAIR	392	339	86.5	53	13.5
ALLEN	287	247	86.1	40	13.9
ANDERSON	102	89	87.3	13	12.7
BALLARD	50	42	84.0	8	16.0
BARREN	230	198	86.1	32	13.9
BATH	136	109	80.1	27	19.9
BELL	982	868	88.4	114	11.6
BOONE	49	46	93.9	3	6.1
BOURBON	84	76	90.5	8	9.5
BOYD	1,105	765	69.2	340	30.8
BOYLE	189	169	89.4	20	10.6
BRACKEN	86	66	76.7	20	23.3
BREATHITT	135	103	76.3	32	23.7
BRECKINRIDGE	398	365	91.7	33	8.3
BULLITT	55	50	90.9	5	9.1
BUTLER	484	445	91.9	39	8.1
CALDWELL	183	172	94.0	11	6.0
CALLOWAY	64	57	89.1	7	10.9
CAMPBELL	1,550	1,370	88.4	180	11.6
CARLISLE	46	41	89.1	5	10.9
CARROLL	41	41	100.0		
CARTER	597	423	70.9	174	29.1
CASEY	461	438	95.0	23	5.0
CHRISTIAN	318	301	94.7	17	5.3
CLARK	130	109	83.8	21	16.2
CLAY	1,263	1,043	82.6	220	17.4
CLINTON	892	780	87.4	112	12.6
CRITTENDEN	203	185	91.1	18	8.9
CUMBERLAND	457	419	91.7	38	8.3
DAVIESS	196	160	81.6	36	18.4
EDMONSON	382	368	96.3	14	3.7
ELLIOTT	31	27	87.1	4	12.9
ESTILL	278	225	80.9	53	19.1
FAYETTE	519	469	90.4	50	9.6
FLEMING	209	173	82.8	36	17.2
FLOYD	1,050	926	88.2	124	11.8
FRANKLIN	216	206	95.4	10	4.6
FULTON	21	19	90.5	2	9.5
GALLATIN	30	30	100.0		
GARRARD	144	130	90.3	14	9.7
GRANT	93	83	89.2	10	10.8
GRAVES	149	146	98.0	3	2.0
GRAYSON	431	386	89.6	45	10.4
GREEN	183	167	91.3	16	8.7
GREENUP	499	344	68.9	155	31.1
HANCOCK	135	108	80.0	27	20.0
HARDIN	189	175	92.6	14	7.4
HARLAN	1,623	1,316	81.1	307	18.9
HARRISON	105	95	90.5	10	9.5
HART	370	335	90.5	35	9.5
HENDERSON	64	55	85.9	9	14.1
HENRY	113	100	88.5	13	11.5
HICKMAN	21	21	100.0		
HOPKINS	190	146	76.8	44	23.2
JACKSON	929	788	84.8	141	15.2
JEFFERSON	7,611	7,076	93.0	535	7.0
JESSAMINE	106	98	92.5	8	7.5
JOHNSON	2,003	1,744	87.1	259	12.9
KENTON	508	443	87.2	65	12.8
KNOTT	108	89	82.4	19	17.6
KNOX	1,180	853	72.3	327	27.7
LARUE	133	128	96.2	5	3.8
LAUREL	1,199	1,030	85.9	169	14.1
LAWRENCE	353	252	71.4	101	28.6
LEE	252	203	80.6	49	19.4

County	Total Vote	John S. Cooper		Roscoe C. Douglas	
		Total	Per Cent	Total	Per Cent
LESLIE	801	689	86.0	112	14.0
LETCHER	1,247	1,091	87.5	156	12.5
LEWIS	471	350	74.3	121	25.7
LINCOLN	288	268	93.1	20	6.9
LIVINGSTON	104	99	95.2	5	4.8
LOGAN	43	40	93.0	3	7.0
LYON	93	90	96.8	3	3.2
MADISON	377	313	83.0	64	17.0
MAGOFFIN	1,285	1,209	94.1	76	5.9
MARION	81	68	84.0	13	16.0
MARSHALL	86	82	95.3	4	4.7
MARTIN	767	613	79.9	154	20.1
MASON	236	203	86.0	33	14.0
MC CRACKEN	184	164	89.1	20	10.9
MC CREARY	857	741	86.5	116	13.5
MC LEAN	101	73	72.3	28	27.7
MEADE	64	54	84.4	10	15.6
MENIFEE	62	45	72.6	17	27.4
MERCER	106	92	86.8	14	13.2
METCALFE	233	216	92.7	17	7.3
MONROE	638	573	89.8	65	10.2
MONTGOMERY	84	63	75.0	21	25.0
MORGAN	152	115	75.7	37	24.3
MUHLENBERG	457	371	81.2	86	18.8
NELSON	147	115	78.2	32	21.8
NICHOLAS	89	67	75.3	22	24.7
OHIO	424	356	84.0	68	16.0
OLDHAM	71	65	91.5	6	8.5
OWEN	66	53	80.3	13	19.7
OWSLEY	458	387	84.5	71	15.5
PENDLETON	90	83	92.2	7	7.8
PERRY	2,126	1,918	90.2	208	9.8
PIKE	3,147	2,763	87.8	384	12.2
POWELL	61	41	67.2	20	32.8
PULASKI	2,265	2,182	96.3	83	3.7
ROBERTSON	71	60	84.5	11	15.5
ROCKCASTLE	1,144	1,038	90.7	106	9.3
ROWAN	387	323	83.5	64	16.5
RUSSELL	558	538	96.4	20	3.6
SCOTT	95	79	83.2	16	16.8
SHELBY	103	96	93.2	7	6.8
SIMPSON	89	84	94.4	5	5.6
SPENCER	66	46	69.7	20	30.3
TAYLOR	235	212	90.2	23	9.8
TODD	52	34	65.4	18	34.6
TRIGG	99	93	93.9	6	6.1
TRIMBLE	20	18	90.0	2	10.0
UNION	63	49	77.8	14	22.2
WARREN	231	196	84.8	35	15.2
WASHINGTON	101	88	87.1	13	12.9
WAYNE	589	523	88.8	66	11.2
WEBSTER	116	91	78.4	25	21.6
WHITLEY	1,441	442	30.7	999	69.3
WOLFE	111	88	79.3	23	20.7
WOODFORD	95	72	75.8	23	24.2
TOTAL	56,019	48,092	85.8	7,927	14.2

County	Total Vote	Democratic		Republican		Other Vote		Per Cent of Two-Party Vote		Dem-Rep Plurality
		Total	Per Cent	Total	Per Cent	Total	Per Cent	Dem	Rep	
ADAIR	4,436	1,731	39.0	2,694	60.7	11	0.2	39.1	60.9	963 R
ALLEN	2,853	979	34.3	1,874	65.7			34.3	65.7	895 R
ANDERSON	2,661	1,529	57.5	1,124	42.2	8	0.3	57.6	42.4	405 D
BALLARD	2,296	1,787	77.8	509	22.2			77.8	22.2	1,278 D
BARREN	5,852	3,267	55.8	2,573	44.0	12	0.2	55.9	44.1	694 D
BATH	2,655	1,418	53.4	1,227	46.2	10	0.4	53.6	46.4	191 D
BELL	6,502	2,062	31.7	4,425	68.1	15	0.2	31.8	68.2	2,363 R
BOONE	2,112	1,239	58.7	866	41.0	7	0.3	58.9	41.1	373 D
BOURBON	3,880	2,316	59.7	1,557	40.1	7	0.2	59.8	40.2	759 D
BOYD	11,537	5,254	45.5	6,258	54.2	25	0.2	45.6	54.4	1,004 R
BOYLE	4,461	2,456	55.1	1,996	44.7	9	0.2	55.2	44.8	460 D
BRACKEN	1,722	825	47.9	894	51.9	3	0.2	48.0	52.0	69 R
BREATHITT	3,221	2,132	66.2	1,085	33.7	4	0.1	66.3	33.7	1,047 D
BRECKINRIDGE	4,333	1,789	41.3	2,536	58.5	8	0.2	41.4	58.6	747 R
BULLITT	1,655	1,063	64.2	590	35.6	2	0.1	64.3	35.7	473 D
BUTLER	3,013	679	22.5	2,334	77.5			22.5	77.5	1,655 R
CALDWELL	2,918	1,285	44.0	1,626	55.7	7	0.2	44.1	55.9	341 R
CALLOWAY	3,928	3,124	79.5	798	20.3	6	0.2	79.7	20.3	2,326 D
CAMPBELL	18,479	7,169	38.8	11,252	60.9	58	0.3	38.9	61.1	4,083 R
CARLISLE	1,444	1,109	76.9	334	23.1	1	0.1	76.9	23.1	775 D
CARROLL	2,528	1,770	70.0	756	29.9	2	0.1	70.1	29.9	1,014 D
CARTER	4,631	1,699	36.7	2,923	63.1	9	0.2	36.8	63.2	1,224 R
CASEY	3,986	1,030	25.8	2,952	74.1	4	0.1	25.9	74.1	1,922 R
CHRISTIAN	6,791	3,130	46.1	3,655	53.8	6	0.1	46.1	53.9	525 R
CLARK	3,485	1,849	53.1	1,628	46.7	8	0.2	53.2	46.8	221 D
CLAY	3,777	590	15.6	3,181	84.2	6	0.2	15.6	84.4	2,591 R
CLINTON	2,429	437	18.0	1,987	81.8	5	0.2	18.0	82.0	1,550 R
CRITTENDEN	2,773	995	35.9	1,776	64.0	2	0.1	35.9	64.1	781 R
CUMBERLAND	2,323	478	20.6	1,844	79.4	1		20.6	79.4	1,366 R
DAVIESS	9,740	5,357	55.0	4,368	44.8	15	0.2	55.1	44.9	989 D
EDMONSON	2,575	733	28.5	1,842	71.5			28.5	71.5	1,109 R
ELLIOTT	1,674	1,315	78.6	357	21.3	2	0.1	78.6	21.4	958 D
ESTILL	3,337	1,366	40.9	1,957	58.6	14	0.4	41.1	58.9	591 R
FAYETTE	18,188	7,768	42.7	10,289	56.6	131	0.7	43.0	57.0	2,521 R
FLEMING	3,870	1,890	48.8	1,959	50.6	21	0.5	49.1	50.9	69 R
FLOYD	9,811	6,144	62.6	3,667	37.4			62.6	37.4	2,477 D
FRANKLIN	5,865	3,937	67.1	1,919	32.7	9	0.2	67.2	32.8	2,018 D
FULTON	2,112	1,734	82.1	377	17.9	1		82.1	17.9	1,357 D
GALLATIN	1,168	779	66.7	388	33.2	1	0.1	66.8	33.2	391 D
GARRARD	3,123	1,248	40.0	1,868	59.8	7	0.2	40.1	59.9	620 R
GRANT	2,567	1,589	61.9	976	38.0	2	0.1	61.9	38.1	613 D
GRAVES	6,684	5,024	75.2	1,650	24.7	10	0.1	75.3	24.7	3,374 D
GRAYSON	4,191	1,565	37.3	2,622	62.6	4	0.1	37.4	62.6	1,057 R
GREEN	3,120	1,258	40.3	1,856	59.5	6	0.2	40.4	59.6	598 R
GREENUP	5,851	2,769	47.3	3,068	52.4	14	0.2	47.4	52.6	299 R
HANCOCK	1,670	763	45.7	902	54.0	5	0.3	45.8	54.2	139 R
HARDIN	4,342	2,182	50.3	2,156	49.7	4	0.1	50.3	49.7	26 D
HARLAN	9,289	3,650	39.3	5,633	60.6	6	0.1	39.3	60.7	1,983 R
HARRISON	3,413	2,328	68.2	1,083	31.7	2	0.1	68.2	31.8	1,245 D
HART	4,067	1,717	42.2	2,347	57.7	3	0.1	42.2	57.8	630 R
HENDERSON	4,833	2,910	60.2	1,855	38.4	68	1.4	61.1	38.9	1,055 D
HENRY	3,488	2,315	66.4	1,171	33.6	2	0.1	66.4	33.6	1,144 D
HICKMAN	1,869	1,522	81.4	344	18.4	3	0.2	81.6	18.4	1,178 D
HOPKINS	7,215	4,325	59.9	2,879	39.9	11	0.2	60.0	40.0	1,446 D
JACKSON	2,583	237	9.2	2,339	90.6	7	0.3	9.2	90.8	2,102 R
JEFFERSON	107,445	43,709	40.7	63,294	58.9	442	0.4	40.8	59.2	19,585 R
JESSAMINE	3,284	1,707	52.0	1,572	47.9	5	0.2	52.1	47.9	135 D
JOHNSON	5,366	1,411	26.3	3,954	73.7	1		26.3	73.7	2,543 R
KENTON	19,190	9,788	51.0	9,344	48.7	58	0.3	51.2	48.8	444 D
KNOTT	2,956	2,222	75.2	734	24.8			75.2	24.8	1,488 D
KNOX	6,051	1,642	27.1	4,390	72.5	19	0.3	27.2	72.8	2,748 R
LARUE	2,447	1,278	52.2	1,164	47.6	5	0.2	52.3	47.7	114 D
LAUREL	5,413	1,478	27.3	3,928	72.6	7	0.1	27.3	72.7	2,450 R
LAWRENCE	3,229	1,449	44.9	1,775	55.0	5	0.2	44.9	55.1	326 R
LEE	1,789	586	32.8	1,201	67.1	2	0.1	32.8	67.2	615 R

54

County	Total Vote	Democratic		Republican		Other Vote		Per Cent of Two-Party Vote		Dem-Rep Plurality
		Total	Per Cent	Total	Per Cent	Total	Per Cent	Dem	Rep	
LESLIE	2,084	201	9.6	1,883	90.4			9.6	90.4	1,682 R
LETCHER	5,463	2,319	42.4	3,125	57.2	19	0.3	42.6	57.4	806 R
LEWIS	3,149	756	24.0	2,390	75.9	3	0.1	24.0	76.0	1,634 R
LINCOLN	4,435	1,980	44.6	2,439	55.0	16	0.4	44.8	55.2	459 R
LIVINGSTON	2,152	1,358	63.1	792	36.8	2	0.1	63.2	36.8	566 D
LOGAN	4,854	3,378	69.6	1,463	30.1	13	0.3	69.8	30.2	1,915 D
LYON	1,847	1,032	55.9	814	44.1	1	0.1	55.9	44.1	218 D
MADISON	9,099	4,275	47.0	4,787	52.6	37	0.4	47.2	52.8	512 R
MAGOFFIN	3,999	1,805	45.1	2,177	54.4	17	0.4	45.3	54.7	372 R
MARION	3,948	2,108	53.4	1,831	46.4	9	0.2	53.5	46.5	277 D
MARSHALL	2,681	1,686	62.9	990	36.9	5	0.2	63.0	37.0	696 D
MARTIN	2,191	342	15.6	1,849	84.4			15.6	84.4	1,507 R
MASON	4,220	1,892	44.8	2,326	55.1	2		44.9	55.1	434 R
MC CRACKEN	9,418	5,569	59.1	3,733	39.6	116	1.2	59.9	40.1	1,836 D
MC CREARY	3,431	559	16.3	2,867	83.6	5	0.1	16.3	83.7	2,308 R
MC LEAN	2,645	1,530	57.8	1,110	42.0	5	0.2	58.0	42.0	420 D
MEADE	1,951	1,142	58.5	809	41.5			58.5	41.5	333 D
MENIFEE	1,134	689	60.8	442	39.0	3	0.3	60.9	39.1	247 D
MERCER	3,446	1,852	53.7	1,590	46.1	4	0.1	53.8	46.2	262 D
METCALFE	2,826	1,198	42.4	1,619	57.3	9	0.3	42.5	57.5	421 R
MONROE	3,322	698	21.0	2,620	78.9	4	0.1	21.0	79.0	1,922 R
MONTGOMERY	2,779	1,539	55.4	1,239	44.6	1		55.4	44.6	300 D
MORGAN	3,441	2,336	67.9	1,102	32.0	3	0.1	67.9	32.1	1,234 D
MUHLENBERG	5,663	2,438	43.1	3,212	56.7	13	0.2	43.2	56.8	774 R
NELSON	4,105	2,284	55.6	1,816	44.2	5	0.1	55.7	44.3	468 D
NICHOLAS	1,941	1,194	61.5	743	38.3	4	0.2	61.6	38.4	451 D
OHIO	4,971	1,877	37.8	3,082	62.0	12	0.2	37.9	62.1	1,205 R
OLDHAM	2,157	1,135	52.6	1,022	47.4			52.6	47.4	113 D
OWEN	2,797	2,286	81.7	502	17.9	9	0.3	82.0	18.0	1,784 D
OWSLEY	1,815	171	9.4	1,633	90.0	11	0.6	9.5	90.5	1,462 R
PENDLETON	2,309	1,080	46.8	1,229	53.2			46.8	53.2	149 R
PERRY	6,327	2,646	41.8	3,658	57.8	23	0.4	42.0	58.0	1,012 R
PIKE	14,655	7,067	48.2	7,548	51.5	40	0.3	48.4	51.6	481 R
POWELL	1,305	622	47.7	677	51.9	6	0.5	47.9	52.1	55 R
PULASKI	9,957	2,270	22.8	7,682	77.2	5	0.1	22.8	77.2	5,412 R
ROBERTSON	1,043	598	57.3	445	42.7			57.3	42.7	153 D
ROCKCASTLE	3,964	959	24.2	3,005	75.8			24.2	75.8	2,046 R
ROWAN	2,777	1,252	45.1	1,519	54.7	6	0.2	45.2	54.8	267 R
RUSSELL	2,875	736	25.6	2,136	74.3	3	0.1	25.6	74.4	1,400 R
SCOTT	3,691	2,323	62.9	1,362	36.9	6	0.2	63.0	37.0	961 D
SHELBY	3,731	2,178	58.4	1,550	41.5	3	0.1	58.4	41.6	628 D
SIMPSON	2,183	1,630	74.7	550	25.2	3	0.1	74.8	25.2	1,080 D
SPENCER	1,262	835	66.2	426	33.8	1	0.1	66.2	33.8	409 D
TAYLOR	3,688	1,551	42.1	2,124	57.6	13	0.4	42.2	57.8	573 R
TODD	2,841	2,048	72.1	793	27.9			72.1	27.9	1,255 D
TRIGG	2,946	2,044	69.4	901	30.6	1		69.4	30.6	1,143 D
TRIMBLE	1,435	1,229	85.6	205	14.3	1	0.1	85.7	14.3	1,024 D
UNION	3,443	2,480	72.0	954	27.7	9	0.3	72.2	27.8	1,526 D
WARREN	9,018	5,259	58.3	3,721	41.3	38	0.4	58.6	41.4	1,538 D
WASHINGTON	3,422	1,619	47.3	1,795	52.5	8	0.2	47.4	52.6	176 R
WAYNE	3,749	1,238	33.0	2,510	67.0	1		33.0	67.0	1,272 R
WEBSTER	3,181	1,965	61.8	1,214	38.2	2	0.1	61.8	38.2	751 D
WHITLEY	6,808	1,532	22.5	5,267	77.4	9	0.1	22.5	77.5	3,735 R
WOLFE	1,527	942	61.7	584	38.2	1	0.1	61.7	38.3	358 D
WOODFORD	2,522	1,211	48.0	1,308	51.9	3	0.1	48.1	51.9	97 R
TOTAL	615,119	285,829	46.5	327,652	53.3	1,638	0.3	46.6	53.4	41,823 R

DEMOCRAT: John Y. Brown
REPUBLICAN: John Sherman Cooper
SOCIALIST: W. A. Sandefur

County	Total Vote	Virgil Chapman		John Y. Brown		Other Vote	
		Total	Per Cent	Total	Per Cent	Total	Per Cent
ADAIR	692	423	61.1	206	29.8	63	9.1
ALLEN	762	626	82.2	127	16.7	9	1.2
ANDERSON	1,070	674	63.0	307	28.7	89	8.3
BALLARD	1,288	582	45.2	644	50.0	62	4.8
BARREN	1,699	838	49.3	739	43.5	122	7.2
BATH	1,334	1,123	84.2	164	12.3	47	3.5
BELL	1,114	481	43.2	599	53.8	34	3.1
BOONE	877	335	38.2	524	59.7	18	2.1
BOURBON	2,217	2,021	91.2	148	6.7	48	2.2
BOYD	2,957	903	30.5	1,933	65.4	121	4.1
BOYLE	1,890	1,024	54.2	797	42.2	69	3.7
BRACKEN	776	541	69.7	190	24.5	45	5.8
BREATHITT	1,892	1,765	93.3	118	6.2	9	0.5
BRECKINRIDGE	1,060	454	42.8	171	16.1	435	41.0
BULLITT	743	147	19.8	513	69.0	83	11.2
BUTLER	793	577	72.8	199	25.1	17	2.1
CALDWELL	891	370	41.5	473	53.1	48	5.4
CALLOWAY	2,109	985	46.7	1,005	47.7	119	5.6
CAMPBELL	5,391	1,095	20.3	4,091	75.9	205	3.8
CARLISLE	821	259	31.5	530	64.6	32	3.9
CARROLL	1,508	1,050	69.6	357	23.7	101	6.7
CARTER	1,187	809	68.2	340	28.6	38	3.2
CASEY	635	503	79.2	106	16.7	26	4.1
CHRISTIAN	2,584	1,566	60.6	895	34.6	123	4.8
CLARK	2,007	1,797	89.5	162	8.1	48	2.4
CLAY	352	255	72.4	88	25.0	9	2.6
CLINTON	379	219	57.8	156	41.2	4	1.1
CRITTENDEN	636	382	60.1	215	33.8	39	6.1
CUMBERLAND	463	397	85.7	49	10.6	17	3.7
DAVIESS	2,907	1,557	53.6	1,207	41.5	143	4.9
EDMONSON	585	424	72.5	139	23.8	22	3.8
ELLIOTT	1,516	1,139	75.1	336	22.2	41	2.7
ESTILL	837	532	63.6	267	31.9	38	4.5
FAYETTE	5,809	3,574	61.5	1,963	33.8	272	4.7
FLEMING	1,002	674	67.3	289	28.8	39	3.9
FLOYD	6,018	663	11.0	5,216	86.7	139	2.3
FRANKLIN	4,031	2,722	67.5	1,116	27.7	193	4.8
FULTON	1,137	566	49.8	535	47.1	36	3.2
GALLATIN	642	419	65.3	195	30.4	28	4.4
GARRARD	759	658	86.7	76	10.0	25	3.3
GRANT	1,321	764	57.8	524	39.7	33	2.5
GRAVES	5,289	2,375	44.9	2,647	50.0	267	5.0
GRAYSON	1,174	613	52.2	335	28.5	226	19.3
GREEN	750	628	83.7	81	10.8	41	5.5
GREENUP	1,490	487	32.7	868	58.3	135	9.1
HANCOCK	314	145	46.2	134	42.7	35	11.1
HARDIN	1,675	256	15.3	298	17.8	1,121	66.9
HARLAN	2,076	746	35.9	1,295	62.4	35	1.7
HARRISON	1,416	1,031	72.8	317	22.4	68	4.8
HART	987	458	46.4	434	44.0	95	9.6
HENDERSON	1,590	877	55.2	579	36.4	134	8.4
HENRY	1,977	1,663	84.1	257	13.0	57	2.9
HICKMAN	1,064	322	30.3	687	64.6	55	5.2
HOPKINS	1,985	953	48.0	934	47.1	98	4.9
JACKSON	199	172	86.4	23	11.6	4	2.0
JEFFERSON	21,720	7,647	35.2	12,629	58.1	1,444	6.6
JESSAMINE	1,640	1,393	84.9	196	12.0	51	3.1
JOHNSON	1,249	170	13.6	975	78.1	104	8.3
KENTON	8,990	1,489	16.6	7,182	79.9	319	3.5
KNOTT	2,914	348	11.9	2,501	85.8	65	2.2
KNOX	878	368	41.9	488	55.6	22	2.5
LARUE	919	490	53.3	284	30.9	145	15.8
LAUREL	975	651	66.8	301	30.9	23	2.4
LAWRENCE	683	396	58.0	224	32.8	63	9.2
LEE	489	373	76.3	102	20.9	14	2.9

County	Total Vote	Virgil Chapman Total	Virgil Chapman Per Cent	John Y. Brown Total	John Y. Brown Per Cent	Other Vote Total	Other Vote Per Cent
LESLIE	130	65	50.0	62	47.7	3	2.3
LETCHER	2,259	205	9.1	1,972	87.3	82	3.6
LEWIS	399	209	52.4	149	37.3	41	10.3
LINCOLN	1,672	1,095	65.5	523	31.3	54	3.2
LIVINGSTON	1,069	452	42.3	557	52.1	60	5.6
LOGAN	3,906	3,618	92.6	249	6.4	39	1.0
LYON	807	483	59.9	296	36.7	28	3.5
MADISON	2,401	1,749	72.8	558	23.2	94	3.9
MAGOFFIN	1,501	827	55.1	609	40.6	65	4.3
MARION	1,375	676	49.2	466	33.9	233	16.9
MARSHALL	1,626	545	33.5	1,022	62.9	59	3.6
MARTIN	231	44	19.0	175	75.8	12	5.2
MASON	894	522	58.4	312	34.9	60	6.7
MC CRACKEN	3,823	1,199	31.4	2,440	63.8	184	4.8
MC CREARY	307	76	24.8	222	72.3	9	2.9
MC LEAN	736	366	49.7	323	43.9	47	6.4
MEADE	895	187	20.9	104	11.6	604	67.5
MENIFEE	446	326	73.1	89	20.0	31	7.0
MERCER	1,160	824	71.0	285	24.6	51	4.4
METCALFE	938	671	71.5	229	24.4	38	4.1
MONROE	711	544	76.5	159	22.4	8	1.1
MONTGOMERY	1,630	1,320	81.0	197	12.1	113	6.9
MORGAN	2,716	2,440	89.8	235	8.7	41	1.5
MUHLENBERG	1,174	341	29.0	776	66.1	57	4.9
NELSON	1,843	1,153	62.6	508	27.6	182	9.9
NICHOLAS	1,005	760	75.6	194	19.3	51	5.1
OHIO	1,009	535	53.0	416	41.2	58	5.7
OLDHAM	823	504	61.2	201	24.4	118	14.3
OWEN	1,844	1,256	68.1	538	29.2	50	2.7
OWSLEY	148	113	76.4	32	21.6	3	2.0
PENDLETON	740	455	61.5	255	34.5	30	4.1
PERRY	2,951	436	14.8	2,315	78.4	200	6.8
PIKE	5,408	588	10.9	4,616	85.4	204	3.8
POWELL	442	337	76.2	82	18.6	23	5.2
PULASKI	1,939	1,009	52.0	890	45.9	40	2.1
ROBERTSON	792	517	65.3	240	30.3	35	4.4
ROCKCASTLE	585	422	72.1	147	25.1	16	2.7
ROWAN	871	371	42.6	475	54.5	25	2.9
RUSSELL	420	296	70.5	118	28.1	6	1.4
SCOTT	1,875	1,461	77.9	324	17.3	90	4.8
SHELBY	1,544	962	62.3	373	24.2	209	13.5
SIMPSON	1,623	1,332	82.1	273	16.8	18	1.1
SPENCER	621	423	68.1	121	19.5	77	12.4
TAYLOR	959	778	81.1	133	13.9	48	5.0
TODD	1,548	1,292	83.5	214	13.8	42	2.7
TRIGG	1,394	1,222	87.7	156	11.2	16	1.1
TRIMBLE	817	642	78.6	153	18.7	22	2.7
UNION	1,074	495	46.1	501	46.6	78	7.3
WARREN	5,668	3,147	55.5	2,405	42.4	116	2.0
WASHINGTON	702	433	61.7	207	29.5	62	8.8
WAYNE	732	517	70.6	195	26.6	20	2.7
WEBSTER	1,215	741	61.0	436	35.9	38	3.1
WHITLEY	744	387	52.0	330	44.4	27	3.6
WOLFE	719	525	73.0	154	21.4	40	5.6
WOODFORD	1,467	1,023	69.7	249	17.0	195	13.3
TOTAL	205,462	102,860	50.1	90,740	44.2	11,862	5.8

OTHER VOTE: Milt Whiteworth 10,852
D. E. McQueary 1010

County	Total Vote	Democratic		Republican		Other Vote		Per Cent of Two-Party Vote		Dem-Rep Plurality
		Total	Per Cent	Total	Per Cent	Total	Per Cent	Dem	Rep	
ADAIR	4,939	1,843	37.3	3,094	62.6	2		37.3	62.7	1,251 R
ALLEN	3,838	1,499	39.1	2,333	60.8	6	0.2	39.1	60.9	834 R
ANDERSON	3,063	1,949	63.6	1,113	36.3	1		63.7	36.3	836 D
BALLARD	3,007	2,464	81.9	542	18.0	1		82.0	18.0	1,922 D
BARREN	6,492	3,656	56.3	2,834	43.7	2		56.3	43.7	822 D
BATH	3,454	2,071	60.0	1,383	40.0			60.0	40.0	688 D
BELL	9,473	4,115	43.4	5,344	56.4	14	0.1	43.5	56.5	1,229 R
BOONE	3,419	2,114	61.8	1,300	38.0	5	0.1	61.9	38.1	814 D
BOURBON	5,227	3,465	66.3	1,757	33.6	5	0.1	66.4	33.6	1,708 D
BOYD	15,269	8,112	53.1	7,129	46.7	28	0.2	53.2	46.8	983 D
BOYLE	5,247	2,877	54.8	2,364	45.1	6	0.1	54.9	45.1	513 D
BRACKEN	3,032	1,665	54.9	1,366	45.1	1		54.9	45.1	299 D
BREATHITT	4,148	3,071	74.0	1,076	25.9	1		74.1	25.9	1,995 D
BRECKINRIDGE	5,004	2,326	46.5	2,672	53.4	6	0.1	46.5	53.5	346 R
BULLITT	2,290	1,476	64.5	808	35.3	6	0.3	64.6	35.4	668 D
BUTLER	3,508	960	27.4	2,542	72.5	6	0.2	27.4	72.6	1,582 R
CALDWELL	3,856	2,003	51.9	1,847	47.9	6	0.2	52.0	48.0	156 D
CALLOWAY	5,346	4,397	82.2	947	17.7	2		82.3	17.7	3,450 D
CAMPBELL	24,525	11,454	46.7	12,964	52.9	107	0.4	46.9	53.1	1,510 R
CARLISLE	2,083	1,769	84.9	312	15.0	2	0.1	85.0	15.0	1,457 D
CARROLL	3,230	2,299	71.2	929	28.8	2	0.1	71.2	28.8	1,370 D
CARTER	6,172	2,646	42.9	3,517	57.0	9	0.1	42.9	57.1	871 R
CASEY	4,864	1,324	27.2	3,525	72.5	15	0.3	27.3	72.7	2,201 R
CHRISTIAN	9,128	5,251	57.5	3,862	42.3	15	0.2	57.6	42.4	1,389 D
CLARK	4,806	3,073	63.9	1,731	36.0	2		64.0	36.0	1,342 D
CLAY	4,389	1,121	25.5	3,254	74.1	14	0.3	25.6	74.4	2,133 R
CLINTON	3,000	519	17.3	2,478	82.6	3	0.1	17.3	82.7	1,959 R
CRITTENDEN	3,367	1,374	40.8	1,987	59.0	6	0.2	40.9	59.1	613 R
CUMBERLAND	2,684	695	25.9	1,987	74.0	2	0.1	25.9	74.1	1,292 R
DAVIESS	13,303	7,813	58.7	5,475	41.2	15	0.1	58.8	41.2	2,338 D
EDMONSON	2,915	920	31.6	1,987	68.2	8	0.3	31.6	68.4	1,067 R
ELLIOTT	2,407	1,951	81.1	450	18.7	6	0.2	81.3	18.7	1,501 D
ESTILL	3,960	1,740	43.9	2,211	55.8	9	0.2	44.0	56.0	471 R
FAYETTE	24,522	11,801	48.1	12,525	51.1	196	0.8	48.5	51.5	724 R
FLEMING	4,695	2,466	52.5	2,218	47.2	11	0.2	52.6	47.4	248 D
FLOYD	11,295	6,703	59.3	4,553	40.3	39	0.3	59.6	40.4	2,150 D
FRANKLIN	8,599	5,962	69.3	2,629	30.6	8	0.1	69.4	30.6	3,333 D
FULTON	2,887	2,379	82.4	506	17.5	2	0.1	82.5	17.5	1,873 D
GALLATIN	1,681	1,274	75.8	407	24.2			75.8	24.2	867 D
GARRARD	3,619	1,601	44.2	2,011	55.6	7	0.2	44.3	55.7	410 R
GRANT	3,689	2,375	64.4	1,307	35.4	7	0.2	64.5	35.5	1,068 D
GRAVES	9,754	8,006	82.1	1,742	17.9	6	0.1	82.1	17.9	6,264 D
GRAYSON	4,944	1,954	39.5	2,987	60.4	3	0.1	39.5	60.5	1,033 R
GREEN	3,795	1,464	38.6	2,324	61.2	7	0.2	38.6	61.4	860 R
GREENUP	7,149	3,926	54.9	3,202	44.8	21	0.3	55.1	44.9	724 D
HANCOCK	2,106	1,034	49.1	1,067	50.7	5	0.2	49.2	50.8	33 R
HARDIN	6,238	3,323	53.3	2,913	46.7	2		53.3	46.7	410 D
HARLAN	13,042	6,231	47.8	6,784	52.0	27	0.2	47.9	52.1	553 R
HARRISON	4,674	3,243	69.4	1,429	30.6	2		69.4	30.6	1,814 D
HART	4,755	2,245	47.2	2,506	52.7	4	0.1	47.3	52.7	261 R
HENDERSON	7,220	5,021	69.5	2,170	30.1	29	0.4	69.8	30.2	2,851 D
HENRY	4,514	3,225	71.4	1,288	28.5	1		71.5	28.5	1,937 D
HICKMAN	2,408	1,891	78.5	514	21.3	3	0.1	78.6	21.4	1,377 D
HOPKINS	8,825	5,763	65.3	3,043	34.5	19	0.2	65.4	34.6	2,720 D
JACKSON	3,161	385	12.2	2,764	87.4	12	0.4	12.2	87.8	2,379 R
JEFFERSON	140,147	59,874	42.7	79,218	56.5	1,055	0.8	43.0	57.0	19,344 R
JESSAMINE	3,786	2,183	57.7	1,595	42.1	8	0.2	57.8	42.2	588 D
JOHNSON	6,052	1,845	30.5	4,192	69.3	15	0.2	30.6	69.4	2,347 R
KENTON	29,289	16,752	57.2	12,443	42.5	94	0.3	57.4	42.6	4,309 D
KNOTT	5,078	3,962	78.0	1,116	22.0			78.0	22.0	2,846 D
KNOX	6,814	2,061	30.2	4,748	69.7	5	0.1	30.3	69.7	2,687 R
LARUE	3,043	1,515	49.8	1,518	49.9	10	0.3	50.0	50.0	3 R
LAUREL	6,136	1,917	31.2	4,209	68.6	10	0.2	31.3	68.7	2,292 R
LAWRENCE	4,395	2,171	49.4	2,214	50.4	10	0.2	49.5	50.5	43 R
LEE	2,273	969	42.6	1,300	57.2	4	0.2	42.7	57.3	331 R

58

U.S. SENATOR: GENERAL ELECTION — 1948

County	Total Vote	Democratic		Republican		Other Vote		Per Cent of Two-Party Vote		Dem-Rep Plurality
		Total	Per Cent	Total	Per Cent	Total	Per Cent	Dem	Rep	
LESLIE	2,963	548	18.5	2,403	81.1	12	0.4	18.6	81.4	1,855 R
LETCHER	7,947	3,757	47.3	4,175	52.5	15	0.2	47.4	52.6	418 R
LEWIS	4,023	1,299	32.3	2,717	67.5	7	0.2	32.3	67.7	1,418 R
LINCOLN	5,401	2,396	44.4	2,995	55.5	10	0.2	44.4	55.6	599 R
LIVINGSTON	2,214	1,484	67.0	729	32.9	1		67.1	32.9	755 D
LOGAN	5,719	4,156	72.7	1,552	27.1	11	0.2	72.8	27.2	2,604 D
LYON	2,032	1,404	69.1	615	30.3	13	0.6	69.5	30.5	789 D
MADISON	9,966	4,864	48.8	5,088	51.1	14	0.1	48.9	51.1	224 R
MAGOFFIN	4,104	2,062	50.2	2,042	49.8			50.2	49.8	20 D
MARION	4,077	2,506	61.5	1,565	38.4	6	0.1	61.6	38.4	941 D
MARSHALL	3,491	2,598	74.4	892	25.6	1		74.4	25.6	1,706 D
MARTIN	2,553	780	30.6	1,762	69.0	11	0.4	30.7	69.3	982 R
MASON	6,098	3,299	54.1	2,791	45.8	8	0.1	54.2	45.8	508 D
MC CRACKEN	14,013	9,783	69.8	4,167	29.7	63	0.4	70.1	29.9	5,616 D
MC CREARY	3,775	663	17.6	3,096	82.0	16	0.4	17.6	82.4	2,433 R
MC LEAN	3,171	1,994	62.9	1,173	37.0	4	0.1	63.0	37.0	821 D
MEADE	2,622	1,698	64.8	919	35.0	5	0.2	64.9	35.1	779 D
MENIFEE	1,488	1,034	69.5	453	30.4	1	0.1	69.5	30.5	581 D
MERCER	4,258	2,373	55.7	1,881	44.2	4	0.1	55.8	44.2	492 D
METCALFE	3,253	1,543	47.4	1,700	52.3	10	0.3	47.6	52.4	157 R
MONROE	3,832	1,082	28.2	2,747	71.7	3	0.1	28.3	71.7	1,665 R
MONTGOMERY	3,829	2,478	64.7	1,344	35.1	7	0.2	64.8	35.2	1,134 D
MORGAN	4,268	3,135	73.5	1,127	26.4	6	0.1	73.6	26.4	2,008 D
MUHLENBERG	7,685	3,860	50.2	3,810	49.6	15	0.2	50.3	49.7	50 D
NELSON	5,173	3,096	59.8	2,073	40.1	4	0.1	59.9	40.1	1,023 D
NICHOLAS	2,674	1,777	66.5	895	33.5	2	0.1	66.5	33.5	882 D
OHIO	5,884	2,413	41.0	3,459	58.8	12	0.2	41.1	58.9	1,046 R
OLDHAM	2,749	1,524	55.4	1,221	44.4	4	0.1	55.5	44.5	303 D
OWEN	3,477	2,739	78.8	734	21.1	4	0.1	78.9	21.1	2,005 D
OWSLEY	2,093	382	18.3	1,711	81.7			18.3	81.7	1,329 R
PENDLETON	3,309	1,816	54.9	1,483	44.8	10	0.3	55.0	45.0	333 D
PERRY	9,147	4,506	49.3	4,610	50.4	31	0.3	49.4	50.6	104 R
PIKE	18,828	10,103	53.7	8,690	46.2	35	0.2	53.8	46.2	1,413 D
POWELL	1,665	933	56.0	729	43.8	3	0.2	56.1	43.9	204 D
PULASKI	11,553	2,799	24.2	8,738	75.6	16	0.1	24.3	75.7	5,939 R
ROBERTSON	1,265	758	59.9	506	40.0	1	0.1	60.0	40.0	252 D
ROCKCASTLE	4,450	1,110	24.9	3,340	75.1			24.9	75.1	2,230 R
ROWAN	3,497	1,869	53.4	1,624	46.4	4	0.1	53.5	46.5	245 D
RUSSELL	3,546	1,023	28.8	2,523	71.2			28.8	71.2	1,500 R
SCOTT	4,840	3,239	66.9	1,594	32.9	7	0.1	67.0	33.0	1,645 D
SHELBY	5,434	3,299	60.7	2,131	39.2	4	0.1	60.8	39.2	1,168 D
SIMPSON	3,366	2,516	74.7	849	25.2	1		74.8	25.2	1,667 D
SPENCER	1,749	1,161	66.4	586	33.5	2	0.1	66.5	33.5	575 D
TAYLOR	4,513	2,223	49.3	2,280	50.5	10	0.2	49.4	50.6	57 R
TODD	3,687	2,745	74.5	929	25.2	13	0.4	74.7	25.3	1,816 D
TRIGG	3,219	2,301	71.5	916	28.5	2	0.1	71.5	28.5	1,385 D
TRIMBLE	1,888	1,585	84.0	302	16.0	1	0.1	84.0	16.0	1,283 D
UNION	4,168	3,140	75.3	1,022	24.5	6	0.1	75.4	24.6	2,118 D
WARREN	10,676	6,075	56.9	4,590	43.0	11	0.1	57.0	43.0	1,485 D
WASHINGTON	3,911	1,903	48.7	2,003	51.2	5	0.1	48.7	51.3	100 R
WAYNE	4,462	1,788	40.1	2,655	59.5	19	0.4	40.2	59.8	867 R
WEBSTER	4,274	3,057	71.5	1,213	28.4	4	0.1	71.6	28.4	1,844 D
WHITLEY	8,121	2,322	28.6	5,781	71.2	18	0.2	28.7	71.3	3,459 R
WOLFE	2,552	1,719	67.4	833	32.6			67.4	32.6	886 D
WOODFORD	3,460	2,006	58.0	1,451	41.9	3	0.1	58.0	42.0	555 D
TOTAL	794,442	408,256	51.4	383,776	48.3	2,410	0.3	51.5	48.5	24,480 D

OTHER VOTE: W. A. Sandefur (Socialist) 1232
David R. Cox (Socialist Labor) 254
H. G. Stanfield (New Progressive) 924
DEMOCRAT: Virgil Chapman
REPUBLICAN: John S. Cooper

County	Total Vote	Earle C. Clements		George G. Hatcher		Other Vote	
		Total	Per Cent	Total	Per Cent	Total	Per Cent
ADAIR	585	457	78.1	92	15.7	36	6.2
ALLEN	767	635	82.8	105	13.7	27	3.5
ANDERSON	978	846	86.5	99	10.1	33	3.4
BALLARD	1,116	814	72.9	240	21.5	62	5.6
BARREN	1,686	993	58.9	551	32.7	142	8.4
BATH	999	701	70.2	255	25.5	43	4.3
BELL	876	814	92.9	36	4.1	26	3.0
BOONE	856	427	49.9	345	40.3	84	9.8
BOURBON	800	463	57.9	307	38.4	30	3.8
BOYD	2,655	1,553	58.5	1,045	39.4	57	2.1
BOYLE	1,103	710	64.4	318	28.8	75	6.8
BRACKEN	519	340	65.5	149	28.7	30	5.8
BREATHITT	2,072	1,949	94.1	76	3.7	47	2.3
BRECKINRIDGE	912	824	90.4	54	5.9	34	3.7
BULLITT	412	304	73.8	63	15.3	45	10.9
BUTLER	799	690	86.4	98	12.3	11	1.4
CALDWELL	644	434	67.4	175	27.2	35	5.4
CALLOWAY	1,351	713	52.8	478	35.4	160	11.8
CAMPBELL	3,697	1,580	42.7	1,457	39.4	660	17.9
CARLISLE	553	364	65.8	140	25.3	49	8.9
CARROLL	1,250	863	69.0	293	23.4	94	7.5
CARTER	1,006	869	86.4	107	10.6	30	3.0
CASEY	369	319	86.4	35	9.5	15	4.1
CHRISTIAN	2,250	1,548	68.8	482	21.4	220	9.8
CLARK	726	258	35.5	440	60.6	28	3.9
CLAY	216	207	95.8	7	3.2	2	0.9
CLINTON	318	164	51.6	147	46.2	7	2.2
CRITTENDEN	585	494	84.4	57	9.7	34	5.8
CUMBERLAND	261	240	92.0	15	5.7	6	2.3
DAVIESS	4,174	2,396	57.4	1,383	33.1	395	9.5
EDMONSON	504	465	92.3	29	5.8	10	2.0
ELLIOTT	1,339	1,247	93.1	62	4.6	30	2.2
ESTILL	457	344	75.3	83	18.2	30	6.6
FAYETTE	2,380	1,569	65.9	628	26.4	183	7.7
FLEMING	802	608	75.8	149	18.6	45	5.6
FLOYD	5,208	1,739	33.4	3,272	62.8	197	3.8
FRANKLIN	3,602	3,003	83.4	489	13.6	110	3.1
FULTON	673	448	66.6	195	29.0	30	4.5
GALLATIN	574	345	60.1	177	30.8	52	9.1
GARRARD	352	280	79.5	60	17.0	12	3.4
GRANT	1,244	576	46.3	597	48.0	71	5.7
GRAVES	3,592	2,768	77.1	713	19.8	111	3.1
GRAYSON	920	784	85.2	90	9.8	46	5.0
GREEN	651	613	94.2	19	2.9	19	2.9
GREENUP	1,346	894	66.4	392	29.1	60	4.5
HANCOCK	215	118	54.9	76	35.3	21	9.8
HARDIN	1,269	883	69.6	311	24.5	75	5.9
HARLAN	1,266	980	77.4	219	17.3	67	5.3
HARRISON	856	588	68.7	204	23.8	64	7.5
HART	787	697	88.6	53	6.7	37	4.7
HENDERSON	1,668	1,227	73.6	322	19.3	119	7.1
HENRY	945	671	71.0	203	21.5	71	7.5
HICKMAN	1,239	706	57.0	427	34.5	106	8.6
HOPKINS	1,763	1,238	70.2	425	24.1	100	5.7
JACKSON	180	169	93.9	8	4.4	3	1.7
JEFFERSON	15,396	13,034	84.7	1,717	11.2	645	4.2
JESSAMINE	1,484	1,210	81.5	208	14.0	66	4.4
JOHNSON	1,296	496	38.3	765	59.0	35	2.7
KENTON	6,054	2,292	37.9	2,770	45.8	992	16.4
KNOTT	3,465	2,426	70.0	885	25.5	154	4.4
KNOX	460	407	88.5	44	9.6	9	2.0
LARUE	1,152	999	86.7	108	9.4	45	3.9
LAUREL	686	633	92.3	43	6.3	10	1.5
LAWRENCE	952	702	73.7	222	23.3	28	2.9
LEE	353	278	78.8	57	16.1	18	5.1

County	Total Vote	Earle C. Clements Total	Per Cent	George G. Hatcher Total	Per Cent	Other Vote Total	Per Cent
LESLIE	108	96	88.9	10	9.3	2	1.9
LETCHER	1,941	1,380	71.1	478	24.6	83	4.3
LEWIS	450	371	82.4	45	10.0	34	7.6
LINCOLN	1,049	693	66.1	289	27.6	67	6.4
LIVINGSTON	684	577	84.4	90	13.2	17	2.5
LOGAN	4,077	3,949	96.9	65	1.6	63	1.5
LYON	599	446	74.5	130	21.7	23	3.8
MADISON	1,370	890	65.0	405	29.6	75	5.5
MAGOFFIN	1,744	1,033	59.2	681	39.0	30	1.7
MARION	1,266	1,019	80.5	182	14.4	65	5.1
MARSHALL	866	648	74.8	185	21.4	33	3.8
MARTIN	265	184	69.4	63	23.8	18	6.8
MASON	782	469	60.0	258	33.0	55	7.0
MC CRACKEN	3,916	2,658	67.9	876	22.4	382	9.8
MC CREARY	228	198	86.8	19	8.3	11	4.8
MC LEAN	639	403	63.1	188	29.4	48	7.5
MEADE	740	601	81.2	103	13.9	36	4.9
MENIFEE	528	426	80.7	78	14.8	24	4.5
MERCER	653	431	66.0	195	29.9	27	4.1
METCALFE	797	687	86.2	86	10.8	24	3.0
MONRÖE	388	358	92.3	20	5.2	10	2.6
MONTGOMERY	1,179	739	62.7	387	32.8	53	4.5
MORGAN	1,954	1,682	86.1	256	13.1	16	0.8
MUHLENBERG	1,054	678	64.3	297	28.2	79	7.5
NELSON	1,782	1,523	85.5	184	10.3	75	4.2
NICHOLAS	634	472	74.4	140	22.1	22	3.5
OHIO	855	673	78.7	119	13.9	63	7.4
OLDHAM	664	436	65.7	200	30.1	28	4.2
OWEN	906	551	60.8	315	34.8	40	4.4
OWSLEY	90	81	90.0	8	8.9	1	1.1
PENDLETON	1,058	688	65.0	252	23.8	118	11.2
PERRY	2,049	1,510	73.7	469	22.9	70	3.4
PIKE	4,918	3,271	66.5	1,473	30.0	174	3.5
POWELL	497	427	85.9	38	7.6	32	6.4
PULASKI	2,331	1,216	52.2	1,069	45.9	46	2.0
ROBERTSON	523	369	70.6	137	26.2	17	3.3
ROCKCASTLE	456	406	89.0	39	8.6	11	2.4
ROWAN	810	652	80.5	131	16.2	27	3.3
RUSSELL	419	229	54.7	186	44.4	4	1.0
SCOTT	940	569	60.5	318	33.8	53	5.6
SHELBY	1,277	831	65.1	368	28.8	78	6.1
SIMPSON	639	529	82.8	78	12.2	32	5.0
SPENCER	278	193	69.4	49	17.6	36	12.9
TAYLOR	743	673	90.6	46	6.2	24	3.2
TODD	1,628	1,315	80.8	212	13.0	101	6.2
TRIGG	1,051	959	91.2	76	7.2	16	1.5
TRIMBLE	753	605	80.3	94	12.5	54	7.2
UNION	2,072	1,764	85.1	165	8.0	143	6.9
WARREN	2,787	2,081	74.7	578	20.7	128	4.6
WASHINGTON	520	418	80.4	73	14.0	29	5.6
WAYNE	976	960	98.4	14	1.4	2	0.2
WEBSTER	1,159	811	70.0	270	23.3	78	6.7
WHITLEY	690	617	89.4	63	9.1	10	1.4
WOLFE	610	510	83.6	78	12.8	22	3.6
WOODFORD	765	421	55.0	311	40.7	33	4.3
TOTAL	161,522	114,482	70.9	38,010	23.5	9,030	5.6

OTHER VOTE: Dennis E. McQueary 4874
James L. Delk 4156

County	Total Vote	Charles I. Dawson Total	Per Cent	James W. Brown Total	Per Cent	Charles E. Whittle Total	Per Cent
ADAIR	296	240	81.1	38	12.8	18	6.1
ALLEN	311	288	92.6	7	2.3	16	5.1
ANDERSON	94	75	79.8	13	13.8	6	6.4
BALLARD	70	62	88.6	8	11.4		
BARREN	402	283	70.4	78	19.4	41	10.2
BATH	117	112	95.7	2	1.7	3	2.6
BELL	1,300	787	60.5	152	11.7	361	27.8
BOONE	60	49	81.7	6	10.0	5	8.3
BOURBON	109	93	85.3	6	5.5	10	9.2
BOYD	867	699	80.6	91	10.5	77	8.9
BOYLE	108	83	76.9	5	4.6	20	18.5
BRACKEN	82	78	95.1	2	2.4	2	2.4
BREATHITT	136	128	94.1	5	3.7	3	2.2
BRECKINRIDGE	338	294	87.0	29	8.6	15	4.4
BULLITT	56	49	87.5	3	5.4	4	7.1
BUTLER	522	418	80.1	23	4.4	81	15.5
CALDWELL	236	192	81.4	34	14.4	10	4.2
CALLOWAY	82	69	84.1	10	12.2	3	3.7
CAMPBELL	1,764	1,210	68.6	322	18.3	232	13.2
CARLISLE	30	16	53.3	13	43.3	1	3.3
CARROLL	43	42	97.7			1	2.3
CARTER	485	408	84.1	19	3.9	58	12.0
CASEY	354	283	79.9	26	7.3	45	12.7
CHRISTIAN	458	365	79.7	88	19.2	5	1.1
CLARK	102	86	84.3	6	5.9	10	9.8
CLAY	539	389	72.2	69	12.8	81	15.0
CLINTON	314	206	65.6	31	9.9	77	24.5
CRITTENDEN	239	199	83.3	28	11.7	12	5.0
CUMBERLAND	669	576	86.1	37	5.5	56	8.4
DAVIESS	285	275	96.5	4	1.4	6	2.1
EDMONSON	1,194	533	44.6	84	7.0	577	48.3
ELLIOTT	26	23	88.5			3	11.5
ESTILL	217	164	75.6	20	9.2	33	15.2
FAYETTE	530	468	88.3	23	4.3	39	7.4
FLEMING	179	162	90.5	6	3.4	11	6.1
FLOYD	810	563	69.5	195	24.1	52	6.4
FRANKLIN	195	187	95.9	3	1.5	5	2.6
FULTON	30	27	90.0	2	6.7	1	3.3
GALLATIN	29	25	86.2	2	6.9	2	6.9
GARRARD	125	107	85.6	8	6.4	10	8.0
GRANT	70	63	90.0	4	5.7	3	4.3
GRAVES	176	126	71.6	36	20.5	14	8.0
GRAYSON	380	268	70.5	59	15.5	53	13.9
GREEN	353	320	90.7	28	7.9	5	1.4
GREENUP	324	242	74.7	37	11.4	45	13.9
HANCOCK	141	118	83.7	16	11.3	7	5.0
HARDIN	180	158	87.8	12	6.7	10	5.6
HARLAN	1,367	840	61.4	253	18.5	274	20.0
HARRISON	106	103	97.2			3	2.8
HART	370	327	88.4	21	5.7	22	5.9
HENDERSON	63	55	87.3	3	4.8	5	7.9
HENRY	141	117	83.0	10	7.1	14	9.9
HICKMAN	22	13	59.1	9	40.9		
HOPKINS	202	179	88.6	9	4.5	14	6.9
JACKSON	413	245	59.3	65	15.7	103	24.9
JEFFERSON	8,482	7,757	91.5	323	3.8	402	4.7
JESSAMINE	122	103	84.4	2	1.6	17	13.9
JOHNSON	1,108	642	57.9	372	33.6	94	8.5
KENTON	487	332	68.2	66	13.6	89	18.3
KNOTT	62	31	50.0	25	40.3	6	9.7
KNOX	861	516	59.9	143	16.6	202	23.5
LARUE	109	96	88.1	8	7.3	5	4.6
LAUREL	637	448	70.3	96	15.1	93	14.6
LAWRENCE	296	232	78.4	40	13.5	24	8.1
LEE	214	169	79.0	25	11.7	20	9.3

County	Total Vote	Charles I. Dawson Total	Charles I. Dawson Per Cent	James W. Brown Total	James W. Brown Per Cent	Charles E. Whittle Total	Charles E. Whittle Per Cent
LESLIE	500	264	52.8	142	28.4	94	18.8
LETCHER	840	537	63.9	225	26.8	78	9.3
LEWIS	442	397	89.8	15	3.4	30	6.8
LINCOLN	365	327	89.6	12	3.3	26	7.1
LIVINGSTON	85	74	87.1	5	5.9	6	7.1
LOGAN	127	120	94.5	1	0.8	6	4.7
LYON	66	66	100.0				
MADISON	292	248	84.9	5	1.7	39	13.4
MAGOFFIN	619	509	82.2	86	13.9	24	3.9
MARION	79	74	93.7	4	5.1	1	1.3
MARSHALL	73	62	84.9	9	12.3	2	2.7
MARTIN	474	256	54.0	164	34.6	54	11.4
MASON	206	183	88.8	9	4.4	14	6.8
MC CRACKEN	194	163	84.0	20	10.3	11	5.7
MC CREARY	546	287	52.6	111	20.3	148	27.1
MC LEAN	107	97	90.7	1	0.9	9	8.4
MEADE	69	57	82.6	8	11.6	4	5.8
MENIFEE	44	38	86.4	2	4.5	4	9.1
MERCER	98	88	89.8	6	6.1	4	4.1
METCALFE	207	160	77.3	28	13.5	19	9.2
MONROE	348	245	70.4	40	11.5	63	18.1
MONTGOMERY	64	60	93.8	1	1.6	3	4.7
MORGAN	120	111	92.5	2	1.7	7	5.8
MUHLENBERG	413	242	58.6	78	18.9	93	22.5
NELSON	131	113	86.3	13	9.9	5	3.8
NICHOLAS	90	89	98.9	1	1.1		
OHIO	1,389	1,036	74.6	186	13.4	167	12.0
OLDHAM	68	63	92.6	3	4.4	2	2.9
OWEN	72	60	83.3	3	4.2	9	12.5
OWSLEY	309	201	65.0	43	13.9	65	21.0
PENDLETON	134	129	96.3	3	2.2	2	1.5
PERRY	1,088	684	62.9	293	26.9	111	10.2
PIKE	2,189	1,207	55.1	576	26.3	406	18.5
POWELL	110	88	80.0	14	12.7	8	7.3
PULASKI	1,369	1,069	78.1	118	8.6	182	13.3
ROBERTSON	63	59	93.7	2	3.2	2	3.2
ROCKCASTLE	549	427	77.8	56	10.2	66	12.0
ROWAN	263	226	85.9	11	4.2	26	9.9
RUSSELL	378	321	84.9	26	6.9	31	8.2
SCOTT	96	82	85.4	5	5.2	9	9.4
SHELBY	171	157	91.8	11	6.4	3	1.8
SIMPSON	93	89	95.7			4	4.3
SPENCER	42	37	88.1	4	9.5	1	2.4
TAYLOR	152	134	88.2	14	9.2	4	2.6
TODD	86	78	90.7			8	9.3
TRIGG	97	90	92.8	7	7.2		
TRIMBLE	22	22	100.0				
UNION	45	39	86.7	1	2.2	5	11.1
WARREN	260	223	85.8	6	2.3	31	11.9
WASHINGTON	112	104	92.9	7	6.3	1	0.9
WAYNE	422	270	64.0	48	11.4	104	24.6
WEBSTER	112	103	92.0	2	1.8	7	6.3
WHITLEY	995	591	59.4	223	22.4	181	18.2
WOLFE	112	105	93.8	4	3.6	3	2.7
WOODFORD	103	87	84.5	4	3.9	12	11.7
TOTAL	47,934	36,461	76.1	5,763	12.0	5,710	11.9

County	Total Vote	Democratic		Republican		Other Vote		Per Cent of Two-Party Vote		Dem-Rep Plurality
		Total	Per Cent	Total	Per Cent	Total	Per Cent	Dem	Rep	
ADAIR	4,539	1,896	41.8	2,632	58.0	11	0.2	41.9	58.1	736 R
ALLEN	3,318	1,396	42.1	1,917	57.8	5	0.2	42.1	57.9	521 R
ANDERSON	2,335	1,666	71.3	664	28.4	5	0.2	71.5	28.5	1,002 D
BALLARD	2,281	1,926	84.4	353	15.5	2	0.1	84.5	15.5	1,573 D
BARREN	5,062	2,635	52.1	2,393	47.3	34	0.7	52.4	47.6	242 D
BATH	2,637	1,631	61.9	995	37.7	11	0.4	62.1	37.9	636 D
BELL	6,965	3,600	51.7	3,317	47.6	48	0.7	52.0	48.0	283 D
BOONE	2,155	1,248	57.9	879	40.8	28	1.3	58.7	41.3	369 D
BOURBON	2,972	1,876	63.1	1,081	36.4	15	0.5	63.4	36.6	795 D
BOYD	10,862	5,373	49.5	5,429	50.0	60	0.6	49.7	50.3	56 R
BOYLE	3,885	2,285	58.8	1,570	40.4	30	0.8	59.3	40.7	715 D
BRACKEN	1,907	1,153	60.5	743	39.0	11	0.6	60.8	39.2	410 D
BREATHITT	3,247	2,589	79.7	652	20.1	6	0.2	79.9	20.1	1,937 D
BRECKINRIDGE	4,226	2,364	55.9	1,847	43.7	15	0.4	56.1	43.9	517 D
BULLITT	1,608	1,140	70.9	464	28.9	4	0.2	71.1	28.9	676 D
BUTLER	3,392	1,168	34.4	2,217	65.4	7	0.2	34.5	65.5	1,049 R
CALDWELL	3,010	1,465	48.7	1,530	50.8	15	0.5	48.9	51.1	65 R
CALLOWAY	3,908	3,160	80.9	734	18.8	14	0.4	81.2	18.8	2,426 D
CAMPBELL	19,403	8,248	42.5	10,790	55.6	365	1.9	43.3	56.7	2,542 R
CARLISLE	1,561	1,317	84.4	242	15.5	2	0.1	84.5	15.5	1,075 D
CARROLL	2,195	1,699	77.4	487	22.2	9	0.4	77.7	22.3	1,212 D
CARTER	4,404	1,884	42.8	2,508	56.9	12	0.3	42.9	57.1	624 R
CASEY	3,692	1,096	29.7	2,590	70.2	6	0.2	29.7	70.3	1,494 R
CHRISTIAN	6,742	3,960	58.7	2,764	41.0	18	0.3	58.9	41.1	1,196 D
CLARK	2,805	1,724	61.5	1,064	37.9	17	0.6	61.8	38.2	660 D
CLAY	3,475	1,004	28.9	2,459	70.8	12	0.3	29.0	71.0	1,455 R
CLINTON	2,461	521	21.2	1,936	78.7	4	0.2	21.2	78.8	1,415 R
CRITTENDEN	2,649	1,106	41.8	1,538	58.1	5	0.2	41.8	58.2	432 R
CUMBERLAND	2,769	827	29.9	1,934	69.8	8	0.3	30.0	70.0	1,107 R
DAVIESS	9,014	4,500	49.9	4,462	49.5	52	0.6	50.2	49.8	38 D
EDMONSON	2,443	892	36.5	1,549	63.4	2	0.1	36.5	63.5	657 R
ELLIOTT	1,860	1,561	83.9	295	15.9	4	0.2	84.1	15.9	1,266 D
ESTILL	3,176	1,431	45.1	1,736	54.7	9	0.3	45.2	54.8	305 R
FAYETTE	14,026	7,113	50.7	6,692	47.7	221	1.6	51.5	48.5	421 D
FLEMING	3,588	2,040	56.9	1,533	42.7	15	0.4	57.1	42.9	507 D
FLOYD	10,971	7,723	70.4	3,151	28.7	97	0.9	71.0	29.0	4,572 D
FRANKLIN	6,864	5,403	78.7	1,411	20.6	50	0.7	79.3	20.7	3,992 D
FULTON	1,833	1,410	76.9	422	23.0	1	0.1	77.0	23.0	988 D
GALLATIN	1,021	767	75.1	252	24.7	2	0.2	75.3	24.7	515 D
GARRARD	2,817	1,225	43.5	1,586	56.3	6	0.2	43.6	56.4	361 R
GRANT	2,201	1,390	63.2	798	36.3	13	0.6	63.5	36.5	592 D
GRAVES	7,907	6,325	80.0	1,552	19.6	30	0.4	80.3	19.7	4,773 D
GRAYSON	3,973	1,737	43.7	2,230	56.1	6	0.2	43.8	56.2	493 R
GREEN	3,504	1,542	44.0	1,955	55.8	7	0.2	44.1	55.9	413 R
GREENUP	5,601	3,002	53.6	2,569	45.9	30	0.5	53.9	46.1	433 D
HANCOCK	2,091	1,035	49.5	1,054	50.4	2	0.1	49.5	50.5	19 R
HARDIN	4,736	2,876	60.7	1,838	38.8	22	0.5	61.0	39.0	1,038 D
HARLAN	10,898	6,378	58.5	4,447	40.8	73	0.7	58.9	41.1	1,931 D
HARRISON	3,002	2,195	73.1	797	26.5	10	0.3	73.4	26.6	1,398 D
HART	3,874	2,097	54.1	1,765	45.6	12	0.3	54.3	45.7	332 D
HENDERSON	6,139	4,003	65.2	2,108	34.3	28	0.5	65.5	34.5	1,895 D
HENRY	3,290	2,315	70.4	943	28.7	32	1.0	71.1	28.9	1,372 D
HICKMAN	1,839	1,452	79.0	384	20.9	3	0.2	79.1	20.9	1,068 D
HOPKINS	6,914	4,724	68.3	2,163	31.3	27	0.4	68.6	31.4	2,561 D
JACKSON	1,962	328	16.7	1,614	82.3	20	1.0	16.9	83.1	1,286 R
JEFFERSON	112,734	56,268	49.9	55,355	49.1	1,111	1.0	50.4	49.6	913 D
JESSAMINE	3,041	1,905	62.6	1,120	36.8	16	0.5	63.0	37.0	785 D
JOHNSON	5,484	2,025	36.9	3,450	62.9	9	0.2	37.0	63.0	1,425 R
KENTON	20,384	10,658	52.3	9,250	45.4	476	2.3	53.5	46.5	1,408 D
KNOTT	4,668	3,881	83.1	769	16.5	18	0.4	83.5	16.5	3,112 D
KNOX	5,463	2,105	38.5	3,306	60.5	52	1.0	38.9	61.1	1,201 R
LARUE	2,694	1,696	63.0	982	36.5	16	0.6	63.3	36.7	714 D
LAUREL	5,542	1,746	31.5	3,778	68.2	18	0.3	31.6	68.4	2,032 R
LAWRENCE	3,367	1,780	52.9	1,568	46.6	19	0.6	53.2	46.8	212 D
LEE	1,944	814	41.9	1,127	58.0	3	0.2	41.9	58.1	313 R

64

County	Total Vote	Democratic Total	Democratic Per Cent	Republican Total	Republican Per Cent	Other Vote Total	Other Vote Per Cent	Per Cent of Two-Party Vote Dem	Per Cent of Two-Party Vote Rep	Dem-Rep Plurality
LESLIE	2,208	443	20.1	1,737	78.7	28	1.3	20.3	79.7	1,294 R
LETCHER	6,885	3,778	54.9	3,068	44.6	39	0.6	55.2	44.8	710 D
LEWIS	3,475	1,171	33.7	2,295	66.0	9	0.3	33.8	66.2	1,124 R
LINCOLN	4,178	2,167	51.9	1,976	47.3	35	0.8	52.3	47.7	191 D
LIVINGSTON	1,796	1,144	63.7	651	36.2	1	0.1	63.7	36.3	493 D
LOGAN	5,676	4,584	80.8	1,080	19.0	12	0.2	80.9	19.1	3,504 D
LYON	1,403	963	68.6	436	31.1	4	0.3	68.8	31.2	527 D
MADISON	6,575	3,400	51.7	3,127	47.6	48	0.7	52.1	47.9	273 D
MAGOFFIN	3,707	2,035	54.9	1,671	45.1	1		54.9	45.1	364 D
MARION	3,438	2,414	70.2	1,007	29.3	17	0.5	70.6	29.4	1,407 D
MARSHALL	2,571	1,905	74.1	653	25.4	13	0.5	74.5	25.5	1,252 D
MARTIN	2,355	695	29.5	1,657	70.4	3	0.1	29.5	70.5	962 R
MASON	3,902	1,955	50.1	1,920	49.2	27	0.7	50.5	49.5	35 D
MC CRACKEN	8,811	5,859	66.5	2,928	33.2	24	0.3	66.7	33.3	2,931 D
MC CREARY	2,706	720	26.6	1,972	72.9	14	0.5	26.7	73.3	1,252 R
MC LEAN	2,170	1,246	57.4	915	42.2	9	0.4	57.7	42.3	331 D
MEADE	1,870	1,261	67.4	606	32.4	3	0.2	67.5	32.5	655 D
MENIFEE	1,363	978	71.8	377	27.7	8	0.6	72.2	27.8	601 D
MERCER	2,938	1,659	56.5	1,265	43.1	14	0.5	56.7	43.3	394 D
METCALFE	3,091	1,457	47.1	1,619	52.4	15	0.5	47.4	52.6	162 R
MONROE	3,080	777	25.2	2,301	74.7	2	0.1	25.2	74.8	1,524 R
MONTGOMERY	2,782	1,735	62.4	1,032	37.1	15	0.5	62.7	37.3	703 D
MORGAN	3,196	2,514	78.7	678	21.2	4	0.1	78.8	21.2	1,836 D
MUHLENBERG	5,781	3,204	55.4	2,491	43.1	86	1.5	56.3	43.7	713 D
NELSON	4,537	2,926	64.5	1,598	35.2	13	0.3	64.7	35.3	1,328 D
NICHOLAS	1,890	1,306	69.1	576	30.5	8	0.4	69.4	30.6	730 D
OHIO	4,930	2,046	41.5	2,861	58.0	23	0.5	41.7	58.3	815 R
OLDHAM	2,106	1,221	58.0	872	41.4	13	0.6	58.3	41.7	349 D
OWEN	2,444	2,041	83.5	395	16.2	8	0.3	83.8	16.2	1,646 D
OWSLEY	1,495	279	18.7	1,210	80.9	6	0.4	18.7	81.3	931 R
PENDLETON	2,393	1,242	51.9	1,141	47.7	10	0.4	52.1	47.9	101 D
PERRY	7,806	4,325	55.4	3,443	44.1	38	0.5	55.7	44.3	882 D
PIKE	16,996	9,471	55.7	7,462	43.9	63	0.4	55.9	44.1	2,009 D
POWELL	1,420	806	56.8	612	43.1	2	0.1	56.8	43.2	194 D
PULASKI	9,592	3,292	34.3	6,292	65.6	8	0.1	34.3	65.7	3,000 R
ROBERTSON	957	568	59.4	384	40.1	5	0.5	59.7	40.3	184 D
ROCKCASTLE	3,459	988	28.6	2,454	70.9	17	0.5	28.7	71.3	1,466 R
ROWAN	2,923	1,602	54.8	1,311	44.9	10	0.3	55.0	45.0	291 D
RUSSELL	2,965	1,123	37.9	1,838	62.0	4	0.1	37.9	62.1	715 R
SCOTT	3,424	2,272	66.4	1,125	32.9	27	0.8	66.9	33.1	1,147 D
SHELBY	3,980	2,433	61.1	1,523	38.3	24	0.6	61.5	38.5	910 D
SIMPSON	2,272	1,759	77.4	508	22.4	5	0.2	77.6	22.4	1,251 D
SPENCER	1,336	850	63.6	480	35.9	6	0.4	63.9	36.1	370 D
TAYLOR	3,428	1,814	52.9	1,604	46.8	10	0.3	53.1	46.9	210 D
TODD	2,885	2,107	73.0	763	26.4	15	0.5	73.4	26.6	1,344 D
TRIGG	2,648	1,861	70.3	784	29.6	3	0.1	70.4	29.6	1,077 D
TRIMBLE	1,419	1,237	87.2	156	11.0	26	1.8	88.8	11.2	1,081 D
UNION	3,482	2,837	81.5	639	18.4	6	0.2	81.6	18.4	2,198 D
WARREN	8,355	4,852	58.1	3,451	41.3	52	0.6	58.4	41.6	1,401 D
WASHINGTON	2,801	1,431	51.1	1,363	48.7	7	0.2	51.2	48.8	68 D
WAYNE	4,099	2,075	50.6	2,010	49.0	14	0.3	50.8	49.2	65 D
WEBSTER	3,038	2,121	69.8	909	29.9	8	0.3	70.0	30.0	1,212 D
WHITLEY	6,168	2,257	36.6	3,893	63.1	18	0.3	36.7	63.3	1,636 R
WOLFE	1,934	1,323	68.4	602	31.1	9	0.5	68.7	31.3	721 D
WOODFORD	2,644	1,421	53.7	907	34.3	316	12.0	61.0	39.0	514 D
TOTAL	617,113	334,249	54.2	278,368	45.1	4,496	0.7	54.6	45.4	55,881 D

DEMOCRAT: Earle C. Clements
REPUBLICAN: Charles I. Dawson
INDEPENDENT: James E. Olsen

County	Total Vote	Democratic		Republican			Per Cent of Two-Party Vote		Dem-Rep Plurality
		Total	Per Cent	Total	Per Cent		Dem	Rep	
ADAIR	5,731	1,985	34.6	3,746	65.4		34.6	65.4	1,761 R
ALLEN	4,579	1,710	37.3	2,869	62.7		37.3	62.7	1,159 R
ANDERSON	3,534	2,010	56.9	1,524	43.1		56.9	43.1	486 D
BALLARD	3,678	2,746	74.7	932	25.3		74.7	25.3	1,814 D
BARREN	8,101	4,223	52.1	3,878	47.9		52.1	47.9	345 D
BATH	3,929	2,182	55.5	1,747	44.5		55.5	44.5	435 D
BELL	11,002	4,737	43.1	6,265	56.9		43.1	56.9	1,528 R
BOONE	4,788	2,493	52.1	2,295	47.9		52.1	47.9	198 D
BOURBON	5,390	3,165	58.7	2,225	41.3		58.7	41.3	940 D
BOYD	20,181	9,820	48.7	10,361	51.3		48.7	51.3	541 R
BOYLE	6,577	3,379	51.4	3,198	48.6		51.4	48.6	181 D
BRACKEN	3,233	1,622	50.2	1,611	49.8		50.2	49.8	11 D
BREATHITT	4,628	3,253	70.3	1,375	29.7		70.3	29.7	1,878 D
BRECKINRIDGE	5,752	2,665	46.3	3,087	53.7		46.3	53.7	422 R
BULLITT	3,292	1,975	60.0	1,317	40.0		60.0	40.0	658 D
BUTLER	4,033	1,090	27.0	2,943	73.0		27.0	73.0	1,853 R
CALDWELL	4,519	2,026	44.8	2,493	55.2		44.8	55.2	467 R
CALLOWAY	7,020	4,977	70.9	2,043	29.1		70.9	29.1	2,934 D
CAMPBELL	29,838	12,749	42.7	17,089	57.3		42.7	57.3	4,340 R
CARLISLE	2,364	1,718	72.7	646	27.3		72.7	27.3	1,072 D
CARROLL	3,438	2,364	68.8	1,074	31.2		68.8	31.2	1,290 D
CARTER	6,990	2,775	39.7	4,215	60.3		39.7	60.3	1,440 R
CASEY	5,231	1,387	26.5	3,844	73.5		26.5	73.5	2,457 R
CHRISTIAN	11,312	6,595	58.3	4,717	41.7		58.3	41.7	1,878 D
CLARK	6,097	3,410	55.9	2,687	44.1		55.9	44.1	723 D
CLAY	5,322	1,231	23.1	4,091	76.9		23.1	76.9	2,860 R
CLINTON	3,434	597	17.4	2,837	82.6		17.4	82.6	2,240 R
CRITTENDEN	3,746	1,360	36.3	2,386	63.7		36.3	63.7	1,026 R
CUMBERLAND	3,181	809	25.4	2,372	74.6		25.4	74.6	1,563 R
DAVIESS	17,574	7,386	42.0	10,188	58.0		42.0	58.0	2,802 R
EDMONSON	3,173	957	30.2	2,216	69.8		30.2	69.8	1,259 R
ELLIOTT	2,581	1,963	76.1	618	23.9		76.1	23.9	1,345 D
ESTILL	4,447	1,840	41.4	2,607	58.6		41.4	58.6	767 R
FAYETTE	31,343	13,837	44.1	17,506	55.9		44.1	55.9	3,669 R
FLEMING	4,809	2,257	46.9	2,552	53.1		46.9	53.1	295 R
FLOYD	12,480	8,295	66.5	4,185	33.5		66.5	33.5	4,110 D
FRANKLIN	10,239	6,973	68.1	3,266	31.9		68.1	31.9	3,707 D
FULTON	3,740	2,609	69.8	1,131	30.2		69.8	30.2	1,478 D
GALLATIN	1,752	1,278	72.9	474	27.1		72.9	27.1	804 D
GARRARD	4,280	1,888	44.1	2,392	55.9		44.1	55.9	504 R
GRANT	3,894	2,249	57.8	1,645	42.2		57.8	42.2	604 D
GRAVES	12,124	9,033	74.5	3,091	25.5		74.5	25.5	5,942 D
GRAYSON	6,173	2,227	36.1	3,946	63.9		36.1	63.9	1,719 R
GREEN	4,505	1,744	38.7	2,761	61.3		38.7	61.3	1,017 R
GREENUP	8,845	4,486	50.7	4,359	49.3		50.7	49.3	127 D
HANCOCK	2,435	1,125	46.2	1,310	53.8		46.2	53.8	185 R
HARDIN	8,277	4,179	50.5	4,098	49.5		50.5	49.5	81 D
HARLAN	16,506	9,338	56.6	7,168	43.4		56.6	43.4	2,170 D
HARRISON	5,123	3,224	62.9	1,899	37.1		62.9	37.1	1,325 D
HART	5,780	2,815	48.7	2,965	51.3		48.7	51.3	150 R
HENDERSON	10,273	5,457	53.1	4,816	46.9		53.1	46.9	641 D
HENRY	4,892	3,271	66.9	1,621	33.1		66.9	33.1	1,650 D
HICKMAN	2,697	1,714	63.6	983	36.4		63.6	36.4	731 D
HOPKINS	11,107	6,933	62.4	4,174	37.6		62.4	37.6	2,759 D
JACKSON	3,458	427	12.3	3,031	87.7		12.3	87.7	2,604 R
JEFFERSON	176,927	75,982	42.9	100,945	57.1		42.9	57.1	24,963 R
JESSAMINE	4,617	2,462	53.3	2,155	46.7		53.3	46.7	307 D
JOHNSON	7,662	2,537	33.1	5,125	66.9		33.1	66.9	2,588 R
KENTON	37,554	18,887	50.3	18,667	49.7		50.3	49.7	220 D
KNOTT	5,186	4,137	79.8	1,049	20.2		79.8	20.2	3,088 D
KNOX	7,869	2,473	31.4	5,396	68.6		31.4	68.6	2,923 R
LARUE	3,769	1,940	51.5	1,829	48.5		51.5	48.5	111 D
LAUREL	7,848	2,121	27.0	5,727	73.0		27.0	73.0	3,606 R
LAWRENCE	5,174	2,515	48.6	2,659	51.4		48.6	51.4	144 R
LEE	2,604	1,056	40.6	1,548	59.4		40.6	59.4	492 R

County	Total Vote	Democratic		Republican		Per Cent of Two-Party Vote		Dem-Rep Plurality
		Total	Per Cent	Total	Per Cent	Dem	Rep	
LESLIE	3,807	615	16.2	3,192	83.8	16.2	83.8	2,577 R
LETCHER	9,122	4,713	51.7	4,409	48.3	51.7	48.3	304 D
LEWIS	4,686	1,441	30.8	3,245	69.2	30.8	69.2	1,804 R
LINCOLN	5,969	2,704	45.3	3,265	54.7	45.3	54.7	561 R
LIVINGSTON	2,574	1,472	57.2	1,102	42.8	57.2	42.8	370 D
LOGAN	7,516	4,830	64.3	2,686	35.7	64.3	35.7	2,144 D
LYON	2,098	1,337	63.7	761	36.3	63.7	36.3	576 D
MADISON	11,540	5,559	48.2	5,981	51.8	48.2	51.8	422 R
MAGOFFIN	4,234	2,161	51.0	2,073	49.0	51.0	49.0	88 D
MARION	5,129	2,844	55.4	2,285	44.6	55.4	44.6	559 D
MARSHALL	4,749	3,186	67.1	1,563	32.9	67.1	32.9	1,623 D
MARTIN	3,559	1,064	29.9	2,495	70.1	29.9	70.1	1,431 R
MASON	6,849	3,314	48.4	3,535	51.6	48.4	51.6	221 R
MC CRACKEN	17,761	11,540	65.0	6,221	35.0	65.0	35.0	5,319 D
MC CREARY	3,993	759	19.0	3,234	81.0	19.0	81.0	2,475 R
MC LEAN	3,645	1,924	52.8	1,721	47.2	52.8	47.2	203 D
MEADE	3,171	1,912	60.3	1,259	39.7	60.3	39.7	653 D
MENIFEE	1,767	1,149	65.0	618	35.0	65.0	35.0	531 D
MERCER	5,100	2,479	48.6	2,621	51.4	48.6	51.4	142 R
METCALFE	3,843	1,626	42.3	2,217	57.7	42.3	57.7	591 R
MONROE	4,536	998	22.0	3,538	78.0	22.0	78.0	2,540 R
MONTGOMERY	4,378	2,437	55.7	1,941	44.3	55.7	44.3	496 D
MORGAN	4,269	2,969	69.5	1,300	30.5	69.5	30.5	1,669 D
MUHLENBERG	9,352	4,732	50.6	4,620	49.4	50.6	49.4	112 D
NELSON	6,199	3,192	51.5	3,007	48.5	51.5	48.5	185 D
NICHOLAS	2,877	1,700	59.1	1,177	40.9	59.1	40.9	523 D
OHIO	6,894	2,573	37.3	4,321	62.7	37.3	62.7	1,748 R
OLDHAM	3,391	1,637	48.3	1,754	51.7	48.3	51.7	117 R
OWEN	3,754	2,850	75.9	904	24.1	75.9	24.1	1,946 D
OWSLEY	2,244	370	16.5	1,874	83.5	16.5	83.5	1,504 R
PENDLETON	3,805	1,922	50.5	1,883	49.5	50.5	49.5	39 D
PERRY	10,443	5,331	51.0	5,112	49.0	51.0	49.0	219 D
PIKE	21,919	12,333	56.3	9,586	43.7	56.3	43.7	2,747 D
POWELL	2,126	1,162	54.7	964	45.3	54.7	45.3	198 D
PULASKI	13,456	3,280	24.4	10,176	75.6	24.4	75.6	6,896 R
ROBERTSON	1,381	786	56.9	595	43.1	56.9	43.1	191 D
ROCKCASTLE	4,619	1,210	26.2	3,409	73.8	26.2	73.8	2,199 R
ROWAN	4,107	2,080	50.6	2,027	49.4	50.6	49.4	53 D
RUSSELL	4,029	1,072	26.6	2,957	73.4	26.6	73.4	1,885 R
SCOTT	5,147	3,020	58.7	2,127	41.3	58.7	41.3	893 D
SHELBY	6,311	3,708	58.8	2,603	41.2	58.8	41.2	1,105 D
SIMPSON	3,785	2,543	67.2	1,242	32.8	67.2	32.8	1,301 D
SPENCER	1,838	1,088	59.2	750	40.8	59.2	40.8	338 D
TAYLOR	5,478	2,349	42.9	3,129	57.1	42.9	57.1	780 R
TODD	4,217	2,839	67.3	1,378	32.7	67.3	32.7	1,461 D
TRIGG	3,566	2,432	68.2	1,134	31.8	68.2	31.8	1,298 D
TRIMBLE	2,141	1,760	82.2	381	17.8	82.2	17.8	1,379 D
UNION	5,192	3,255	62.7	1,937	37.3	62.7	37.3	1,318 D
WARREN	13,865	6,724	48.5	7,141	51.5	48.5	51.5	417 R
WASHINGTON	4,315	1,995	46.2	2,320	53.8	46.2	53.8	325 R
WAYNE	5,775	2,356	40.8	3,419	59.2	40.8	59.2	1,063 R
WEBSTER	5,106	3,334	65.3	1,772	34.7	65.3	34.7	1,562 D
WHITLEY	9,585	2,683	28.0	6,902	72.0	28.0	72.0	4,219 R
WOLFE	2,344	1,481	63.2	863	36.8	63.2	36.8	618 D
WOODFORD	4,035	2,154	53.4	1,881	46.6	53.4	46.6	273 D
TOTAL	960,228	465,652	48.5	494,576	51.5	48.5	51.5	28,924 R

DEMOCRAT: Thomas R. Underwood
REPUBLICAN: John S. Cooper

County	Total Vote	Democratic		Republican		Per Cent of Two-Party Vote		Dem-Rep Plurality
		Total	Per Cent	Total	Per Cent	Dem	Rep	
ADAIR	5,385	2,208	41.0	3,177	59.0	41.0	59.0	969 R
ALLEN	3,901	1,685	43.2	2,216	56.8	43.2	56.8	531 R
ANDERSON	3,113	2,031	65.2	1,082	34.8	65.2	34.8	949 D
BALLARD	3,589	3,041	84.7	548	15.3	84.7	15.3	2,493 D
BARREN	7,523	4,511	60.0	3,012	40.0	60.0	40.0	1,499 D
BATH	3,225	1,938	60.1	1,287	39.9	60.1	39.9	651 D
BELL	9,242	4,491	48.6	4,751	51.4	48.6	51.4	260 R
BOONE	3,804	2,285	60.1	1,519	39.9	60.1	39.9	766 D
BOURBON	4,530	2,821	62.3	1,709	37.7	62.3	37.7	1,112 D
BOYD	16,203	8,580	53.0	7,623	47.0	53.0	47.0	957 D
BOYLE	5,419	3,141	58.0	2,278	42.0	58.0	42.0	863 D
BRACKEN	2,294	1,291	56.3	1,003	43.7	56.3	43.7	288 D
BREATHITT	4,089	2,956	72.3	1,133	27.7	72.3	27.7	1,823 D
BRECKINRIDGE	5,161	2,675	51.8	2,486	48.2	51.8	48.2	189 D
BULLITT	2,690	1,774	65.9	916	34.1	65.9	34.1	858 D
BUTLER	3,584	1,302	36.3	2,282	63.7	36.3	63.7	980 R
CALDWELL	4,083	2,323	56.9	1,760	43.1	56.9	43.1	563 D
CALLOWAY	6,754	5,431	80.4	1,323	19.6	80.4	19.6	4,108 D
CAMPBELL	20,828	9,787	47.0	11,041	53.0	47.0	53.0	1,254 R
CARLISLE	2,217	1,800	81.2	417	18.8	81.2	18.8	1,383 D
CARROLL	2,970	2,253	75.9	717	24.1	75.9	24.1	1,536 D
CARTER	5,754	2,495	43.4	3,259	56.6	43.4	56.6	764 R
CASEY	4,833	1,446	29.9	3,387	70.1	29.9	70.1	1,941 R
CHRISTIAN	8,239	5,266	63.9	2,973	36.1	63.9	36.1	2,293 D
CLARK	4,795	2,838	59.2	1,957	40.8	59.2	40.8	881 D
CLAY	4,123	1,105	26.8	3,018	73.2	26.8	73.2	1,913 R
CLINTON	2,965	760	25.6	2,205	74.4	25.6	74.4	1,445 R
CRITTENDEN	3,530	1,605	45.5	1,925	54.5	45.5	54.5	320 R
CUMBERLAND	3,087	935	30.3	2,152	69.7	30.3	69.7	1,217 R
DAVIESS	12,833	6,316	49.2	6,517	50.8	49.2	50.8	201 R
EDMONSON	2,937	1,032	35.1	1,905	64.9	35.1	64.9	873 R
ELLIOTT	2,216	1,649	74.4	567	25.6	74.4	25.6	1,082 D
ESTILL	3,563	1,666	46.8	1,897	53.2	46.8	53.2	231 R
FAYETTE	24,369	11,294	46.3	13,075	53.7	46.3	53.7	1,781 R
FLEMING	4,050	2,225	54.9	1,825	45.1	54.9	45.1	400 D
FLOYD	11,019	6,769	61.4	4,250	38.6	61.4	38.6	2,519 D
FRANKLIN	9,108	6,961	76.4	2,147	23.6	76.4	23.6	4,814 D
FULTON	3,182	2,477	77.8	705	22.2	77.8	22.2	1,772 D
GALLATIN	1,465	1,107	75.6	358	24.4	75.6	24.4	749 D
GARRARD	3,555	1,732	48.7	1,823	51.3	48.7	51.3	91 R
GRANT	3,134	2,047	65.3	1,087	34.7	65.3	34.7	960 D
GRAVES	12,359	10,115	81.8	2,244	18.2	81.8	18.2	7,871 D
GRAYSON	5,323	2,116	39.8	3,207	60.2	39.8	60.2	1,091 R
GREEN	3,918	1,715	43.8	2,203	56.2	43.8	56.2	488 R
GREENUP	7,782	4,366	56.1	3,416	43.9	56.1	43.9	950 D
HANCOCK	1,872	973	52.0	899	48.0	52.0	48.0	74 D
HARDIN	6,856	3,973	57.9	2,883	42.1	57.9	42.1	1,090 D
HARLAN	12,845	7,586	59.1	5,259	40.9	59.1	40.9	2,327 D
HARRISON	4,425	3,000	67.8	1,425	32.2	67.8	32.2	1,575 D
HART	4,899	2,634	53.8	2,265	46.2	53.8	46.2	369 D
HENDERSON	8,061	5,338	66.2	2,723	33.8	66.2	33.8	2,615 D
HENRY	4,189	3,053	72.9	1,136	27.1	72.9	27.1	1,917 D
HICKMAN	2,654	2,119	79.8	535	20.2	79.8	20.2	1,584 D
HOPKINS	9,121	6,199	68.0	2,922	32.0	68.0	32.0	3,277 D
JACKSON	3,007	518	17.2	2,489	82.8	17.2	82.8	1,971 R
JEFFERSON	146,454	72,375	49.4	74,079	50.6	49.4	50.6	1,704 R
JESSAMINE	3,785	2,200	58.1	1,585	41.9	58.1	41.9	615 D
JOHNSON	6,082	2,392	39.3	3,690	60.7	39.3	60.7	1,298 R
KENTON	26,721	14,676	54.9	12,045	45.1	54.9	45.1	2,631 D
KNOTT	4,489	3,415	76.1	1,074	23.9	76.1	23.9	2,341 D
KNOX	6,517	2,754	42.3	3,763	57.7	42.3	57.7	1,009 R
LARUE	3,380	1,906	56.4	1,474	43.6	56.4	43.6	432 D
LAUREL	6,459	2,068	32.0	4,391	68.0	32.0	68.0	2,323 R
LAWRENCE	4,216	2,151	51.0	2,065	49.0	51.0	49.0	86 D
LEE	2,111	988	46.8	1,123	53.2	46.8	53.2	135 R

County	Total Vote	Democratic		Republican		Per Cent of Two-Party Vote		Dem-Rep Plurality
		Total	Per Cent	Total	Per Cent	Dem.	Rep.	
LESLIE	2,556	512	20.0	2,044	80.0	20.0	80.0	1,532 R
LETCHER	8,008	4,150	51.8	3,858	48.2	51.8	48.2	292 D
LEWIS	3,914	1,263	32.3	2,651	67.7	32.3	67.7	1,388 R
LINCOLN	4,702	2,460	52.3	2,242	47.7	52.3	47.7	218 D
LIVINGSTON	2,461	1,776	72.2	685	27.8	72.2	27.8	1,091 D
LOGAN	6,649	5,119	77.0	1,530	23.0	77.0	23.0	3,589 D
LYON	1,995	1,458	73.1	537	26.9	73.1	26.9	921 D
MADISON	9,387	5,132	54.7	4,255	45.3	54.7	45.3	877 D
MAGOFFIN	3,609	1,797	49.8	1,812	50.2	49.8	50.2	15 R
MARION	4,383	2,762	63.0	1,621	37.0	63.0	37.0	1,141 D
MARSHALL	4,801	3,671	76.5	1,130	23.5	76.5	23.5	2,541 D
MARTIN	2,893	976	33.7	1,917	66.3	33.7	66.3	941 R
MASON,.	5,442	2,881	52.9	2,561	47.1	52.9	47.1	320 D
MC CRACKEN	16,781	12,371	73.7	4,410	26.3	73.7	26.3	7,961 D
MC CREARY	3,044	764	25.1	2,280	74.9	25.1	74.9	1,516 R
MC LEAN	3,055	1,765	57.8	1,290	42.2	57.8	42.2	475 D
MEADE	2,788	1,824	65.4	964	34.6	65.4	34.6	860 D
MENIFEE	1,513	1,003	66.3	510	33.7	66.3	33.7	493 D
MERCER	4,637	2,571	55.4	2,066	44.6	55.4	44.6	505 D
METCALFE	3,642	1,793	49.2	1,849	50.8	49.2	50.8	56 R
MONROE	3,793	1,193	31.5	2,600	68.5	31.5	68.5	1,407 R
MONTGOMERY	3,353	2,049	61.1	1,304	38.9	61.1	38.9	745 D
MORGAN	3,529	2,564	72.7	965	27.3	72.7	27.3	1,599 D
MUHLENBERG	8,453	4,875	57.7	3,578	42.3	57.7	42.3	1,297 D
NELSON	5,349	3,154	59.0	2,195	41.0	59.0	41.0	959 D
NICHOLAS	2,264	1,546	68.3	718	31.7	68.3	31.7	828 D
OHIO	6,111	2,638	43.2	3,473	56.8	43.2	56.8	835 R
OLDHAM	3,120	1,722	55.2	1,398	44.8	55.2	44.8	324 D
OWEN	3,330	2,724	81.8	606	18.2	81.8	18.2	2,118 D
OWSLEY	1,644	345	21.0	1,299	79.0	21.0	79.0	954 R
PENDLETON	3,106	1,724	55.5	1,382	44.5	55.5	44.5	342 D
PERRY	8,012	3,878	48.4	4,134	51.6	48.4	51.6	256 R
PIKE	18,353	10,802	58.9	7,551	41.1	58.9	41.1	3,251 D
POWELL	2,002	1,177	58.8	825	41.2	58.8	41.2	352 D
PULASKI	11,833	3,438	29.1	8,395	70.9	29.1	70.9	4,957 R
ROBERTSON	1,059	680	64.2	379	35.8	64.2	35.8	301 D
ROCKCASTLE	3,635	1,142	31.4	2,493	68.6	31.4	68.6	1,351 R
ROWAN	3,745	2,047	54.7	1,698	45.3	54.7	45.3	349 D
RUSSELL	3,565	1,144	32.1	2,421	67.9	32.1	67.9	1,277 R
SCOTT	3,914	2,582	66.0	1,332	34.0	66.0	34.0	1,250 D
SHELBY	5,401	3,545	65.6	1,856	34.4	65.6	34.4	1,689 D
SIMPSON	3,104	2,294	73.9	810	26.1	73.9	26.1	1,484 D
SPENCER	1,566	1,030	65.8	536	34.2	65.8	34.2	494 D
TAYLOR	5,049	2,378	47.1	2,671	52.9	47.1	52.9	293 R
TODD	3,659	2,817	77.0	842	23.0	77.0	23.0	1,975 D
TRIGG	3,229	2,329	72.1	900	27.9	72.1	27.9	1,429 D
TRIMBLE	1,952	1,657	84.9	295	15.1	84.9	15.1	1,362 D
UNION	4,388	3,142	71.6	1,246	28.4	71.6	28.4	1,896 D
WARREN	10,527	5,976	56.8	4,551	43.2	56.8	43.2	1,425 D
WASHINGTON	3,526	1,818	51.6	1,708	48.4	51.6	48.4	110 D
WAYNE	4,522	2,078	46.0	2,444	54.0	46.0	54.0	366 R
WEBSTER	4,495	3,269	72.7	1,226	27.3	72.7	27.3	2,043 D
WHITLEY	7,532	2,646	35.1	4,886	64.9	35.1	64.9	2,240 R
WOLFE	1,623	1,125	69.3	498	30.7	69.3	30.7	627 D
WOODFORD	3,168	1,854	58.5	1,314	41.5	58.5	41.5	540 D
TOTAL	797,057	434,109	54.5	362,948	45.5	54.5	45.5	71,161 D

DEMOCRAT: Alben W. Barkley
REPUBLICAN: John S. Cooper

County	Total Vote	Earle C. Clements		Joe B. Bates		Other Vote	
		Total	Per Cent	Total	Per Cent	Total	Per Cent
ADAIR	2,103	864	41.1	1,223	58.2	16	0.8
ALLEN	1,524	578	37.9	933	61.2	13	0.9
ANDERSON	1,995	1,269	63.6	723	36.2	3	0.2
BALLARD	2,428	1,298	53.5	1,125	46.3	5	0.2
BARREN	3,379	1,896	56.1	1,460	43.2	23	0.7
BATH	2,315	1,116	48.2	1,186	51.2	13	0.6
BELL	2,367	1,358	57.4	985	41.6	24	1.0
BOONE	1,926	1,232	64.0	676	35.1	18	0.9
BOURBON	2,601	1,796	69.1	780	30.0	25	1.0
BOYD	4,530	2,046	45.2	2,457	54.2	27	0.6
BOYLE	3,394	1,926	56.7	1,436	42.3	32	0.9
BRACKEN	1,177	720	61.2	441	37.5	16	1.4
BREATHITT	4,164	2,389	57.4	1,768	42.5	7	0.2
BRECKINRIDGE	2,672	1,428	53.4	1,226	45.9	18	0.7
BULLITT	1,867	867	46.4	992	53.1	8	0.4
BUTLER	1,183	709	59.9	462	39.1	12	1.0
CALDWELL	2,048	1,177	57.5	863	42.1	8	0.4
CALLOWAY	4,668	2,400	51.4	2,256	48.3	12	0.3
CAMPBELL	5,379	3,999	74.3	1,264	23.5	116	2.2
CARLISLE	1,701	695	40.9	1,002	58.9	4	0.2
CARROLL	2,018	1,242	61.5	763	37.8	13	0.6
CARTER	2,275	456	20.0	1,817	79.9	2	0.1
CASEY	1,113	541	48.6	560	50.3	12	1.1
CHRISTIAN	5,065	3,210	63.4	1,836	36.2	19	0.4
CLARK	2,734	1,784	65.3	917	33.5	33	1.2
CLAY	654	197	30.1	455	69.6	2	0.3
CLINTON	550	171	31.1	377	68.5	2	0.4
CRITTENDEN	1,234	669	54.2	563	45.6	2	0.2
CUMBERLAND	827	280	33.9	540	65.3	7	0.8
DAVIESS	4,825	3,604	74.7	1,140	23.6	81	1.7
EDMONSON	883	500	56.6	372	42.1	11	1.2
ELLIOTT	2,255	997	44.2	1,257	55.7	1	
ESTILL	1,318	697	52.9	602	45.7	19	1.4
FAYETTE	11,444	7,851	68.6	3,344	29.2	249	2.2
FLEMING	2,417	1,103	45.6	1,290	53.4	24	1.0
FLOYD	7,298	4,019	55.1	3,219	44.1	60	0.8
FRANKLIN	7,898	4,003	50.7	3,816	48.3	79	1.0
FULTON	2,097	953	45.4	1,134	54.1	10	0.5
GALLATIN	1,029	441	42.9	575	55.9	13	1.3
GARRARD	1,211	845	69.8	359	29.6	7	0.6
GRANT	1,791	991	55.3	782	43.7	18	1.0
GRAVES	8,235	3,753	45.6	4,449	54.0	33	0.4
GRAYSON	1,811	1,015	56.0	786	43.4	10	0.6
GREEN	1,155	653	56.5	502	43.5		
GREENUP	3,491	808	23.1	2,671	76.5	12	0.3
HANCOCK	618	432	69.9	178	28.8	8	1.3
HARDIN	3,744	2,428	64.9	1,298	34.7	18	0.5
HARLAN	2,929	1,652	56.4	1,230	42.0	47	1.6
HARRISON	2,509	1,513	60.3	986	39.3	10	0.4
HART	2,118	1,036	48.9	1,080	51.0	2	0.1
HENDERSON	4,844	3,358	69.3	1,365	28.2	121	2.5
HENRY	2,473	1,623	65.6	821	33.2	29	1.2
HICKMAN	2,359	619	26.2	1,730	73.3	10	0.4
HOPKINS	5,063	2,820	55.7	2,191	43.3	52	1.0
JACKSON	450	103	22.9	346	76.9	1	0.2
JEFFERSON	48,123	41,334	85.9	5,587	11.6	1,202	2.5
JESSAMINE	2,629	1,564	59.5	1,021	38.8	44	1.7
JOHNSON	1,621	652	40.2	965	59.5	4	0.2
KENTON	9,470	7,313	77.2	2,040	21.5	117	1.2
KNOTT	3,860	1,734	44.9	2,100	54.4	26	0.7
KNOX	1,291	612	47.4	672	52.1	7	0.5
LARUE	1,947	899	46.2	1,032	53.0	16	0.8
LAUREL	2,006	705	35.1	1,285	64.1	16	0.8
LAWRENCE	1,847	608	32.9	1,234	66.8	5	0.3
LEE	728	377	51.8	348	47.8	3	0.4

70

County	Total Vote	Earle C. Clements Total	Per Cent	Joe B. Bates Total	Per Cent	Other Vote Total	Per Cent
LESLIE	364	66	18.1	295	81.0	3	0.8
LETCHER	2,754	1,664	60.4	1,062	38.6	28	1.0
LEWIS	1,125	235	20.9	882	78.4	8	0.7
LINCOLN	2,102	1,191	56.7	884	42.1	27	1.3
LIVINGSTON	1,934	1,135	58.7	796	41.2	3	0.2
LOGAN	5,773	4,666	80.8	1,080	18.7	27	0.5
LYON	1,734	834	48.1	889	51.3	11	0.6
MADISON	4,245	2,996	70.6	1,210	28.5	39	0.9
MAGOFFIN	1,763	697	39.5	1,062	60.2	4	0.2
MARION	2,557	1,656	64.8	889	34.8	12	0.5
MARSHALL	3,419	2,369	69.3	1,031	30.2	19	0.6
MARTIN	501	228	45.5	271	54.1	2	0.4
MASON	2,842	1,497	52.7	1,308	46.0	37	1.3
MC CRACKEN	8,718	6,711	77.0	1,958	22.5	49	0.6
MC CREARY	490	161	32.9	326	66.5	3	0.6
MC LEAN	1,207	862	71.4	334	27.7	11	0.9
MEADE	1,721	1,048	60.9	670	38.9	3	0.2
MENIFEE	1,037	382	36.8	651	62.8	4	0.4
MERCER	2,345	1,433	61.1	905	38.6	7	0.3
METCALFE	1,966	1,111	56.5	851	43.3	4	0.2
MONROE	964	482	50.0	478	49.6	4	0.4
MONTGOMERY	2,749	1,444	52.5	1,281	46.6	24	0.9
MORGAN	3,440	1,702	49.5	1,724	50.1	14	0.4
MUHLENBERG	3,465	2,189	63.2	1,258	36.3	18	0.5
NELSON	3,185	2,432	76.4	736	23.1	17	0.5
NICHOLAS	1,127	680	60.3	441	39.1	6	0.5
OHIO	1,813	1,078	59.5	716	39.5	19	1.0
OLDHAM	1,407	979	69.6	418	29.7	10	0.7
OWEN	2,452	1,266	51.6	1,161	47.3	25	1.0
OWSLEY	234	79	33.8	154	65.8	1	0.4
PENDLETON	1,760	1,198	68.1	524	29.8	38	2.2
PERRY	2,940	1,843	62.7	1,087	37.0	10	0.3
PIKE	6,720	4,287	63.8	2,383	35.5	50	0.7
POWELL	1,073	519	48.4	538	50.1	16	1.5
PULASKI	3,481	1,200	34.5	2,269	65.2	12	0.3
ROBERTSON	729	413	56.7	305	41.8	11	1.5
ROCKCASTLE	938	473	50.4	461	49.1	4	0.4
ROWAN	1,666	630	37.8	1,033	62.0	3	0.2
RUSSELL	978	351	35.9	617	63.1	10	1.0
SCOTT	1,942	1,220	62.8	697	35.9	25	1.3
SHELBY	3,281	1,812	55.2	1,456	44.4	13	0.4
SIMPSON	2,326	1,493	64.2	816	35.1	17	0.7
SPENCER	1,036	609	58.8	423	40.8	4	0.4
TAYLOR	1,981	965	48.7	1,014	51.2	2	0.1
TODD	3,323	1,680	50.6	1,637	49.3	6	0.2
TRIGG	1,972	887	45.0	1,080	54.8	5	0.3
TRIMBLE	1,130	751	66.5	371	32.8	8	0.7
UNION	3,433	2,728	79.5	675	19.7	30	0.9
WARREN	7,663	4,282	55.9	3,305	43.1	76	1.0
WASHINGTON	1,743	1,110	63.7	630	36.1	3	0.2
WAYNE	1,580	888	56.2	681	43.1	11	0.7
WEBSTER	2,472	1,681	68.0	775	31.4	16	0.6
WHITLEY	1,514	639	42.2	865	57.1	10	0.7
WOLFE	1,616	471	29.1	1,141	70.6	4	0.2
WOODFORD	2,181	1,022	46.9	1,136	52.1	23	1.1
TOTAL	358,589	218,353	60.9	136,533	38.1	3,703	1.0

OTHER VOTE: James L. Delk 3703

County	Total Vote	Thruston B. Morton		Julian H. Golden		Other Vote	
		Total	Per Cent	Total	Per Cent	Total	Per Cent
ADAIR	423	328	77.5	82	19.4	13	3.1
ALLEN	306	280	91.5	14	4.6	12	3.9
ANDERSON	116	94	81.0	20	17.2	2	1.7
BALLARD	58	41	70.7	15	25.9	2	3.4
BARREN	250	205	82.0	43	17.2	2	0.8
BATH	78	63	80.8	8	10.3	7	9.0
BELL	1,461	438	30.0	993	68.0	30	2.1
BOONE	89	74	83.1	9	10.1	6	6.7
BOURBON	110	71	64.5	22	20.0	17	15.5
BOYD	1,380	1,050	76.1	195	14.1	135	9.8
BOYLE	120	89	74.2	13	10.8	18	15.0
BRACKEN	78	57	73.1	14	17.9	7	9.0
BREATHITT	156	124	79.5	19	12.2	13	8.3
BRECKINRIDGE	471	450	95.5	17	3.6	4	0.8
BULLITT	76	64	84.2	11	14.5	1	1.3
BUTLER	563	497	88.3	41	7.3	25	4.4
CALDWELL	299	214	71.6	60	20.1	25	8.4
CALLOWAY	88	74	84.1	13	14.8	1	1.1
CAMPBELL	1,458	1,059	72.6	127	8.7	272	18.7
CARLISLE	35	21	60.0	10	28.6	4	11.4
CARROLL	55	51	92.7	4	7.3		
CARTER	737	561	76.1	149	20.2	27	3.7
CASEY	454	314	69.2	96	21.1	44	9.7
CHRISTIAN	333	249	74.8	74	22.2	10	3.0
CLARK	137	89	65.0	27	19.7	21	15.3
CLAY	873	427	48.9	411	47.1	35	4.0
CLINTON	391	130	33.2	233	59.6	28	7.2
CRITTENDEN	287	221	77.0	52	18.1	14	4.9
CUMBERLADN	437	226	51.7	194	44.4	17	3.9
DAVIESS	547	447	81.7	57	10.4	43	7.9
EDMONSON	462	410	88.7	36	7.8	16	3.5
ELLIOTT	24	19	79.2	4	16.7	1	4.2
ESTILL	397	267	67.3	58	14.6	72	18.1
FAYETTE	1,038	739	71.2	149	14.4	150	14.5
FLEMING	222	184	82.9	33	14.9	5	2.3
FLOYD	710	491	69.2	164	23.1	55	7.7
FRANKLIN	228	214	93.9	10	4.4	4	1.8
FULTON	40	30	75.0	8	20.0	2	5.0
GALLATIN	29	28	96.6	1	3.4		
GARRARD	130	115	88.5	5	3.8	10	7.7
GRANT	76	54	71.1	13	17.1	9	11.8
GRAVES	119	94	79.0	20	16.8	5	4.2
GRAYSON	615	564	91.7	32	5.2	19	3.1
GREEN	274	224	81.8	37	13.5	13	4.7
GREENUP	616	364	59.1	194	31.5	58	9.4
HANCOCK	186	151	81.2	17	9.1	18	9.7
HARDIN	243	208	85.6	30	12.3	5	2.1
HARLAN	1,650	683	41.4	838	50.8	129	7.8
HARRISON	108	70	64.8	21	19.4	17	15.7
HART	292	254	87.0	33	11.3	5	1.7
HENDERSON	159	130	81.8	23	14.5	6	3.8
HENRY	129	107	82.9	7	5.4	15	11.6
HICKMAN	29	21	72.4	7	24.1	1	3.4
HOPKINS	375	350	93.3	20	5.3	5	1.3
JACKSON	974	331	34.0	588	60.4	55	5.6
JEFFERSON	13,907	12,267	88.2	390	2.8	1,250	9.0
JESSAMINE	101	61	60.4	18	17.8	22	21.8
JOHNSON	869	558	64.2	195	22.4	116	13.3
KENTON	410	301	73.4	51	12.4	58	14.1
KNOTT	55	35	63.6	12	21.8	8	14.5
KNOX	1,154	454	39.3	640	55.5	60	5.2
LARUE	87	76	87.4	8	9.2	3	3.4
LAUREL	1,196	541	45.2	600	50.2	55	4.6
LAWRENCE	446	294	65.9	100	22.4	52	11.7
LEE	261	158	60.5	72	27.6	31	11.9

County	Total Vote	Thruston B. Morton Total	Per Cent	Julian H. Golden Total	Per Cent	Other Vote Total	Per Cent
LESLIE	987	285	28.9	656	66.5	46	4.7
LETCHER	691	364	52.7	264	38.2	63	9.1
LEWIS	497	389	78.3	62	12.5	46	9.3
LINCOLN	273	205	75.1	49	17.9	19	7.0
LIVINGSTON	123	116	94.3	5	4.1	2	1.6
LOGAN	80	71	88.8	8	10.0	1	1.3
LYON	64	53	82.8	11	17.2		
MADISON	386	295	76.4	41	10.6	50	13.0
MAGOFFIN	412	292	70.9	92	22.3	28	6.8
MARION	79	66	83.5	10	12.7	3	3.8
MARSHALL	189	157	83.1	26	13.8	6	3.2
MARTIN	444	223	50.2	158	35.6	63	14.2
MASON	238	202	84.9	25	10.5	11	4.6
MC CRACKEN	739	661	89.4	56	7.6	22	3.0
MC CREARY	1,361	560	41.1	629	46.2	172	12.6
MC LEAN	147	135	91.8	5	3.4	7	4.8
MEADE	74	63	85.1	10	13.5	1	1.4
MENIFEE	46	27	58.7	15	32.6	4	8.7
MERCER	191	177	92.7	11	5.8	3	1.6
METCALFE	248	224	90.3	20	8.1	4	1.6
MONROE	393	250	63.6	128	32.6	15	3.8
MONTGOMERY	83	67	80.7	11	13.3	5	6.0
MORGAN	150	113	75.3	33	22.0	4	2.7
MUHLENBERG	439	346	78.8	70	15.9	23	5.2
NELSON	133	117	88.0	12	9.0	4	3.0
NICHOLAS	57	38	66.7	6	10.5	13	22.8
OHIO	1,071	888	82.9	113	10.6	70	6.5
OLDHAM	135	121	89.6	12	8.9	2	1.5
OWEN	81	65	80.2	7	8.6	9	11.1
OWSLEY	329	184	55.9	115	35.0	30	9.1
PENDLETON	291	189	64.9	63	21.6	39	13.4
PERRY	1,216	647	53.2	430	35.4	139	11.4
PIKE	1,689	1,034	61.2	461	27.3	194	11.5
POWELL	173	108	62.4	36	20.8	29	16.8
PULASKI	1,710	1,345	78.7	345	20.2	20	1.2
ROBERTSON	69	65	94.2	2	2.9	2	2.9
ROCKCASTLE	654	387	59.2	240	36.7	27	4.1
ROWAN	255	199	78.0	39	15.3	17	6.7
RUSSELL	392	276	70.4	98	25.0	18	4.6
SCOTT	53	38	71.7	10	18.9	5	9.4
SHELBY	160	130	81.3	26	16.3	4	2.5
SIMPSON	90	81	90.0	7	7.8	2	2.2
SPENCER	60	48	80.0	8	13.3	4	6.7
TAYLOR	258	229	88.8	28	10.9	1	0.4
TODD	59	36	61.0	19	32.2	4	6.8
TRIGG	100	74	74.0	23	23.0	3	3.0
TRIMBLE	25	18	72.0	4	16.0	3	12.0
UNION	68	57	83.8	9	13.2	2	2.9
WARREN	362	314	86.7	33	9.1	15	4.1
WASHINGTON	127	121	95.3	5	3.9	1	0.8
WAYNE	489	345	70.6	140	28.6	4	0.8
WEBSTER	112	87	77.7	15	13.4	10	8.9
WHITLEY	1,302	476	36.6	777	59.7	49	3.8
WOLFE	97	55	56.7	36	37.1	6	6.2
WOODFORD	81	70	86.4	5	6.2	6	7.4
TOTAL	59,509	42,038	70.6	12,976	21.8	4,495	7.6

OTHER VOTE: Granville Thomas 4495

73

County	Total Vote	Democratic		Republican		Per Cent of Two-Party Vote		Dem-Rep Plurality
		Total	Per Cent	Total	Per Cent	Dem	Rep	
ADAIR	6,382	2,631	41.2	3,751	58.8	41.2	58.8	1,120 R
ALLEN	4,960	1,991	40.1	2,969	59.9	40.1	59.9	978 R
ANDERSON	3,820	2,168	56.8	1,652	43.2	56.8	43.2	516 D
BALLARD	3,743	3,088	82.5	655	17.5	82.5	17.5	2,433 D
BARREN	8,985	5,208	58.0	3,777	42.0	58.0	42.0	1,431 D
BATH	3,890	2,224	57.2	1,666	42.8	57.2	42.8	558 D
BELL	10,804	4,679	43.3	6,125	56.7	43.3	56.7	1,446 R
BOONE	5,852	3,259	55.7	2,593	44.3	55.7	44.3	666 D
BOURBON	5,434	3,340	61.5	2,094	38.5	61.5	38.5	1,246 D
BOYD	19,289	8,964	46.5	10,325	53.5	46.5	53.5	1,361 R
BOYLE	6,590	3,517	53.4	3,073	46.6	53.4	46.6	444 D
BRACKEN	3,087	1,709	55.4	1,378	44.6	55.4	44.6	331 D
BREATHITT	5,208	3,230	62.0	1,978	38.0	62.0	38.0	1,252 D
BRECKINRIDGE	6,494	3,067	47.2	3,427	52.8	47.2	52.8	360 R
BULLITT	4,133	2,406	58.2	1,727	41.8	58.2	41.8	679 D
BUTLER	4,331	1,277	29.5	3,054	70.5	29.5	70.5	1,777 R
CALDWELL	4,929	2,616	53.1	2,313	46.9	53.1	46.9	303 D
CALLOWAY	8,057	6,292	78.1	1,765	21.9	78.1	21.9	4,527 D
CAMPBELL	27,412	12,290	44.8	15,122	55.2	44.8	55.2	2,832 R
CARLISLE	2,521	2,060	81.7	461	18.3	81.7	18.3	1,599 D
CARROLL	3,164	2,251	71.1	913	28.9	71.1	28.9	1,338 D
CARTER	7,884	3,148	39.9	4,736	60.1	39.9	60.1	1,588 R
CASEY	5,511	1,596	29.0	3,915	71.0	29.0	71.0	2,319 R
CHRISTIAN	11,105	6,678	60.1	4,427	39.9	60.1	39.9	2,251 D
CLARK	6,307	3,737	59.3	2,570	40.7	59.3	40.7	1,167 D
CLAY	5,553	1,039	18.7	4,514	81.3	18.7	81.3	3,475 R
CLINTON	3,917	772	19.7	3,145	80.3	19.7	80.3	2,373 R
CRITTENDEN	3,945	1,610	40.8	2,335	59.2	40.8	59.2	725 R
CUMBERLAND	3,374	1,000	29.6	2,374	70.4	29.6	70.4	1,374 R
DAVIESS	17,580	7,751	44.1	9,829	55.9	44.1	55.9	2,078 R
EDMONSON	3,697	1,136	30.7	2,561	69.3	30.7	69.3	1,425 R
ELLIOTT	2,979	2,065	69.3	914	30.7	69.3	30.7	1,151 D
ESTILL	4,708	1,974	41.9	2,734	58.1	41.9	58.1	760 R
FAYETTE	34,759	14,803	42.6	19,956	57.4	42.6	57.4	5,153 R
FLEMING	5,016	2,663	53.1	2,353	46.9	53.1	46.9	310 D
FLOYD	13,431	8,254	61.5	5,177	38.5	61.5	38.5	3,077 D
FRANKLIN	9,788	6,562	67.0	3,226	33.0	67.0	33.0	3,336 D
FULTON	3,797	3,058	80.5	739	19.5	80.5	19.5	2,319 D
GALLATIN	1,657	1,233	74.4	424	25.6	74.4	25.6	809 D
GARRARD	4,035	1,844	45.7	2,191	54.3	45.7	54.3	347 R
GRANT	3,663	2,285	62.4	1,378	37.6	62.4	37.6	907 D
GRAVES	13,243	10,228	77.2	3,015	22.8	77.2	22.8	7,213 D
GRAYSON	6,477	2,099	32.4	4,378	67.6	32.4	67.6	2,279 R
GREEN	4,557	1,761	38.6	2,796	61.4	38.6	61.4	1,035 R
GREENUP	10,216	5,122	50.1	5,094	49.9	50.1	49.9	28 D
HANCOCK	2,300	1,101	47.9	1,199	52.1	47.9	52.1	98 R
HARDIN	9,194	4,767	51.8	4,427	48.2	51.8	48.2	340 D
HARLAN	14,596	7,079	48.5	7,517	51.5	48.5	51.5	438 R
HARRISON	5,359	3,582	66.8	1,777	33.2	66.8	33.2	1,805 D
HART	6,349	3,355	52.8	2,994	47.2	52.8	47.2	361 D
HENDERSON	10,086	6,123	60.7	3,963	39.3	60.7	39.3	2,160 D
HENRY	4,651	3,207	69.0	1,444	31.0	69.0	31.0	1,763 D
HICKMAN	2,948	2,358	80.0	590	20.0	80.0	20.0	1,768 D
HOPKINS	11,484	7,136	62.1	4,348	37.9	62.1	37.9	2,788 D
JACKSON	4,141	513	12.4	3,628	87.6	12.4	87.6	3,115 R
JEFFERSON	198,207	85,779	43.3	112,428	56.7	43.3	56.7	26,649 R
JESSAMINE	4,061	2,165	53.3	1,896	46.7	53.3	46.7	269 D
JOHNSON	7,798	2,486	31.9	5,312	68.1	31.9	68.1	2,826 R
KENTON	33,790	17,877	52.9	15,913	47.1	52.9	47.1	1,964 D
KNOTT	5,362	4,027	75.1	1,335	24.9	75.1	24.9	2,692 D
KNOX	8,457	2,601	30.8	5,856	69.2	30.8	69.2	3,255 R
LARUE	3,874	1,969	50.8	1,905	49.2	50.8	49.2	64 D
LAUREL	8,509	2,377	27.9	6,132	72.1	27.9	72.1	3,755 R
LAWRENCE	5,260	2,535	48.2	2,725	51.8	48.2	51.8	190 R
LEE	2,570	1,012	39.4	1,558	60.6	39.4	60.6	546 R

74

County	Total Vote	Democratic		Republican			Per Cent of Two-Party Vote		Dem-Rep Plurality
		Total	Per Cent	Total	Per Cent		Dem	Rep	
LESLIE	3,997	549	13.7	3,448	86.3		13.7	86.3	2,899 R
LETCHER	9,255	4,396	47.5	4,859	52.5		47.5	52.5	463 R
LEWIS	4,704	1,563	33.2	3,141	66.8		33.2	66.8	1,578 R
LINCOLN	6,172	3,008	48.7	3,164	51.3		48.7	51.3	156 R
LIVINGSTON	2,924	1,917	65.6	1,007	34.4		65.6	34.4	910 D
LOGAN	7,744	5,343	69.0	2,401	31.0		69.0	31.0	2,942 D
LYON	2,390	1,568	65.6	822	34.4		65.6	34.4	746 D
MADISON	11,381	5,848	51.4	5,533	48.6		51.4	48.6	315 D
MAGOFFIN	4,369	2,298	52.6	2,071	47.4		52.6	47.4	227 D
MARION	5,563	3,268	58.7	2,295	41.3		58.7	41.3	973 D
MARSHALL	6,160	4,501	73.1	1,659	26.9		73.1	26.9	2,842 D
MARTIN	3,453	746	21.6	2,707	78.4		21.6	78.4	1,961 R
MASON	7,178	3,836	53.4	3,342	46.6		53.4	46.6	494 D
MC CRACKEN	20,208	14,461	71.6	5,747	28.4		71.6	28.4	8,714 D
MC CREARY	4,292	852	19.9	3,440	80.1		19.9	80.1	2,588 R
MC LEAN	3,739	2,090	55.9	1,649	44.1		55.9	44.1	441 D
MEADE	3,503	2,124	60.6	1,379	39.4		60.6	39.4	745 D
MENIFEE	1,828	1,151	63.0	677	37.0		63.0	37.0	474 D
MERCER	5,673	2,929	51.6	2,744	48.4		51.6	48.4	185 D
METCALFE	4,263	2,058	48.3	2,205	51.7		48.3	51.7	147 R
MONROE	4,692	1,278	27.2	3,414	72.8		27.2	72.8	2,136 R
MONTGOMERY	4,517	2,713	60.1	1,804	39.9		60.1	39.9	909 D
MORGAN	4,789	3,176	66.3	1,613	33.7		66.3	33.7	1,563 D
MUHLENBERG	9,595	5,008	52.2	4,587	47.8		52.2	47.8	421 D
NELSON	6,926	3,829	55.3	3,097	44.7		55.3	44.7	732 D
NICHOLAS	2,525	1,671	66.2	854	33.8		66.2	33.8	817 D
OHIO	7,430	2,932	39.5	4,498	60.5		39.5	60.5	1,566 R
OLDHAM	3,767	1,887	50.1	1,880	49.9		50.1	49.9	7 D
OWEN	3,616	2,896	80.1	720	19.9		80.1	19.9	2,176 D
OWSLEY	2,156	322	14.9	1,834	85.1		14.9	85.1	1,512 R
PENDLETON	3,980	2,106	52.9	1,874	47.1		52.9	47.1	232 D
PERRY	10,619	4,853	45.7	5,766	54.3		45.7	54.3	913 R
PIKE	22,522	12,038	53.4	10,484	46.6		53.4	46.6	1,554 D
POWELL	2,571	1,363	53.0	1,208	47.0		53.0	47.0	155 D
PULASKI	13,690	3,994	29.2	9,696	70.8		29.2	70.8	5,702 R
ROBERTSON	1,342	805	60.0	537	40.0		60.0	40.0	268 D
ROCKCASTLE	4,911	1,328	27.0	3,583	73.0		27.0	73.0	2,255 R
ROWAN	4,749	2,594	54.6	2,155	45.4		54.6	45.4	439 D
RUSSELL	4,145	1,325	32.0	2,820	68.0		32.0	68.0	1,495 R
SCOTT	4,635	2,932	63.3	1,703	36.7		63.3	36.7	1,229 D
SHELBY	6,529	4,089	62.6	2,440	37.4		62.6	37.4	1,649 D
SIMPSON	4,120	2,910	70.6	1,210	29.4		70.6	29.4	1,700 D
SPENCER	2,016	1,254	62.2	762	37.8		62.2	37.8	492 D
TAYLOR	6,148	2,679	43.6	3,469	56.4		43.6	56.4	790 R
TODD	4,288	3,023	70.5	1,265	29.5		70.5	29.5	1,758 D
TRIGG	3,570	2,488	69.7	1,082	30.3		69.7	30.3	1,406 D
TRIMBLE	2,198	1,813	82.5	385	17.5		82.5	17.5	1,428 D
UNION	4,705	3,474	73.8	1,231	26.2		73.8	26.2	2,243 D
WARREN	14,592	7,714	52.9	6,878	47.1		52.9	47.1	836 D
WASHINGTON	4,516	2,263	50.1	2,253	49.9		50.1	49.9	10 D
WAYNE	5,642	2,265	40.1	3,377	59.9		40.1	59.9	1,112 R
WEBSTER	4,828	3,278	67.9	1,550	32.1		67.9	32.1	1,728 D
WHITLEY	9,928	2,733	27.5	7,195	72.5		27.5	72.5	4,462 R
WOLFE	2,549	1,651	64.8	898	35.2		64.8	35.2	753 D
WOODFORD	3,943	1,998	50.7	1,945	49.3		50.7	49.3	53 D
TOTAL	1,006,825	499,922	49.7	506,903	50.3		49.7	50.3	6,981 R

DEMOCRAT: Earle C. Clements
REPUBLICAN: Thruston B. Morton

County	Total Vote	Democratic		Republican		Per Cent of Two-Party Vote		Dem-Rep Plurality
		Total	Per Cent	Total	Per Cent	Dem	Rep	
ADAIR	6,447	2,516	39.0	3,931	61.0	39.0	61.0	1,415 R
ALLEN	4,934	1,910	38.7	3,024	61.3	38.7	61.3	1,114 R
ANDERSON	3,853	2,082	54.0	1,771	46.0	54.0	46.0	311 D
BALLARD	3,778	2,995	79.3	783	20.7	79.3	20.7	2,212 D
BARREN	8,995	4,976	55.3	4,019	44.7	55.3	44.7	957 D
BATH	3,915	2,108	53.8	1,807	46.2	53.8	46.2	301 D
BELL	10,883	4,526	41.6	6,357	58.4	41.6	58.4	1,831 R
BOONE	5,930	2,925	49.3	3,005	50.7	49.3	50.7	80 R
BOURBON	5,458	3,091	56.6	2,367	43.4	56.6	43.4	724 D
BOYD	19,453	8,582	44.1	10,871	55.9	44.1	55.9	2,289 R
BOYLE	6,656	3,291	49.4	3,365	50.6	49.4	50.6	74 R
BRACKEN	3,128	1,539	49.2	1,589	50.8	49.2	50.8	50 R
BREATHITT	5,236	3,076	58.7	2,160	41.3	58.7	41.3	916 D
BRECKINRIDGE	6,276	2,870	45.7	3,406	54.3	45.7	54.3	536 R
BULLITT	4,160	2,323	55.8	1,837	44.2	55.8	44.2	486 D
BUTLER	4,335	1,166	26.9	3,169	73.1	26.9	73.1	2,003 R
CALDWELL	4,938	2,472	50.1	2,466	49.9	50.1	49.9	6 D
CALLOWAY	8,055	5,965	74.1	2,090	25.9	74.1	25.9	3,875 D
CAMPBELL	27,729	11,015	39.7	16,714	60.3	39.7	60.3	5,699 R
CARLISLE	2,524	1,960	77.7	564	22.3	77.7	22.3	1,396 D
CARROLL	3,199	2,124	66.4	1,075	33.6	66.4	33.6	1,049 D
CARTER	7,899	3,010	38.1	4,889	61.9	38.1	61.9	1,879 R
CASEY	5,585	1,521	27.2	4,064	72.8	27.2	72.8	2,543 R
CHRISTIAN	11,126	6,395	57.5	4,731	42.5	57.5	42.5	1,664 D
CLARK	6,423	3,459	53.9	2,964	46.1	53.9	46.1	495 D
CLAY	5,662	990	17.5	4,672	82.5	17.5	82.5	3,682 R
CLINTON	3,958	701	17.7	3,257	82.3	17.7	82.3	2,556 R
CRITTENDEN	3,927	1,515	38.6	2,412	61.4	38.6	61.4	897 R
CUMBERLAND	3,375	955	28.3	2,420	71.7	28.3	71.7	1,465 R
DAVIESS	17,573	6,881	39.2	10,692	60.8	39.2	60.8	3,811 R
EDMONSON	3,695	1,101	29.8	2,594	70.2	29.8	70.2	1,493 R
ELLIOTT	3,004	2,007	66.8	997	33.2	66.8	33.2	1,010 D
ESTILL	4,717	1,870	39.6	2,847	60.4	39.6	60.4	977 R
FAYETTE	34,842	13,494	38.7	21,348	61.3	38.7	61.3	7,854 R
FLEMING	5,021	2,466	49.1	2,555	50.9	49.1	50.9	89 R
FLOYD	13,555	7,862	58.0	5,693	42.0	58.0	42.0	2,169 D
FRANKLIN	9,805	6,181	63.0	3,624	37.0	63.0	37.0	2,557 D
FULTON	3,804	2,896	76.1	908	23.9	76.1	23.9	1,988 D
GALLATIN	1,678	1,162	69.2	516	30.8	69.2	30.8	646 D
GARRARD	4,038	1,783	44.2	2,255	55.8	44.2	55.8	472 R
GRANT	3,761	2,170	57.7	1,591	42.3	57.7	42.3	579 D
GRAVES	13,202	9,844	74.6	3,358	25.4	74.6	25.4	6,486 D
GRAYSON	6,456	1,942	30.1	4,514	69.9	30.1	69.9	2,572 R
GREEN	4,575	1,721	37.6	2,854	62.4	37.6	62.4	1,133 R
GREENUP	10,305	5,035	48.9	5,270	51.1	48.9	51.1	235 R
HANCOCK	2,293	1,031	45.0	1,262	55.0	45.0	55.0	231 R
HARDIN	9,246	4,396	47.5	4,850	52.5	47.5	52.5	454 R
HARLAN	14,869	6,679	44.9	8,190	55.1	44.9	55.1	1,511 R
HARRISON	5,468	3,444	63.0	2,024	37.0	63.0	37.0	1,420 D
HART	6,364	3,209	50.4	3,155	49.6	50.4	49.6	54 D
HENDERSON	10,131	5,684	56.1	4,447	43.9	56.1	43.9	1,237 D
HENRY	4,666	3,029	64.9	1,637	35.1	64.9	35.1	1,392 D
HICKMAN	2,936	2,208	75.2	728	24.8	75.2	24.8	1,480 D
HOPKINS	11,456	6,722	58.7	4,734	41.3	58.7	41.3	1,988 D
JACKSON	4,245	500	11.8	3,745	88.2	11.8	88.2	3,245 R
JEFFERSON	198,414	84,555	42.6	113,859	57.4	42.6	57.4	29,304 R
JESSAMINE	4,029	1,946	48.3	2,083	51.7	48.3	51.7	137 R
JOHNSON	7,908	2,415	30.5	5,493	69.5	30.5	69.5	3,078 R
KENTON	34,235	15,625	45.6	18,610	54.4	45.6	54.4	2,985 R
KNOTT	5,411	3,848	71.1	1,563	28.9	71.1	28.9	2,285 D
KNOX	8,504	2,461	28.9	6,043	71.1	28.9	71.1	3,582 R
LARUE	3,929	1,796	45.7	2,133	54.3	45.7	54.3	337 R
LAUREL	8,550	2,276	26.6	6,274	73.4	26.6	73.4	3,998 R
LAWRENCE	5,284	2,460	46.6	2,824	53.4	46.6	53.4	364 R
LEE	2,602	968	37.2	1,634	62.8	37.2	62.8	666 R

U.S. SENATOR: GENERAL ELECTION (SHORT TERM) — 1956

County	Total Vote	Democratic		Republican		Other Vote		Per Cent of Two-Party Vote		Dem-Rep Plurality
		Total	Per Cent	Total	Per Cent	Total	Per Cent	Dem	Rep	
LESLIE	4,055	457	11.3	3,598	88.7			11.3	88.7	3,141 R
LETCHER	9,354	4,125	44.1	5,229	55.9			44.1	55.9	1,104 R
LEWIS	4,719	1,517	32.1	3,202	67.9			32.1	67.9	1,685 R
LINCOLN	6,226	2,831	45.5	3,395	54.5			45.5	54.5	564 R
LIVINGSTON	2,939	1,835	62.4	1,104	37.6			62.4	37.6	731 D
LOGAN	7,705	5,121	66.5	2,584	33.5			66.5	33.5	2,537 D
LYON	2,412	1,497	62.1	915	37.9			62.1	37.9	582 D
MADISON	11,362	5,546	48.8	5,816	51.2			48.8	51.2	270 R
MAGOFFIN	4,391	2,216	50.5	2,175	49.5			50.5	49.5	41 D
MARION	5,639	3,064	54.3	2,575	45.7			54.3	45.7	489 D
MARSHALL	6,124	4,216	68.8	1,908	31.2			68.8	31.2	2,308 D
MARTIN	3,471	698	20.1	2,773	79.9			20.1	79.9	2,075 R
MASON	7,219	3,613	50.0	3,606	50.0			50.0	50.0	7 D
MC CRACKEN	20,272	13,748	67.8	6,524	32.2			67.8	32.2	7,224 D
MC CREARY	4,354	731	16.8	3,623	83.2			16.8	83.2	2,892 R
MC LEAN	3,745	1,985	53.0	1,760	47.0			53.0	47.0	225 D
MEADE	3,550	1,994	56.2	1,556	43.8			56.2	43.8	438 D
MENIFEE	1,828	1,103	60.3	725	39.7			60.3	39.7	378 D
MERCER	5,722	2,679	46.8	3,043	53.2			46.8	53.2	364 R
METCALFE	4,251	1,962	46.2	2,289	53.8			46.2	53.8	327 R
MONROE	4,713	1,231	26.1	3,482	73.9			26.1	73.9	2,251 R
MONTGOMERY	4,616	2,533	54.9	2,083	45.1			54.9	45.1	450 D
MORGAN	4,781	3,043	63.6	1,738	36.4			63.6	36.4	1,305 D
MUHLENBERG	9,725	4,735	48.7	4,990	51.3			48.7	51.3	255 R
NELSON	6,997	3,524	50.4	3,473	49.6			50.4	49.6	51 D
NICHOLAS	2,542	1,605	63.1	937	36.9			63.1	36.9	668 D
OHIO	7,390	2,711	36.7	4,679	63.3			36.7	63.3	1,968 R
OLDHAM	3,802	1,855	48.8	1,947	51.2			48.8	51.2	92 R
OWEN	3,607	2,745	76.1	862	23.9			76.1	23.9	1,883 D
OWSLEY	2,204	298	13.5	1,906	86.5			13.5	86.5	1,608 R
PENDLETON	3,991	1,954	49.0	2,037	51.0			49.0	51.0	83 R
PERRY	10,692	4,488	42.0	6,204	58.0			42.0	58.0	1,716 R
PIKE	22,522	11,634	51.7	10,888	48.3			51.7	48.3	746 D
POWELL	2,566	1,299	50.6	1,267	49.4			50.6	49.4	32 D
PULASKI	14,300	3,533	24.7	10,767	75.3			24.7	75.3	7,234 R
ROBERTSON	1,358	765	56.3	593	43.7			56.3	43.7	172 D
ROCKCASTLE	4,957	1,273	25.7	3,684	74.3			25.7	74.3	2,411 R
ROWAN	4,673	2,369	50.7	2,304	49.3			50.7	49.3	65 D
RUSSELL	4,217	1,284	30.4	2,933	69.6			30.4	69.6	1,649 R
SCOTT	4,557	2,689	59.0	1,868	41.0			59.0	41.0	821 D
SHELBY	6,527	3,817	58.5	2,710	41.5			58.5	41.5	1,107 D
SIMPSON	4,073	2,730	67.0	1,343	33.0			67.0	33.0	1,387 D
SPENCER	2,007	1,172	58.4	835	41.6			58.4	41.6	337 D
TAYLOR	6,154	2,457	39.9	3,697	60.1			39.9	60.1	1,240 R
TODD	4,306	2,927	68.0	1,379	32.0			68.0	32.0	1,548 D
TRIGG	3,619	2,408	66.5	1,211	33.5			66.5	33.5	1,197 D
TRIMBLE	2,197	1,726	78.6	471	21.4			78.6	21.4	1,255 D
UNION	4,619	3,010	65.2	1,609	34.8			65.2	34.8	1,401 D
WARREN	14,557	7,175	49.3	7,382	50.7			49.3	50.7	207 R
WASHINGTON	4,511	2,121	47.0	2,390	53.0			47.0	53.0	269 R
WAYNE	5,692	2,185	38.4	3,507	61.6			38.4	61.6	1,322 R
WEBSTER	4,808	3,100	64.5	1,708	35.5			64.5	35.5	1,392 D
WHITLEY	10,070	2,619	26.0	7,451	74.0			26.0	74.0	4,832 R
WOLFE	2,565	1,575	61.4	990	38.6			61.4	38.6	585 D
WOODFORD	3,984	1,887	47.4	2,097	52.6			47.4	52.6	210 R
TOTAL	1,011,645	473,140	46.8	538,505	53.2			46.8	53.2	65,365 R

DEMOCRAT: Lawrence W. Wetherby
REPUBLICAN: John S. Cooper

County	Total Vote	Keen Johnson		John Y. Brown		Other Vote	
		Total	Per Cent	Total	Per Cent	Total	Per Cent
ADAIR	1,136	692	60.9	427	37.6	17	1.5
ALLEN	804	689	85.7	100	12.4	15	1.9
ANDERSON	1,225	731	59.7	483	39.4	11	0.9
BALLARD	775	383	49.4	375	48.4	17	2.2
BARREN	1,376	1,079	78.4	252	18.3	45	3.3
BATH	1,045	712	68.1	317	30.3	16	1.5
BELL	1,318	982	74.5	254	19.3	82	6.2
BOONE	2,233	1,103	49.4	1,031	46.2	99	4.4
BOURBON	885	436	49.3	425	48.0	24	2.7
BOYD	1,762	1,128	64.0	572	32.5	62	3.5
BOYLE	1,531	727	47.5	783	51.1	21	1.4
BRACKEN	539	289	53.6	223	41.4	27	5.0
BREATHITT	2,055	1,751	85.2	289	14.1	15	0.7
BRECKINRIDGE	1,602	964	60.2	621	38.8	17	1.1
BULLITT	998	438	43.9	547	54.8	13	1.3
BUTLER	647	488	75.4	150	23.2	9	1.4
CALDWELL	1,024	717	70.0	298	29.1	9	0.9
CALLOWAY	1,419	1,027	72.4	379	26.7	13	0.9
CAMPBELL	3,160	1,560	49.4	1,450	45.9	150	4.7
CARLISLE	476	307	64.5	166	34.9	3	0.6
CARROLL	1,238	761	61.5	458	37.0	19	1.5
CARTER	1,094	618	56.5	450	41.1	26	2.4
CASEY	798	474	59.4	315	39.5	9	1.1
CHRISTIAN	2,286	1,855	81.1	397	17.4	34	1.5
CLARK	974	443	45.5	518	53.2	13	1.3
CLAY	491	435	88.6	43	8.8	13	2.6
CLINTON	500	343	68.6	150	30.0	7	1.4
CRITTENDEN	531	321	60.5	205	38.6	5	0.9
CUMBERLAND	303	257	84.8	41	13.5	5	1.7
DAVIESS	2,170	1,481	68.2	620	28.6	69	3.2
EDMONSON	595	454	76.3	130	21.8	11	1.8
ELLIOTT	1,127	766	68.0	345	30.6	16	1.4
ESTILL	1,138	533	46.8	598	52.5	7	0.6
FAYETTE	8,273	2,261	27.3	5,915	71.5	97	1.2
FLEMING	886	595	67.2	271	30.6	20	2.3
FLOYD	3,966	2,127	53.6	1,680	42.4	159	4.0
FRANKLIN	6,219	3,131	50.3	2,813	45.2	275	4.4
FULTON	1,004	581	57.9	386	38.4	37	3.7
GALLATIN	500	327	65.4	164	32.8	9	1.8
GARRARD	531	356	67.0	171	32.2	4	0.8
GRANT	845	520	61.5	291	34.4	34	4.0
GRAVES	2,470	1,319	53.4	1,066	43.2	85	3.4
GRAYSON	1,092	789	72.3	290	26.6	13	1.2
GREEN	734	556	75.7	168	22.9	10	1.4
GREENUP	1,448	958	66.2	446	30.8	44	3.0
HANCOCK	299	189	63.2	105	35.1	5	1.7
HARDIN	2,137	1,055	49.4	1,012	47.4	70	3.3
HARLAN	2,210	1,571	71.1	538	24.3	101	4.6
HARRISON	1,006	629	62.5	363	36.1	14	1.4
HART	1,356	1,017	75.0	312	23.0	27	2.0
HENDERSON	2,819	1,379	48.9	1,210	42.9	230	8.2
HENRY	1,310	625	47.7	655	50.0	30	2.3
HICKMAN	956	445	46.5	496	51.9	15	1.6
HOPKINS	2,525	1,684	66.7	758	30.0	83	3.3
JACKSON	403	251	62.3	140	34.7	12	3.0
JEFFERSON	28,579	15,831	55.4	11,282	39.5	1,466	5.1
JESSAMINE	1,258	556	44.2	673	53.5	29	2.3
JOHNSON	1,135	668	58.9	441	38.9	26	2.3
KENTON	4,720	2,121	44.9	2,348	49.7	251	5.3
KNOTT	2,381	952	40.0	1,311	55.1	118	5.0
KNOX	699	481	68.8	177	25.3	41	5.9
LARUE	1,058	694	65.6	354	33.5	10	0.9
LAUREL	990	704	71.1	244	24.6	42	4.2
LAWRENCE	1,073	803	74.8	258	24.0	12	1.1
LEE	746	455	61.0	242	32.4	49	6.6

County	Total Vote	Keen Johnson Total	Keen Johnson Per Cent	John Y. Brown Total	John Y. Brown Per Cent	Other Vote Total	Other Vote Per Cent
LESLIE	378	273	72.2	94	24.9	11	2.9
LETCHER	1,317	700	53.2	542	41.2	75	5.7
LEWIS	576	484	84.0	83	14.4	9	1.6
LINCOLN	1,123	585	52.1	519	46.2	19	1.7
LIVINGSTON	851	536	63.0	307	36.1	8	0.9
LOGAN	2,942	2,719	92.4	208	7.1	15	0.5
LYON	621	439	70.7	180	29.0	2	0.3
MADISON	3,319	2,535	76.4	758	22.8	26	0.8
MAGOFFIN	2,070	817	39.5	1,175	56.8	78	3.8
MARION	996	368	36.9	595	59.7	33	3.3
MARSHALL	854	452	52.9	377	44.1	25	2.9
MARTIN	343	229	66.8	100	29.2	14	4.1
MASON	1,019	763	74.9	230	22.6	26	2.6
MC CRACKEN	2,082	1,292	62.1	754	36.2	36	1.7
MC CREARY	390	316	81.0	59	15.1	15	3.8
MC LEAN	576	371	64.4	184	31.9	21	3.6
MEADE	860	473	55.0	373	43.4	14	1.6
MENIFEE	750	299	39.9	436	58.1	15	2.0
MERCER	1,190	411	34.5	765	64.3	14	1.2
METCALFE	1,325	808	61.0	496	37.4	21	1.6
MONROE	638	537	84.2	93	14.6	8	1.3
MONTGOMERY	1,857	763	41.1	1,044	56.2	50	2.7
MORGAN	1,559	1,165	74.7	358	23.0	36	2.3
MUHLENBERG	1,398	995	71.2	391	28.0	12	0.9
NELSON	1,773	1,159	65.4	567	32.0	47	2.7
NICHOLAS	394	215	54.6	170	43.1	9	2.3
OHIO	757	588	77.7	130	17.2	39	5.2
OLDHAM	1,064	555	52.2	500	47.0	9	0.8
OWEN	1,338	652	48.7	654	48.9	32	2.4
OWSLEY	218	158	72.5	52	23.9	8	3.7
PENDLETON	724	470	64.9	227	31.4	27	3.7
PERRY	1,717	780	45.4	908	52.9	29	1.7
PIKE	4,615	1,954	42.3	2,531	54.8	130	2.8
POWELL	430	236	54.9	189	44.0	5	1.2
PULASKI	2,407	1,792	74.4	575	23.9	40	1.7
ROBERTSON	427	249	58.3	168	39.3	10	2.3
ROCKCASTLE	852	555	65.1	283	33.2	14	1.6
ROWAN	1,034	567	54.8	446	43.1	21	2.0
RUSSELL	731	508	69.5	204	27.9	19	2.6
SCOTT	1,614	653	40.5	940	58.2	21	1.3
SHELBY	1,867	991	53.1	857	45.9	19	1.0
SIMPSON	1,170	1,034	88.4	111	9.5	25	2.1
SPENCER	538	239	44.4	288	53.5	11	2.0
TAYLOR	1,133	732	64.6	388	34.2	13	1.1
TODD	1,547	1,279	82.7	253	16.4	15	1.0
TRIGG	1,186	1,025	86.4	149	12.6	12	1.0
TRIMBLE	690	462	67.0	219	31.7	9	1.3
UNION	1,901	1,259	66.2	548	28.8	94	4.9
WARREN	2,559	1,739	68.0	751	29.3	69	2.7
WASHINGTON	1,330	557	41.9	743	55.9	30	2.3
WAYNE	1,064	679	63.8	360	33.8	25	2.3
WEBSTER	1,720	921	53.5	737	42.8	62	3.6
WHITLEY	1,076	827	76.9	233	21.7	16	1.5
WOLFE	1,182	553	46.8	585	49.5	44	3.7
WOODFORD	1,538	505	32.8	1,018	66.2	15	1.0
TOTAL	194,503	112,797	58.0	75,897	39.0	5,809	3.0

OTHER VOTE: James L. Delk 1517
Jesse N. R. Cecil 2083
Wilton B. Cupp 2209

County	Total Vote	Democratic		Republican		Per Cent of Two-Party Vote		Dem-Rep Plurality
		Total	Per Cent	Total	Per Cent	Dem	Rep	
ADAIR	6,694	1,949	29.1	4,745	70.9	29.1	70.9	2,796 R
ALLEN	4,937	1,536	31.1	3,401	68.9	31.1	68.9	1,865 R
ANDERSON	3,964	1,646	41.5	2,318	58.5	41.5	58.5	672 R
BALLARD	3,694	2,301	62.3	1,393	37.7	62.3	37.7	908 D
BARREN	9,510	4,258	44.8	5,252	55.2	44.8	55.2	994 R
BATH	3,761	1,690	44.9	2,071	55.1	44.9	55.1	381 R
BELL	11,319	4,657	41.1	6,662	58.9	41.1	58.9	2,005 R
BOONE	7,589	2,889	38.1	4,700	61.9	38.1	61.9	1,811 R
BOURBON	5,355	2,651	49.5	2,704	50.5	49.5	50.5	53 R
BOYD	19,602	7,945	40.5	11,657	59.5	40.5	59.5	3,712 R
BOYLE	6,587	2,422	36.8	4,165	63.2	36.8	63.2	1,743 R
BRACKEN	3,205	1,189	37.1	2,016	62.9	37.1	62.9	827 R
BREATHITT	5,103	2,960	58.0	2,143	42.0	58.0	42.0	817 D
BRECKINRIDGE	6,791	2,654	39.1	4,137	60.9	39.1	60.9	1,483 R
BULLITT	5,069	2,128	42.0	2,941	58.0	42.0	58.0	813 R
BUTLER	4,470	860	19.2	3,610	80.8	19.2	80.8	2,750 R
CALDWELL	5,449	2,007	36.8	3,442	63.2	36.8	63.2	1,435 R
CALLOWAY	7,840	4,048	51.6	3,792	48.4	51.6	48.4	256 D
CAMPBELL	30,577	12,953	42.4	17,624	57.6	42.4	57.6	4,671 R
CARLISLE	2,612	1,592	60.9	1,020	39.1	60.9	39.1	572 D
CARROLL	3,223	1,927	59.8	1,296	40.2	59.8	40.2	631 D
CARTER	8,315	2,993	36.0	5,322	64.0	36.0	64.0	2,329 R
CASEY	6,107	1,196	19.6	4,911	80.4	19.6	80.4	3,715 R
CHRISTIAN	11,706	6,103	52.1	5,603	47.9	52.1	47.9	500 D
CLARK	6,238	2,566	41.1	3,672	58.9	41.1	58.9	1,106 R
CLAY	6,131	1,329	21.7	4,802	78.3	21.7	78.3	3,473 R
CLINTON	3,992	583	14.6	3,409	85.4	14.6	85.4	2,826 R
CRITTENDEN	4,019	1,232	30.7	2,787	69.3	30.7	69.3	1,555 R
CUMBERLAND	3,283	669	20.4	2,614	79.6	20.4	79.6	1,945 R
DAVIESS	22,479	8,511	37.9	13,968	62.1	37.9	62.1	5,457 R
EDMONSON	3,774	940	24.9	2,834	75.1	24.9	75.1	1,894 R
ELLIOTT	2,455	1,523	62.0	932	38.0	62.0	38.0	591 D
ESTILL	4,815	1,420	29.5	3,395	70.5	29.5	70.5	1,975 R
FAYETTE	40,607	13,228	32.6	27,379	67.4	32.6	67.4	14,151 R
FLEMING	4,836	1,986	41.1	2,850	58.9	41.1	58.9	864 R
FLOYD	14,333	8,676	60.5	5,657	39.5	60.5	39.5	3,019 D
FRANKLIN	10,992	5,461	49.7	5,531	50.3	49.7	50.3	70 R
FULTON	4,021	2,260	56.2	1,761	43.8	56.2	43.8	499 D
GALLATIN	1,680	926	55.1	754	44.9	55.1	44.9	172 D
GARRARD	4,492	1,601	35.6	2,891	64.4	35.6	64.4	1,290 R
GRANT	3,939	1,650	41.9	2,289	58.1	41.9	58.1	639 R
GRAVES	12,319	7,194	58.4	5,125	41.6	58.4	41.6	2,069 D
GRAYSON	6,846	2,075	30.3	4,771	69.7	30.3	69.7	2,696 R
GREEN	5,078	1,395	27.5	3,683	72.5	27.5	72.5	2,288 R
GREENUP	11,211	4,863	43.4	6,348	56.6	43.4	56.6	1,485 R
HANCOCK	2,416	945	39.1	1,471	60.9	39.1	60.9	526 R
HARDIN	10,846	4,124	38.0	6,722	62.0	38.0	62.0	2,598 R
HARLAN	15,932	7,775	48.8	8,157	51.2	48.8	51.2	382 R
HARRISON	5,647	3,006	53.2	2,641	46.8	53.2	46.8	365 D
HART	6,456	2,660	41.2	3,796	58.8	41.2	58.8	1,136 R
HENDERSON	10,491	5,165	49.2	5,326	50.8	49.2	50.8	161 R
HENRY	4,521	2,219	49.1	2,302	50.9	49.1	50.9	83 R
HICKMAN	3,043	1,740	57.2	1,303	42.8	57.2	42.8	437 D
HOPKINS	11,749	6,173	52.5	5,576	47.5	52.5	47.5	597 D
JACKSON	4,235	410	9.7	3,825	90.3	9.7	90.3	3,415 R
JEFFERSON	231,818	93,872	40.5	137,946	59.5	40.5	59.5	44,074 R
JESSAMINE	4,413	1,625	36.8	2,788	63.2	36.8	63.2	1,163 R
JOHNSON	7,628	2,148	28.2	5,480	71.8	28.2	71.8	3,332 R
KENTON	39,034	16,722	42.8	22,312	57.2	42.8	57.2	5,590 R
KNOTT	5,193	3,350	64.5	1,843	35.5	64.5	35.5	1,507 D
KNOX	8,232	2,389	29.0	5,843	71.0	29.0	71.0	3,454 R
LARUE	3,929	1,316	33.5	2,613	66.5	33.5	66.5	1,297 R
LAUREL	9,368	2,026	21.6	7,342	78.4	21.6	78.4	5,316 R
LAWRENCE	5,445	2,242	41.2	3,203	58.8	41.2	58.8	961 R
LEE	2,891	891	30.8	2,000	69.2	30.8	69.2	1,109 R

County	Total Vote	Democratic Total	Democratic Per Cent	Republican Total	Republican Per Cent	Per Cent of Two-Party Vote Dem	Per Cent of Two-Party Vote Rep	Dem-Rep Plurality
LESLIE	4,561	731	16.0	3,830	84.0	16.0	84.0	3,099 R
LETCHER	8,343	3,773	45.2	4,570	54.8	45.2	54.8	797 R
LEWIS	5,297	1,490	28.1	3,807	71.9	28.1	71.9	2,317 R
LINCOLN	5,972	1,969	33.0	4,003	67.0	33.0	67.0	2,034 R
LIVINGSTON	3,043	1,451	47.7	1,592	52.3	47.7	52.3	141 R
LOGAN	8,543	4,194	49.1	4,349	50.9	49.1	50.9	155 R
LYON	2,356	1,293	54.9	1,063	45.1	54.9	45.1	230 D
MADISON	12,205	5,145	42.2	7,060	57.8	42.2	57.8	1,915 R
MAGOFFIN	5,046	2,261	44.8	2,785	55.2	44.8	55.2	524 R
MARION	6,057	3,470	57.3	2,587	42.7	57.3	42.7	883 D
MARSHALL	6,722	3,087	45.9	3,635	54.1	45.9	54.1	548 R
MARTIN	3,671	940	25.6	2,731	74.4	25.6	74.4	1,791 R
MASON	7,318	2,998	41.0	4,320	59.0	41.0	59.0	1,322 R
MC CRACKEN	21,243	10,821	50.9	10,422	49.1	50.9	49.1	399 D
MC CREARY	4,428	690	15.6	3,738	84.4	15.6	84.4	3,048 R
MC LEAN	3,969	1,653	41.6	2,316	58.4	41.6	58.4	663 R
MEADE	4,045	1,878	46.4	2,167	53.6	46.4	53.6	289 R.
MENIFEE	1,683	812	48.2	871	51.8	48.2	51.8	59 R
MERCER	5,971	2,133	35.7	3,838	64.3	35.7	64.3	1,705 R
METCALFE	3,529	1,283	36.4	2,246	63.6	36.4	63.6	963 R
MONROE	5,080	860	16.9	4,220	83.1	16.9	83.1	3,360 R
MONTGOMERY	4,774	2,156	45.2	2,618	54.8	45.2	54.8	462 R
MORGAN	4,329	2,517	58.1	1,812	41.9	58.1	41.9	705 D
MUHLENBERG	10,447	4,377	41.9	6,070	58.1	41.9	58.1	1,693 R
NELSON	7,626	3,844	50.4	3,782	49.6	50.4	49.6	62 D
NICHOLAS	2,386	1,250	52.4	1,136	47.6	52.4	47.6	114 D
OHIO	7,547	2,267	30.0	5,280	70.0	30.0	70.0	3,013 R
OLDHAM	4,091	1,597	39.0	2,494	61.0	39.0	61.0	897 R
OWEN	3,480	1,955	56.2	1,525	43.8	56.2	43.8	430 D
OWSLEY	2,515	346	13.8	2,169	86.2	13.8	86.2	1,823 R
PENDLETON	3,673	1,399	38.1	2,274	61.9	38.1	61.9	875 R
PERRY	10,526	4,617	43.9	5,909	56.1	43.9	56.1	1,292 R
PIKE	22,672	12,222	53.9	10,450	46.1	53.9	46.1	1,772 D
POWELL	2,574	1,090	42.3	1,484	57.7	42.3	57.7	394 R
PULASKI	14,933	2,443	16.4	12,490	83.6	16.4	83.6	10,047 R
ROBERTSON	1,208	576	47.7	632	52.3	47.7	52.3	56 R
ROCKCASTLE	4,986	1,030	20.7	3,956	79.3	20.7	79.3	2,926 R
ROWAN	4,919	2,112	42.9	2,807	57.1	42.9	57.1	695 R
RUSSELL	4,697	1,014	21.6	3,683	78.4	21.6	78.4	2,669 R
SCOTT	4,637	2,222	47.9	2,415	52.1	47.9	52.1	193 R
SHELBY	6,594	2,984	45.3	3,610	54.7	45.3	54.7	626 R
SIMPSON	4,220	2,322	55.0	1,898	45.0	55.0	45.0	424 D
SPENCER	2,069	878	42.4	1,191	57.6	42.4	57.6	313 R
TAYLOR	6,608	1,830	27.7	4,778	72.3	27.7	72.3	2,948 R
TODD	4,472	2,536	56.7	1,936	43.3	56.7	43.3	600 D
TRIGG	3,809	2,129	55.9	1,680	44.1	55.9	44.1	449 D
TRIMBLE	2,269	1,399	61.7	870	38.3	61.7	38.3	529 D
UNION	5,036	3,116	61.9	1,920	38.1	61.9	38.1	1,196 D
WARREN	15,638	6,461	41.3	9,177	58.7	41.3	58.7	2,716 R
WASHINGTON	4,829	1,919	39.7	2,910	60.3	39.7	60.3	991 R
WAYNE	5,775	1,705	29.5	4,070	70.5	29.5	70.5	2,365 R
WEBSTER	5,425	2,959	54.5	2,466	45.5	54.5	45.5	493 D
WHITLEY	10,064	2,467	24.5	7,597	75.5	24.5	75.5	5,130 R
WOLFE	2,722	1,353	49.7	1,369	50.3	49.7	50.3	16 R
WOODFORD	3,979	1,366	34.3	2,613	65.7	34.3	65.7	1,247 R
TOTAL	1,088,917	444,830	40.9	644,087	59.1	40.9	59.1	199,257 R

DEMOCRAT: Keen Johnson
REPUBLICAN: John S. Cooper

www.ingramcontent.com/pod-product-compliance
Lightning Source LLC
Chambersburg PA
CBHW081403270326
41930CB00015B/3398